Ocean Sailing

Ocean Sailing

The offshore cruising experience
with real-life practical advice from

Paul Heiney

with members of

Royal Cruising Club
Ocean Cruising Club
Cruising Club of America

ROYAL CRUISING CLUB
PILOTAGE FOUNDATION

ADLARD
COLES

LONDON • OXFORD • NEW YORK • NEW DELHI • SYDNEY

ADLARD COLES
Bloomsbury Publishing Plc
50 Bedford Square, London, WC1B 3DP, UK

BLOOMSBURY, ADLARD COLES and the Adlard Coles logo are trademarks of
Bloomsbury Publishing Plc

First published in Great Britain 2019

A catalogue record for this book is available from the British Library

Library of Congress Cataloguing-in-Publication data has been applied for

ISBN: HB: 978-1-4729-5539-5; eBook: 978-1-4729-5538-8

2 4 6 8 10 9 7 5 3 1

Designed and typeset by Susan McIntyre
Typeset in Berkeley Old Style and Gill Sans
Printed and bound in China by Toppan Leefung Printing

CAUTION

Whilst the RCC Pilotage Foundation, the author and the publishers have used reasonable endeavours to ensure the accuracy of the content of this book, it contains selected information and thus is not definitive. It does not contain all known information on the subject in hand and should not be relied on alone for navigational use: it should only be used in conjunction with official hydrographical data.

The RCC Pilotage Foundation, the authors and the publishers believe that the information that they have included is a useful aid to prudent navigation. But the safety of a vessel depends ultimately on the judgement of the skipper, who should assess all information, published or unpublished.

The information provided in this publication may be out of date and may be changed or updated without notice. The RCC Pilotage Foundation cannot accept any liability for any error, omission or failure to update such information.

To the extent permitted by law the RCC Pilotage Foundation, the author and the publishers do not accept liability for any loss and/or damage howsoever caused that may arise from reliance on information contained in this publication.

ROYAL CRUISING CLUB
PILOTAGE FOUNDATION

This book is published on behalf of the Royal Cruising Club Pilotage Foundation, rccpf.org.uk, a voluntary and charitable organisation run by cruising sailors, mostly members of the Royal Cruising Club, to provide passage planning and pilotage information. It was established in 1976 and has grown rapidly since, and there is now hardly a cruising area of the world for which it does not provide information via its commercial publishers or its website. For more remote and unvisited parts of the world, many of its pilotage notes are available as free downloads. Its pilot books and website are updated and their website should be one of the first ports of call for anyone planning to go ocean sailing.

Acknowledgements

This book has been made possible by the co-operation of three clubs, the Royal Cruising Club, the Ocean Cruising Club and the Cruising Club of America, and the Pilotage Foundation is grateful for their support. Many of their members have freely shared their accounts of their ocean voyages and their experiences under sail, in the hope that the wider sailing community will benefit.

In compiling this book, I am grateful for the assistance of Doug Bruce of the CCA, the Commodores and committees of the RCC and the OCC for their support, and to Jane Russell, editor-in-chief of the Pilotage Foundation. Also to Janet Murphy, Clara Jump and the team at Bloomsbury for their support and expertise.

Paul Heiney

The Royal Cruising Club

This was founded on a small scale in 1880 as an association of people who shared an interest in cruising in small yachts, and that remains its core objective but now embracing yachts of all sizes and types.

Its members, who number 400, sail far and wide and it is not unusual for them to report in any given year on their voyages to Greenland, the higher Arctic, the Pacific Islands, Cape Horn and almost every corner of the world that can be reached by boat. Many members have earned their place in cruising history, and the story of the development of ocean sailing can be said to have been partly written by members of the RCC.

Members record their voyages in an annual publication called *Roving Commissions*, which is available for the public to purchase as a hardback book, or there is a free download at www.rcc.org.uk/rovingcommissions.aspx. Here you will be able to electronically search all the journals back to 1883, which, taken together, form a vivid portrait of cruising life over almost a century and a half.

Membership of the RCC is by invitation.

The Ocean Cruising Club

The OCC has a worldwide membership of nearly 3,000, and their distinctive blue-and-yellow flag with its flying fish emblem can be seen on every ocean of the world. They are proud to describe themselves as a community of adventurous cruisers, and welcome all who do the same. Their members come from 61 countries, though the majority are based in the UK, Ireland and North America, and most of the 300+ new joiners welcomed during 2018 were active sailors.

The club was founded in 1954 by Humphrey Barton, an accomplished cruising sailor, to provide a meeting place for like-minded people who sailed the oceans. To qualify for Full Membership, it was necessary to have sailed non-stop between two ports at least 1,000 miles apart in a vessel of not more than 70ft overall. That remains unchanged to this day, although a second category of Associate Membership has been added for those with serious aspirations to qualify fully.

The OCC's twice-yearly journal *Flying Fish* carries accounts of members' voyages, including some truly amazing adventures. Visit oceancruisingclub.org/Flying-Fish-Archive to browse issues back to 1990, soon to extend back to the journal's inception in 1964. Together with the Cruising Forum at forum.oceancruisingclub.org, it is a hugely valuable planning resource available to all cruisers, members and non-members alike.

The Cruising Club of America

This is an international organisation, founded in 1922, now with over 1,300 members, many of whom have considerable ocean-going experience. They pride them-selves on seamanship, and their willingness to share their enthusiasm with others. They make annual awards for exceptional passagemaking and demonstrations of seamanship. Their Blue Water Medal is highly prized in the worldwide cruising community. Membership is by invitation and they note that: 'Since the Club's inception there have been two qualifications for membership: a member must be a complete seaman, and they must be a good shipmate.'

One of the club's main objectives remains the fostering of the highest standards of seamanship and safety at sea, and they organise a variety of seminars and publications on this theme. There is also much useful information to be found on their website, ranging from sea safety to radio communications, available to non-members at www.cruisingclub.org/what-cca.

Contents

Introduction ... 1

1 On the Ocean ~ *a taste of what's in store* ... 5

2 Where in the World Shall We Go? ~ *making plans, and making your choice* ... 9

3 It's Time to Buy ~ *is there a perfect boat for ocean sailing?* ... 66

4 The Boats They Chose ~ *there are any number of craft in which you can go offshore sailing* ... 88

5 How Much to go Ocean Sailing? ~ ...*'all of what you have, plus a little bit more'* ... 126

6 Can the Kids Come Too? ~ *you can't leave them behind, but how do you take your kids to sea?* ... 144

7 Too Old to Go? ~ *does ocean-going come with an upper age limit?* ... 164

8 Keep in Touch ~ ...*with folks back home, and with the weather* ... 173

9 The Complete Engineer ~ *be a jack of all trades – and master of them all* ... 198

10 Look After Yourself ~ *keeping well and staying safe* ... 211

11 When Things Go Wrong ~ *sooner or later you'll have a mishap. Why not think it through now?* ... 226

12 And When It's All Over ~ *coming down to earth and hitting dry land* ... 261

Final words ... 271

Bibliography ... 273

Index ... 276

The horizon beckons – the start of a great ocean sailing adventure. (VINCENT CHIRIE)

Introduction

It is one thing to cast off your mooring lines and head across the bay towards a quiet harbour, or slowly drift along the coastline you know so well till you find a familiar place to drop the hook for the night. It is quite another to cast off those same lines and head out to sea with the intention of crossing an ocean. There are certainties in being close to home, of being in familiar waters. We know how the tide runs, what the changing sky tells us about the weather. There is the comfort of the sight of land, and we know where safety is to be found in familiar anchorages and harbours. If we get tired, we are never more than a few hours from rest. It is true that coastal sailing can be intricate, needs plenty of planning and care in its execution, and can certainly provide enough nail-biting moments, often when we least need them. But the fact remains that these are home waters; the kind of places we understand.

The ocean is a different kind of place and alien to most of us. We know, of course, that it is the same kind of watery sea that laps on our home shores. But the ocean is unrestricted by cliffs, sandbanks and land mass, and those of us who have never sailed there might wonder if it behaves in a different and more threatening kind of way. Home waters are friendly; the mysterious ocean makes us wary. So we remain suspicious because we can't be certain of its ways, because we've never been there. We simply know that when those early navigators sailed far into the unknown and inscribed their charts 'here be dragons', they may have been right. And although we believe it to be nonsense, a primitive thought still lingers that it might just be possible to sail too far and fall off the edge of the world. And so we come to the conclusion that the ocean is a mysterious, dangerous, and an unfathomable kind of place, as far removed from the security of home waters as it is possible for a sailor to be. It is a small step from there to a belief that it presents physical challenges that are way beyond our reach, requires boats and equipment far beyond our pockets, and it puts our lives in grave danger with every roll of that never-ending ocean swell. The great oceans of the world are not for modest sailors like us.

But what if the ocean isn't like that at all? What if it is a rather more benign place than we imagine? What if the 70 per cent of this planet that we call 'ocean' can offer a new kind of sailing experience, with unexpected rewards? The sheer vastness of the oceans and the sense of isolation will unnerve some people, but far more will find the independence and self-sufficiency inspiring. Those who worry about being overtaken by bad weather will find, more often than not, that much more of their time is spent trying to make progress in light weather. And those who do get caught out may well discover that though the storm itself might be testing, the fear of being driven ashore or into shallow, breaking waters found closer to land is no threat to them here. The big seas roll on, but not always in a dangerous kind of way. And when land does eventually appear across the bow, as it surely will, and the temptation comes to shout out loud 'Land ahoy!', as generations of sailors have done, then imagine the satisfaction of an arrival on distant foreign shores. These are among the true rewards that await the ocean sailor. If none of this convinces you, then you might turn to statistics to confirm your suspicions. Except there don't seem to be any. The rescues that involve sailors being plucked mid-ocean seem to be so few that no one has gathered them. Of course, the ones that do occur can create lurid headlines, but they are thankfully few and far between.

But yet another lingering doubt emerges – your boat might not be up to it. It is true that ocean-going boats are getting bigger with every year that passes, and it is easy to assume that this is for reasons of safety. Surely, the bigger the boat, the safer we will be?

Not so. The bigger the boat, the more comfortable you might be, but you won't necessarily be any safer. In fact, big volume boats with cabins the width of a hotel foyer might offer more opportunities to stumble and fall when the going gets rough. The small boat sailor who is never more than a step from a safe handhold might decide he has the better boat for the job. History proves the safety of small boats through the amazing voyages that were made in the pioneering days of ocean sailing. The boat you choose will probably be one that suits your pocket, but if that pocket is a small one with not much spare change, it is no reason for ocean adventuring to be denied to you, as we will discover.

If this book has one mission, it is to persuade you that there is nothing particularly difficult or threatening about ocean sailing. It requires thought and preparation, but it does not ask you to be superhuman. The stories you will read here are the experiences of 'ordinary' cruising sailors who, one day, dropped the lines and headed towards the distant horizon and returned safe and sound having had the experience of a lifetime. But they approached it with due care and with respect. Respect for the sea is

There will be special moments of quiet reflection on any ocean passage (left)... (PARTRIDGE)

...and times when ocean sailing seems to be the hardest work (below)...

possibly the most unconsidered safety device you can have on board. If you treat the ocean with indifference, as you might a tarmac motorway, it will sooner or later take an opportunity to remind you that it should be approached with due seriousness. Successful ocean sailors understand that and do not take the seas for granted.

This is not a book that will teach you how to sail. You will find nothing here on setting trysails, dowsing spinnakers, or the difference between a beat and a reach, or how to gybe. Before considering an ocean passage, it must be assumed that all these things are part of your language and experience. Reefing, for example, must be as instinctive as taking a breath. To set sail otherwise would be to play that dangerous card of showing the sea disrespect.

The mechanical aspects of sailing are not difficult to grasp, nor the routine maintenance of a boat, and this book assumes that you have already done so. But more difficult for newcomers to ocean sailing to discover is the answer to the question, 'What is ocean sailing really like?' How does it differ from coastal sailing? You might love your weekends afloat, but wonder how that would translate when the days turn into weeks and months. Would it be selfish to take my children on what is really my adventure?

And where would we go? The ocean is a mighty place so in which direction should we head, and what will it be like when we get there? How much do I need to live on, and how do I keep in touch with the folks back home? Or have I left it too late and I'm too old for ocean sailing? The experiences of others are to be found within this book.

In your average yacht club bar, the number of people with ocean experience is likely to be quite small. In those casual conversations that are ignited by coming alongside in harbours and marinas, again you'd be lucky to find anyone who had crossed the Indian Ocean, for example. When you're planning an ocean passage, you can feel frighteningly alone.

So in this book we have brought together the people who can help you. Here you will find some of the world's most widely travelled cruising sailors who are ready to share with you their vast experience. They can tell you what it is really like, the mistakes they made, the satisfactions they gleaned, as well as the thrills and the spills. They are mostly members of three great cruising organisations: the Royal Cruising Club, the Ocean Cruising Club and the Cruising Club of America. I cannot estimate how many ocean miles members of these three have under their belts. Of course, ask a group of sailors any question and you'll get a raft of answers. Often, there are no rights and wrongs. Which is why, in this book, you'll find a wide variety of opinion underlining the fact that when it comes to ocean sailing there are no hard and fast rules. The best we can do is share experience and say, 'Well, that worked for us.'

Once you take to the oceans, you are automatically enrolled in the greatest club of them all, even greater than the above, and that is the Cruising Community. It doesn't matter what you are already a member of, or which flag you fly, you are now one of the gang of ocean sailors and the level of support you can expect to find if you are in need can be overwhelming at times. You will make stronger friendships in a shorter time than you imagined possible. Everyone who sails the oceans will not hesitate to share their experiences, or offer their advice, or come and give you help when you need it most. It is notable that of all the people I invited to contribute to this book, none hesitated. All gave their time freely to help others. That's the cruising experience in action.

All those whose stories you will read here have cruised widely, lived to tell the tale, and are now ready and willing to share with you their secrets of ocean sailing.

Your voyage of a lifetime begins here.

1 On the Ocean

A taste of what's in store

At this early stage in planning your voyage, you may not be able to imagine what it is like to be alone on the ocean with only your crew mates for company. Even with plenty of coastal sea miles under your belt, nothing really prepares you for this. All you know is that it is going to be a very different experience.

Tom and Vicky Jackson are two of the world's most experienced cruising sailors. They have won awards from the RCC, the OCC, and have been awarded the CCA's Blue Water Medal – a rare honour. Their boat is a 50-year-old wooden sloop which, so far, has carried them 200,000 miles across every ocean in the world. Nevertheless, despite all the modern cruising comforts that are available, the facilities on their classic boat, *Sunstone*, are only as sophisticated as they feel they need, and no more. Theirs is ocean sailing at its purest, and this is how they sail.

'We have sailed passages of 500 to 1,500 miles with *Sunstone* many times. Our longest single passage was 5,200 miles over 37 days from Simonstown in South Africa to Fremantle in Western Australia. More recently we have criss-crossed the Pacific Ocean. Twice in the past five years we have sailed from our home base in New Zealand north to Alaska and British Columbia and back. The Pacific Ocean is big – it is over 6,000 miles from New Zealand to Alaska.

Pre-passage preparations are important. Typically, in Tofino on the west coast of Canada, we filled all the food containers, stacked the tins locker, put UHT milk, orange juice and tonic into the bilges, as well as some beer and wine. Then we wrapped everything in plastic bags in case it should get wet. We filled and tied down the diesel cans, and walked the decks inspecting everything carefully. We set out rags and towels in case of drips. On the penultimate day, we bought fresh produce and bread to see us through the next month or more. *Sunstone* has a tiny fridge. Fruit is stored in open plastic boxes, veggies in paper, and bread is double-wrapped in plastic bags with

Vicky Jackson, mid-ocean – 'acutely aware of the sea and the sky.' (JACKSON)

the air sucked out. Finally, we topped up the water tanks. We have no water maker – water is probably our defining limit for long passages.

We avoid eating out in the days before departure and eat simple fare on board. Too often a final meal ashore can lead to stomach upsets and/or seasickness for the first days at sea. We get a final, long night's sleep. However, we nearly always make an early start to get into the open ocean and the passage routines as soon as possible. The last few items on lists are never crossed off, but if the weather is right – go!

Life on a passage makes you acutely aware of the sea and sky; especially if, as we do, you "stand watches" on deck, in the cockpit. We have no protection from wind and spray in the cockpit so perhaps, more than many others, we are intimately connected with the elements around us. We become "cloud connoisseurs", bird watchers, readers of the waves and swell. We feel the change in the temperature of the sea water, the wind increasing on our faces. We consider the sail plan with the wind we have and for the expected conditions. We watch the sun rise and set. We marvel at the orange moon that becomes a silver globe or a crescent sliver in a blue-black sky.

The 24-hour cycle rolls round. Unlike life ashore, when it is possible to stop what you are doing and go somewhere else, or change your schedule, or seek help, that is not possible

Tom Jackson enjoys a mid-tropical rain squall. Valuable for washing and replenishing water supplies. (JACKSON)

when you are hundreds or thousands of miles from land or other people. You have to cope. Scotty cannot beam you up.

The sailing part of passagemaking is about trimming, taking reefs, rolling up the headsail, changing the headsail, setting up the pole, taking the main down in a blow. For long periods we may sit in the cockpit contemplating the ocean, the waves, the clouds and the sea birds, even reading a bit. Then there is a burst of physical activity. With modern aids, navigation does not take up much time, but we do record the GPS position and conditions on deck, and we make a pencil dot on the paper chart at every change of watch. It is reassuring to see the lengthening line of dots creeping towards our destination! Each day is set into watches and routines. We always use the same watch system; each 24 hours has six watches of 3, 4 and 5 hours.

The 24-hour watch system on board *Sunstone*:

0800 – 1300	Vicky
1300 – 1800	Tom
1800 – 2200	Vicky
2200 – 0100	Tom
0100 – 0400	Vicky
0400 – 0800	Tom

We get grimy. We have never rationed water for drinking, but we do ration it for washing!

Tom Jackson enjoying the fruits of the ocean. On long ocean passages, fresh food is always a bonus. (JACKSON)

We revert to an old-fashioned flannel wash and a head in a bucket for hair washing – but not often. We have to conserve our 220 litres (58 US gallons) of water and 200 litres of fuel, as well as all other consumables.

Passagemaking is about self-reliance. Whatever is forgotten cannot be bought. The food has to last. We do not report into a net, we have no radio schedules. We get weather from GRIB files and we can send and receive emails via SailMail with the SSB radio. So we are not entirely alone, although no one knows exactly where we are. That is how we like it. We have made our choices and it is up to us to live with them. We do have an EPIRB, but we have some doubts about calling for rescue. We have decided to be out in the ocean, for our own experience and pleasure, and we are not sure that we should put other lives at risk to come and find us.

Off watch, we usually fall into deep sleep quickly. That is important. We always build up a sleep deficit with naps of only 2 or 2½ hours, three times a day. In the tropics, with a water temperature of 30°C/86°F, we can fall into our bunk quickly with few clothes to remove, but the bunk is hot and sweaty even with a fan. When in Alaska, the water temperature drops to 4°C/39°F and there are some seven layers of clothes to take off, leaving at least two on, before climbing into a big sleeping bag and curling into a tight ball to try to get warm. Dressing takes 15 minutes or more, with many thermal layers, mid-layer jacket and salopettes, oilskins, boots, hats and gloves to put on before venturing on deck.

For us, passagemaking is about two people, sailing and living close together, relying on and supporting each other, but not seeing much of each other! It is about full moons, big horizons, a starry sky, colourful sunsets, soft-hued sunrises, dolphins playing in the bow wave, a wandering albatross soaring and swooping over the wave tops. But it is also about dark squally clouds, a tropical downpour, frightening bolts of lightning, a ship not changing course. The pace of life is slow. Time passes but is unimportant; in many ways it hardly exists. Days and nights go by. Slowly, a small yacht on a big ocean gets closer to her destination.'

2 Where in the World Shall We Go?

Making plans, and making your choice

Unroll a map of the world, and start to dream. This is how it begins, often with no more than a passing thought, which grows, and before you know where you are you are overwhelmed by a deep and urgent desire to cast off from the shore and point the bows of your ship towards a new and undiscovered world that will lead you, you hope, towards a new life. There is a lot about planning an ocean voyage that is about rebirth, and there are few people who set off across the oceans of the world and don't return without an entirely new view of their lives, and themselves. Ocean sailing can be a profound and life-changing experience.

But that doesn't come automatically. Just because you've fitted out your boat with every bit of kit in the world, spent all your savings on every feature a yacht can possibly have, it doesn't necessarily mean the achieving of your dream is guaranteed. You cannot buy success in ocean sailing; it doesn't work that way. It is as much an exercise of the mind as the body, and that is why, in the early stages, you must give deep thought as to what your hopes and expectations are. And only when you are settled in your own mind as to what you want to achieve should you drop the lines and wave the shore goodbye. The kit you buy and the gizmos you screw on to your craft will not make the slightest difference to the success of your voyage if you have not fully thought through why you are doing this, and where you really want to go.

I have met many people who admit to wanting to cross oceans, but have no idea where to head. I've heard a lot of casual talk of 'Oh, we'll do a circumnavigation…', as if it's the easiest thing in the world. '…and perhaps take in Antarctica. And we've always wanted to see Galapagos. And then there's Greenland…' And on they go in an uninformed and indecisive way, largely unaware of what these destinations demand. It may work for some, but it's doubtful whether it's a good starting point. It's true that many set off to ramble round the world, dropping the hook wherever it suits them, expecting to stay somewhere a couple of weeks. Sometimes they end up in the same harbour for half a season and love it. But these nomads are few and far between. Most

Dreams like this only come true with careful planning – Kite, *in Cocos Keeling.* (JAKE ADAMS)

of us have to fit ocean sailing into the well-established structures of our working and family lives. No matter how hard we try to rid ourselves of shoreside commitments, they are always at the backs of our minds and, unlike the ever-wandering albatross, there is always some kind of timetable to which we have to adhere.

If you are of the sea-gypsy inclination, with no constraints of any kind, off you go. You'll have a great time and most of us will envy you. The rest of us, on the other hand, need to give it more careful thought and at the very top of the list of questions we need to answer is: 'Where, exactly, do I want to go, and why do I want to go there?'

It might seem as if you are strapping yourself into a straitjacket by deciding these things too soon. Aren't these restrictions the very things you are going to sea to avoid? But consider the thought that 'if you have *no* plan, you get *no*where'.

For example, you have the idea that you want to cross the Atlantic, sail to the Caribbean and live the good life there before setting off for the white coral beaches of the Pacific islands. Sounds lovely. But if you don't leave your home port at the right time of year, don't consider the dangers of the hurricane season in the western Atlantic, don't consider the effort and expense of the Panama Canal, never think for one minute how you are going to deal with the Pacific cyclone season, you are going to be spending an awful lot of time wishing you'd dedicated a bit more effort to planning your route. And finally, how are you going to get home again? And can all that be done in the timescale you have set yourself?

For all these reasons, the vast majority of successful ocean sailing starts at home, at your desk or screen, with a notebook and pencil by your side. There is not one minute of this time that will be wasted.

Start a Library

Get some books on your shelf, or on your tablet if that is what you prefer – it's not an argument I want to get into, but for vital sources of information the durability of paper both at home and at sea takes some beating.

You need some solid sources of reference in order to start planning an ocean passage and, surprisingly, you may not need all that many of them – not for starters anyway. What you need to be able to tap into is the accumulated knowledge of generations of sailors who have been sailing the oceans, taking notes, spotting patterns and then handing them down for others to refine as further knowledge is acquired. Some of this knowledge has been gathered over centuries. Remember, the whole point of passage planning is to make it easier on yourself. You can come out of the harbour and point your boat in any direction you like, but if one direction makes for an easier passage than the other, why not take it? You need to plan in order to know in which direction to point your bows, and also know what time of year to attempt it.

Without doubt, the most authoritative book will be *Ocean Passages for the World* published by the UK Hydrographic Office. In 2018, this book (NP136) was split into two sections, one covering the Atlantic Ocean, the other for the rest of the world. These come with a hefty price tag but are available as e-books.

They are considerable works of reference and include weather, currents, swells and seasonal variations. However, much of the content is directed at commercial shipping and in all likelihood it will be the major shipping routes that you will want to avoid.

You will make many new friends along the way. (RUSCOE)

The good news is that sailing routes are still described in detail and this will be your point of reference. By careful reading there is much to be gleaned, and the wind and weather patterns that dictated the routes of old square-riggers still apply today, although thankfully our windward ability is much improved. Bearing all these things in mind, this book is a useful resource.

To accompany it, you need a set of pilot charts. These too are essential for successful passage planning and contain a vast amount of meteorological data, which can be read at a glance once you 'have your eye in' for the way it is presented. They are issued in five volumes: North Atlantic, South Atlantic, North Pacific, South Pacific and Indian Ocean.

A pilot chart will show you wind, weather and current patterns (and ice limits if appropriate), barometric pressures, wave heights, visibility and sea temperatures for each month of the year. How much more could you ask for on one sheet of paper? Across the chart are scattered 'wind roses', one for every 5° section of the chart, from which it is possible to read the percentage of gales and calms, and also the strength, direction and frequency of the wind at the time of year chosen. This makes it quite easy for the navigator to take his pencil and draw a line through those places where he is most likely to find favourable weather, or avoid beating to windward, to which ocean sailors are rightly averse. These are not forecasts, of course, but averages gathered over many decades, and while you may be unlucky, a pilot chart will give you a reasonable indication of what you are likely to expect.

HOW TO READ WIND ROSES

Wind roses are printed for every 5° square on most pilot charts. Look at the arrows that fly into the central 'hub'. These show the directions from which a particular wind will blow, and the longer the arrow, the more dominant that wind direction will be. If you want to be a bit more precise, you can use a pair of dividers to measure from the edge of the circle to the end of the arrow (but don't include the feathers) and somewhere on the chart you will find a facility to turn the length you have measured into a percentage. In areas where there are strong prevailing winds for long periods of time (for example, the Caribbean), the arrows would be very long. In that case, they are shortened and a number inserted, which indicates a percentage. You can now count the feathers, and each represents one force on the Beaufort scale. The number in the centre is the percentage of calms.

However, there are national variations and wind roses can be drawn in differing ways by different countries – the above describes what is shown on UK Admiralty charts. If you are using pilot charts from other sources, it is wise to check the keys to the symbols for each.

Pilot charts are published by national Hydrographic Offices, and by some independent publishers (see bibliography, page 273). You will also find them online (although they might be infuriatingly difficult to read on anything but a large screen) and are contained in some navigational software. Note that all the pilot charts published by the US government are available as free downloads. Whichever pilot chart package you use, taken together with *Ocean Passages for the World*, it represents a formidable arsenal of ocean planning data.

You should have a broad understanding in your head of the ways in which the winds blow across the oceans. These are the driving forces, the engine if you like, of not only the ocean's weather systems but the climate of the entire planet. They are of profound importance and key to understanding why some ocean crossings are benign affairs while others can be simply dangerous.

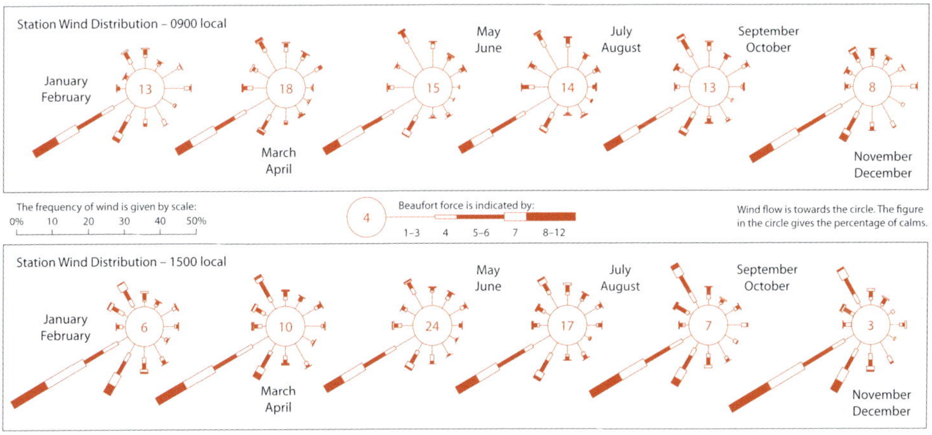

Wind roses provide a good sense of the average conditions you can expect, and are found on pilot charts published for every ocean of the world. (MARK SILVER)

Although the prevailing winds of the world may vary from day to day or week to week, in broad outline they have stuck to the same patterns for thousands of years.

Here's an exercise: you remember those globes that once upon a time every schoolroom had? If you can, grab hold of one – they make inflatable ones, so this need not be expensive. Now, feel the circularity of the Earth in your hands, sense its shape. When you are ocean sailing, you really do have the whole world, or at least its seas, at your disposal.

Now imagine the winds blowing around the planet. Get a fat marker pen and draw the following on the globe.

The Doldrums

We'll start with the quieter spots. Starting at the Equator and running for roughly 5° to 10° either side of the line – depending on the season (see below) – are the Doldrums, properly called the Intertropical Convergence Zone (ITCZ). These present a huge stumbling block for anyone wanting to sail from one side of the Equator to the other. When you find yourself in the Doldrums, you are stuck in an area of low pressure caused by the extreme heat found on the Equator, which causes the very hot air to rise. The heat and humidity, coupled with the strength of the overhead sun, makes the Doldrums an oppressive place to be. Because of the hot, moist and rising air, the Doldrums can produce some of the most spectacular skies imaginable, with towering black clouds between which violent thunderstorms spark away all night. When the upper airflow is disrupted, squalls appear at sea level, often with winds of great strength. But these don't last for very long, perhaps less than 20 minutes, and many sailors choose to ignore them and let them blow through. Although they do bring some wind to an otherwise calm seascape, the wind rotates around the squall in a circle as it passes. If you sail to every wind shift, you might find yourself back where you started, having expended a lot of sweaty effort only to end up exactly where you were. Some squalls bring deluges of rain, which can be collected to fill water tanks. Crews use this as an opportunity for an on-deck shower, but be mindful that these downpours, although sharp, can be very short-lived and the skipper might ignore your request to use some precious tank water to wash the last of the soap from your body when the squall has turned itself off earlier than you hoped. Those who are wise to the ways of squalls learn to catch some in a bucket to avoid a soapy conclusion to their shower.

There are no precise forecasts to be had that might help you with a speedy passage through the Doldrums which shift as quickly as a feather in a breeze, either north or south, or narrowing to a handful of miles or stretching over hundreds. The only principles you can apply with reasonable certainty are that in February and March they tend to lie further north and might be only a few miles wide. In July and August they can extend up to 20° north. The Doldrums vary considerably in width; for example, in the Atlantic they become narrower the further west you are, and by the time you get towards the South American coast they cease to exist. When choosing a spot on the Equator to aim for, the old sailing ship advice in *Ocean Passages for the World* still seems to hold good.

The horse latitudes

This strange name has uncertain origins. Historically, it might have been the point in a long voyage where lack of drinking water forced the crews to throw livestock, including horses, over the side. Or, a ship was said to be 'horsed' when it was making more progress by drifting with the current than it would if relying on a fickle wind. Take your pick.

The horse latitudes still present an easy trap into which the ocean sailor can fall; yet another place of calms and variable weather. They are created at the centre of high-pressure areas – the opposite of the Doldrums, which are features of low pressure. Since they are formed by cooler upper air drifting downwards (creating the higher pressure), and since cool, descending air loses its moisture content as it warms, the air in the horse latitudes can feel fresher – again, the very opposite of the Doldrums.

These high-pressure areas sit in the middle of the North and South Atlantic oceans, the North and South Pacific oceans and the Indian Ocean. Sailing into the centre of one of these is to effectively hit the buffers. You might as well consider yourself parked up. The first part of your planning should be to ensure you don't fall into their trap. It is, for example, because of the mid-Atlantic horse latitudes that a straight line taken from the Caribbean to NW Europe might lead to a frustrating passage.

The Trade winds

We should look kindly on those tricky horse latitudes and Doldrums for they create the convenient Trade winds, and these are the ocean sailor's best friend. Indeed, they have been the navigator's greatest ally ever since we first started to cross oceans, making the world into a place of trade and commerce.

Air will flow from high pressure towards low. Hence – to take the North Atlantic as an example – air will tend to move from the centre of the mid-Atlantic high, often called the Azores High, towards the equatorial Doldrums, and on the northern flank will move towards the lower pressure areas usually to be found towards the poles. But the winds don't take a simple north/south shortcut. Because of the spinning of the Earth the flow is deflected, with the result that we get prevailing south-westerlies in the North Atlantic while the north-east Trade winds appear on the southern side of the high, and these are the breezes on which you hitch a ride from the Canaries or the Cape Verdes to the Caribbean. In the southern hemisphere, the first reliable winds you are likely to meet south of the Equator will be the south-east Trades, followed by the calm latitudes in the centre of the South Atlantic High, before reaching westerlies once again on the far side.

It follows that in planning an ocean passage you must make the most efficient use of what these weather patterns offer you, otherwise you will be banging your head against a brick wall. Of course, none of this is to guarantee that in areas of prevailing westerlies, for example, you will be wafted by a westerly breeze for days on end, for transient weather systems can alter the established patterns. But if anything about the world's weather is reasonably reliable, it is the Trade winds.

Ocean currents

These are also the ocean sailor's greatest friends and are a direct result of the power of the wind to drive the surface water. If you look at a map of the Trade winds, and then the ocean currents, you will find they follow remarkably similar paths. Again, using the North Atlantic as an example, starting from NW Europe, you find the Canary Current, which flows from somewhere on the latitude of Gibraltar towards the Canaries before crossing the Atlantic westbound as the North Equatorial Current, driven by the Trade winds. When the current meets the north-east coast of South America it splits, one arm pouring into the Caribbean Sea until it is deflected north-eastwards by Central America, the other heading north-westwards towards Florida where the two streams reunite, creating a 'river' of warm water some 60 miles wide – the Gulf Stream. At this point, off Florida, it is transporting some 30 million cubic metres of sea water per second, which increases to 150 million cubic metres by the time the stream is approaching Canada. Then, driven by the prevailing westerly winds under whose influence it now finds itself, it travels towards NW Europe, dividing once again into the North Atlantic Drift, which heads towards Iceland, and a southern arm, which continues south-easterly to form the Canary Current, which is where we came in. Similar patterns are seen in the other oceans of the world.

However, not all ocean currents are entirely good news. Fast-moving water can be dangerous to navigate in wind-over-tide conditions, and steep and vicious seas can be the result. Also, where the warm waters of the Gulf Stream meet the chillier waters flowing from the polar regions, these places are the breeding ground for deep depressions, with which sailors are all too familiar.

Cyclones, hurricanes and typhoons

These are a vital part of any ocean planning and you must know the times of year at which they occur, and where you are most likely to encounter them.

They are all the same meteorological phenomenon, together known as tropical cyclones, and are organised, rotating systems of clouds and wind in a closed circulation, born in tropical waters before spinning into subtropical or even temperate areas. The only difference between the three is where you are likely to encounter them. If they occur in the North Atlantic or in the central and eastern North Pacific, they are called hurricanes. In the South Pacific and Indian Ocean, they are called tropical cyclones. In the western North Pacific, they are known as typhoons. Only the South Atlantic is free from these types of storms, although it has others.

The seeds of these nasty storms are sown in tropically warm waters, which give them their fuel. The initiating disturbance can be quite modest. In the case of Caribbean hurricanes, it can be an almost insignificant depression off the Cape Verde islands in the eastern Atlantic, but by the time it has crossed the ocean it has gathered strength to form a storm of destructive potential.

The times of year in which these storms occur are well recognised but it must be remembered that the weather does not read the calendar and out-of-season hurricanes

FOR ROUGH GUIDANCE, THE STORM SEASONS ARE:	
The Caribbean	June to November
Eastern Pacific	May to November
Western North Pacific	June to November
Western South Pacific	November to April
North Indian Ocean	June to November
South Indian Ocean	November to April

can occur in any year. A decent guide to the tropical storm seasons can be gleaned from insurers who will often not provide cover for certain periods of the year unless stringent conditions are met.

These dates are given only for the purpose of back-of-the-envelope planning and much more detailed guidance will be found in the reference books mentioned above.

You now have a broad overview of the kinds of aids and obstacles that ocean weather and currents present. Now, holding the globe in your hand with the prevailing winds and currents marked on it, it is time to decide where to go.

Measuring distances on charts

When you place the dividers on the Panama Canal and wonder how far it is to New Zealand, you have to be aware of the chart projection you are using and how one chart can differ from another. Also, if you punch the co-ordinates of your destination in the plotter/GPS, what course is it really suggesting? And is the course it offers the shortest route? Over small distances, and in tropical waters, none of this matters. Certainly, it is hardly of significance in the coastal sailing you are familiar with. But if you are contemplating passages of ocean length, especially in higher latitudes, it can make a considerable difference to the distance you have to sail, so you need to understand the difference between rhumb line and great circle distances, and Mercator and gnomonic charts.

Mercator charts are a projection of the globe on to a flat sheet of paper where all the lines of latitude and longitude cross at right angles. The problem with this projection is distortion the further north and south you go. The classic example of this is to compare the area of Greenland with that of Africa on a Mercator map of the world. You will find them to be roughly the same size. In fact, Greenland has a surface area 14 times smaller than that of Africa.

Instead of plotting your course on a Mercator chart, try drawing it on a gnomonic chart. To imagine a gnomonic chart, think of a transparent globe of the Earth with a pinpoint of light at its centre. Then place a sheet of paper on the surface of the globe, in our case somewhere mid-North Atlantic, and the projection on to the sheet of paper gives you a gnomonic projection. Your plotter/GPS may allow you to switch between rhumb line and great circle distances and courses and you should understand the difference between the two. In essence, on a Mercator chart the lines of latitude and longitude are parallel and at 90° to each other, making plotting a rhumb line simple.

On a gnomonic chart, plotting straight lines gives you the great circle course and distance, which at high latitudes can be significantly shorter than the rhumb line.

The distances given in this book are rhumb line distances, the ones you will measure on a Mercator chart. All distances are approximate, for guidance.

Determining the best and easiest ocean route to take is a complex business by the time you have factored in wind and current and allowed for seasonal storms. I recommend you also have a copy of *World Cruising Routes* by Jimmy Cornell, who has done the task of digesting all this information for you, but always with the cruising sailor and not the commercial ship's master at the back of his mind. This book takes you up, down and round about all the major ocean routes of the world and it is difficult to imagine a passage that has not been covered.

If you want a taster of all the places the world has to offer, Jimmy Cornell's *World Cruising Destinations* gives informative snapshots that will help you quickly decide if an Atlantic crossing to the Grenadines might be a better bet than the Greenland voyage you had in mind.

But for more detail, advice, and some harbour information, I recommend the *Atlantic Crossing Guide* and *Pacific Crossing Guide* (RCC Pilotage Foundation, published by Adlard Coles). These contain not only advice on timings and passage planning, but useful information on landfall.

Of course, for harbour to harbour cruising when you arrive at your destination, you will need local pilot books and charts, but we are concerned here with the business of getting there, of crossing oceans. As you might expect, software developers have effectively brought together much of the data contained in these books, so instead of having to trace optimum routes with a pencil and hoping you have got it right, software comes to your aid. These packages can do all this for you and some are available as a free trial download. Some require an internet connection and others can be used offline. Some are more directed at ocean racers who will be seeking tactical information as well. Also, there are software packages that allow you to add current weather information downloaded as GRIB files while at sea and this adds yet another parameter into the software's decision-making process.

The World's Great Ocean Passages

You might feel like a pioneer setting sail into uncharted waters but there are now few places where cruising yachts are not found. That's not to say you're going to find the oceans crowded, but without doubt there are distinct parts of the world that draw cruising people to them, and usually for good reason. And the roads that take us there, the tracks across the oceans that keels and rudders have drawn, are there because they have stood the test of time, and one of them is likely to be your eventual choice. Below are some of the most common and you will see also the real-life experiences of those who have sailed them. Of course, like a motorway trip, you can dive off and explore, but those all-powerful winds and currents tend to keep ocean sailors to well-cruised paths and only at the eventual destinations do most people find the freedom to explore. Ocean passages are our business here.

THE NORTH ATLANTIC

This voyage takes in a richness of cultures, landscapes and seascapes. It has just about everything. In the far north there are the wildernesses of Greenland, the volcanic mystery of Iceland. Continuing clockwise, for that is the only way to sail these waters, you come to NW Europe and a wide variety of landscapes, harbours and anchorages that stretch all the way from northern Norway to the hot spots of southern Portugal.

Venture further south and you can make a brief contact with the African continent, perhaps taking in the volcanic islands of the Canaries and Cape Verdes before swinging westwards to the idylls of the Caribbean. Sailing on, clockwise, driven by the helpful winds and currents, the eastern seaboard of the United States beckons with all the variety it has to offer between steamy Florida and foggy Maine. Then onwards to the chilly, pine-clad hills and harbours of Nova Scotia, then Newfoundland with its edge-of-the-world feel.

If you go the full circle, imagine the wealth of experience to be harvested from the variety of cultures and climates you will meet along the way. For the northern hemisphere sailor, this is about as good as ocean sailing can be. And you have the option to add even more interest by taking in the lush Azores islands en route from the Caribbean to Northern Europe or the Mediterranean.

When to go

DISTANCES	
UK to Canaries	1,500nm
Canaries to Cape Verde	800nm
Cape Verde to Caribbean	2,200nm
Caribbean to New York	2,000nm
New York to Newfoundland	1,000nm
Newfoundland to UK	2,000nm

The timing of the North Atlantic circuit is built around a safe mid-ocean crossing from the Canaries or Cape Verdes to the Caribbean. Everything follows from that.

Clearly, the North Atlantic hurricane season (midsummer to late November) has to be avoided so that makes departure possible from mid-November onwards. Some like to make the passage as early as they can in order to arrive in time for Christmas, but that is to risk fickle Trade winds, which may not have fully set in by then. There is a risk of calms, or even head winds, at the start of a passage made that early. Those who leave a month later, even into January, can usually reckon on more reliable and stronger Trade winds. Some advise that for the most reliable winds, a departure from the Cape Verdes is the best bet, also resulting in a shorter crossing: Cape Verde to Grenada is 2,200nm compared with a crossing from the Canaries at 2,700nm.

Working backwards from there, you could, in theory, leave from NW Europe for the Canaries as late as October, but that would mean a direct passage with no stops, which is to miss a lot of the richness to be derived from this circuit. Those who have enjoyed this leg tend to cruise southwards, crossing Biscay before the autumn storms, and gradually relax into the rhythm of the voyage.

A major decision awaits you in the Caribbean for you will now have to commit to either attempting the full Atlantic circuit in one year, or spreading it over two or even three. Many have done it in one, but that allows little time to linger, for once you are moving towards April you should have the American mainland firmly in your sights and you should be hitching a ride on the Gulf Stream, which will sweep you up the coast of the US. Once there, the time you are able to spend is determined by your departure date from Maine, or from even further north if you are thinking of making your departure from Nova Scotia. The depressions that are the remnants of the Caribbean hurricanes will still pack a punch and come at you with some force and it is clearly best not to be caught in one of these in mid-Atlantic, and certainly not in the Gulf Stream, where wind over strong current can create treacherous seas that have been known to overwhelm yachts. You can reckon on mid-July being the time to be looking over your shoulder and thinking of heading eastwards, or even six weeks earlier if you are planning on a Bermuda to Azores passage. Of course, with reliable weather forecasting, you can run and hide when you are coastal sailing the eastern seaboard of America, but once you are committed to a North Atlantic crossing you are at the weather's mercy. Sailing the North Atlantic in July and August is a bit of a gambler's game. Deep depressions are far from certain, and some years there are none at all but it would be a foolish sailor who gambled on an easy passage at this time of year.

Many complete the Atlantic circuit by leaving from the Caribbean for Bermuda or the Azores. Having worked your way northwards, the best time to leave from Florida, for example, would be in May, and certainly before the end of June when the hurricane season starts to wind itself up.

If you leave the North American continent in early July with favourable winds and the help of the Gulf Stream and North Atlantic Drift, you should easily be back in the UK by the beginning of August. Which will be roughly a year after you set out. And, boy, will you feel good.

The classic Atlantic circuit breaks nicely into two halves, allowing for a full circuit to be comfortably achieved within a year.

NW Europe to the Caribbean

This is a well-trodden and popular route. For those with time, there is much enjoyable cruising to be had down the coasts of Spain and Portugal, possibly calling at Madeira before the Canaries to restock and prepare for the crossing. It is also worth a diversion to the coast of Africa, where Morocco offers interesting harbours and their associated cultures. If sailing on to the Cape Verde islands, there is much inventive cruising to be had there, especially since an increase in prosperity and an associated boom in tourism has made them increasingly friendly and safe islands to visit. Mindelo, in particular, offers a fine marina, chandlery and many services.

Nothing about the weather is certain but, broadly speaking, once a southbound yacht has crossed the Bay of Biscay unscathed, there is a strong chance of a downwind trip all the way across the Atlantic.

The popular route from NW Europe to the Caribbean was taken by Donald Tew and his mother, Helen. The story is an unusual one. Helen Tew's father, a distinguished yachtsman himself, Commander Douglas Graham, made an epic transatlantic crossing in establishing a singlehanded speed record in 1934, which was not beaten until the 1960s. It was always to her regret that, unlike her father, she had never sailed the

Atlantic. Her father had, in fact, promised to take her on a transatlantic voyage, but never did.

However, aboard a 64-year-old 26ft gaff cutter, *Mary Helen*, she eventually made the voyage in late 2000, aged 88, with her eldest son, Donald. She was at sea for over 26 days and although she occasionally used a wheelchair when ashore, she was quite happy in the cockpit of this small boat, in command, at the helm. She died at the age of 92, having fulfilled a lifelong ambition.

The route they chose was the classic one: UK to Spain, Portugal, Canaries, thence to Antigua. The boat itself was equipped with all essentials, but few luxuries. She is a deeply traditional craft sailed in an extremely traditional way and underlines the fact that you don't need the latest and glossiest yacht for a successful ocean voyage. Donald Tew writes:

'The first essential was to ensure the boat was in a seaworthy condition to undertake the trip so we gave *Mary Helen* a major refit with new decks, garboards, transom, keel bolts, engine etc. (The boat was built the year Helen married, asking wedding guests for money to help build her rather than conventional wedding presents.) A radar was fitted, an EPIRB, and a liferaft, which I didn't stow on deck because a very large sea in storm conditions could sweep the ship. If this happens the sea will clear the deck of everything. The power of water is phenomenal and should never be underestimated. I would recommend liferaft storage below with easy access. In storm conditions the raft should be stored in the cockpit, well lashed down.

Donald Tew and his mother, aged 89, transatlantic-bound on their 64-year-old gaff cutter.

Charts were bought to cover the likely route and any possible changes. We had three handheld GPSs, together with a sextant and tables. A Walker log was also on board despite the fact that there was an electronic log. A well designed and properly prepared older wooden vessel is perhaps a better choice than some of the cheaper modern plastic boats that can flex. Also, a wooden boat will fare better if an object is hit at sea: plastic may well split whereas wood will contain damage in the area hit. Again, a through-deck mast is probably better than one stepped on deck because if a mast goes over the side a through-deck mast gives a better prospect of a jury-rigged set-up.

For planning we had all the relevant RCC Pilotage Foundation books and found them extremely helpful in deciding where we should put in en route south. The details of ports and their facilities made route planning south much easier.

I set a departure date that was not going to be missed. All tin labels were removed and the contents marked in indelible ink. Eggs were smeared with Vaseline to ensure they lasted. Extra water in two-litre plastic bottles (approx. 40) was stowed about the vessel, thus splitting the water supply into many sources in case of some loss. A couple of two-gallon cans of water were stowed in the cockpit locker for emergency getaway in the liferaft. Many cartons of orange juice were bought to protect against scurvy. Regarding water, work out how long the voyage will take and then double the amount accordingly; you can never have too much water although it will need rationing. The amounts should be: as much as wanted to drink, half a glass for teeth cleaning and none for washing. Baby wipes do a very good job.

When it came to bad weather, I had the attitude "can I deal with it?" For example, being pooped, broached, rolled over, fore hatch and skylight breached, and hitting submerged objects. I had wooden boards made to cover such holes with sufficient fastenings and two heavy weather boards made to fit the companionway doors in case of pooping. All yachts should carry these to protect the dog house windows and others along the coach roof and they should be deployed in gale force winds. I was once caught in an out of season hurricane off Bermuda and they were not used until after we had been damaged. I learned a lesson then.

My attitude is that if you make sure you look after your boat, then she will look after you. Be prepared to heave-to early with bows about 35 degrees to the wind, fore-reaching. After that, you have to run off before the wind, trailing warps in a loop preferably with canvas tied around them. It is essential to keep speed down to prevent running down the face of a breaking sea. In other words, try and get the seas to rise up behind you and pass under you. I would not advise a sea anchor for two reasons: you have to go forward to set it and in very bad conditions this should be avoided. Also chafe can be a problem. If it is going to fail it will do so at the worst possible moment.

In the end, only three problems arose. One was not fitting two copper rings on the mast to prevent gaff jaws chafing, and the second was not checking that we could take a third reef – this we found out en route to Lanzarote. And the goose neck broke after leaving La Gomera. However, I managed to lash it to the mast for the passage south to the point where we turned west and thereafter did not need the mainsail in the Trade winds.

When we got to English Harbour, Antigua, my mother said, "Pass me the log book, Donald." In there she wrote, "At last, all blights forgiven." Then, looking skywards, she said, "Sucks to you Dad, I've done it now."

As for me, it was the extreme satisfaction of doing the whole circuit as I achieved both my aims. I had crossed the Atlantic in my own boat and, most importantly, enabled my mother to achieve her dream.

My advice? Grab a chance and you will not be sorry for a "might have been".

From the USA to NW Europe

DISTANCES	
Halifax to Land's End (UK)	2,400nm
St John's to Cork (Ireland)	1,800nm
St John's to Iceland (Reykjavik)	1,400nm
Iceland to Scotland (Stornoway)	600nm

For the fastest passages, a course should be made that does not risk stumbling into the Azores high-pressure area. Although tempting to sail in warmer waters, the Azores High can occupy a large proportion of the mid-Atlantic at this time of year, and is to be avoided.

Passages from the American continent to Europe use routes north of roughly 42°. Of all the well-planned transatlantic passages, these are likely to be the most problematical with the possibility of deep depressions, fog and even ice. By way of compensation, these tend to be fast passages with a high incidence of following winds and help from the Gulf Stream and North Atlantic Drift. Most sensible people will attempt it in the summer months but need to be aware that the path of the northwards-rambling Caribbean hurricanes – which show themselves at these latitudes as nasty little depressions – often take a route that sees them skirt the coasts of Nova Scotia and follow pretty much a great circle route eastwards, often diverting north towards Iceland, or taking a more southerly route towards the UK, depending on the position of the North Atlantic jet stream. Certainly, June and early July are the safest summer months if you want to avoid these storms.

A passage along the US coast, followed by Nova Scotia and then Newfoundland, is attractive and there is some wonderful exploration to enjoy, and some splendid harbours, not to mention the seafood. But the passagemaker needs to be aware that the Nantucket Shoals and the Grand Banks of Newfoundland are considerable hazards to navigation. The Grand Banks, in particular, are renowned for their fog, which can linger for days if not weeks. In fact, fog is known locally as 'Newfoundland sunshine'. A glance at the pilot chart will also show that there is a possibility of encountering ice, especially in the summer months when, of course, the Arctic glaciers are calving. These bergs have been carried south on the Labrador Current after the spring thaw and the pilot chart will show that the Mean Maximum Iceberg Limit will reach as far south as 40°N. However, that figure represents the mean maximum limit and at this latitude icebergs will be very few and far between. Even so, up-to-date ice reports should be consulted.

An arbitrary waypoint at 40°N, 50°W can be used as a starting point, which would reduce the chances of meeting these hazards on a west to east Atlantic crossing.

Debi Dennis and Jack Markin chose this route in their Ohlson 38, *Iroquois*, carrying with them their philosophy that 'sailing allows one's world to shrink to just the area of the boat, where everything matters a lot and the rest of the world doesn't. It's extreme mindfulness. At sea our position never changes. We are always in the centre of a disc, with the horizon always the same distance in every direction. The delight is that within the stationary there is constant movement and change. We are moving and so is everything around us. Sailing the ocean in a small boat is an act of faith, but it's not blind faith.'

Their preparations were very thorough and appropriate to their choice of route.

Debi: 'We are romantics. I thought I would have peaceful starry nights occasionally, and although I was afraid of them I also kind of wanted to see an iceberg. Neither of those happened though. It was almost always cloudy or foggy. I thought the low-pressure systems that regularly pass through the area might be difficult, but I really had no idea just how uncomfortable it would turn out to be. I was worried about getting enough sleep with only two of us aboard but we surprised ourselves with our stamina.'

Jack: 'Like Debi I had never experienced winds greater than 25–30 knots so I had no idea how uncomfortable sustained winds greater than that are. I did not know if we would be able to remain hove to for extended periods, but was pleased that we were able to do so as it became our primary tactic for storm management.'

Debi: 'To prepare for it, we first focused on the boat. We spent every winter weekend for three years working on her, going through every part of every system until we were familiar with the whole boat. Our goal was to simplify and minimise maintenance. We removed the electric water pump and installed new hand pumps. We replaced all the light bulbs with LEDs. We had the engine, shaft seal and all through-hulls replaced. We installed a chart plotter, wind, depth and speed instruments, a new VHF radio, and an AIS. We also installed a Monitor windvane and a below-decks autopilot. We removed all deck hardware, painted with nonskid and re-bedded everything. We had the hull underbody blasted clean to the fibreglass, then faired it and sealed it with epoxy. We had new standing and running rigging installed including an inner forestay and new sails. Pretty much we remade the whole boat. It was very well built, but it was 40 years old.

To plan the actual first voyage, we studied weather and routes. We used gnomonic charts to plan waypoints and transferred them to a navigation chart. At the last minute we bought immersion survival suits at the urging of family. We prepared a ditch (grab) bag and reviewed emergency procedures. We studied other people's provision lists and then created our own based on what we like to eat, then bought enough for six weeks (we expected to take about four). We bought full length underwear, wool socks, hats and gloves as well as new foul weather bibs and jackets. We reviewed and organised our tool bags, calculated water, diesel and propane usage and stocked what we could carry, anticipating possible rationing once under way. We tried to imagine what it would be like and what kind of problems we might encounter and how we might cope with them.

We put "every hour and every dollar" into the planning. It's hard to say exactly how much time but it was a lot. For the last three months both of us spent probably 20–30 hours a week making lists, purchasing supplies, and preparing ourselves. The month before we left was spent full-time on final boat preparations and provisioning. Many sailors shared their experiences with us in countless conversations on docks, at boat shows, on the telephone and through email. Our sailing library had over 75 books, many of them from the 1950s, 60s and 70s, which were more in line with the vintage of our boat.

We didn't really need to set a date to leave, but we knew we wanted to go once the spring storms settled down, which usually happens mid-June, so we picked a date and asked a weather router to help us choose a departure window. That didn't work out as

Debi and Jack's Iroquois *– 'We put every hour and every dollar into the preparation.'*

we would have liked, but we probably didn't understand how they operate. In the end we just left and it probably wasn't the best day to go because we quickly ran into adverse conditions, which made us both very seasick.

The day we left was a combination of stress, acceptance and then anticipation and this had a detrimental impact on how we felt for the first few days of the passage, and contributed to our stopping in Nova Scotia and restarting the passage after five days of rest. This enabled us to fix some minor problems that would have made the actual passage more difficult. At some point you need to accept that you're on your own and you just have to deal with whatever comes along.

Our first storm was in the Gulf Stream. The waves were the biggest we had seen. Once it was over we were confident that we could complete the voyage. During that storm the attachment for the pulley leading the Monitor windvane steering lines to the steering wheel pulled out of the cockpit coaming and needed to be rebolted. This was in 45 knot winds and 15–20-foot seas. It was good that we had the bolts, and a fully charged cordless drill on board, and we knew where everything was. What could have been a crisis was just difficult and somewhat exciting. Over time, we learned to never ignore any problem, issue or repair because today's task is tomorrow's crisis.

Our great memory of that trip is the feeling of complete connection between ourselves, the boat and the wind and water. That and seeing the land we had set out for, not because the trip was complete but because we had arrived at the intended destination thanks to the strength of the boat and ourselves and the luck we helped to make.'

THE SOUTH ATLANTIC OCEAN

The eastern coast of the South Atlantic is rarely cruised. The Namibian coast is well known for poor visibility due to large concentrations of sand in the air and there are numerous offshore hazards to trap the unwary. It is nicknamed the 'skeleton coast' and described by early Portuguese sailors as 'The Gates of Hell'. You get the idea.

DISTANCES

Cape Verde islands to Salvador (Brazil)	2,000nm
Salvador to the River Plate	1,600nm
River Plate to Cape Horn	1,300nm
Cape Town to the Caribbean (Grenada)	5,400nm
Falkland Islands to Cape Town	3,400nm

But out at sea, the eastern side of the South Atlantic enjoys a south-east Trade wind, generated by the high-pressure area that sits firmly in mid-ocean. This makes it an easy passage, for example, from South Africa to the Caribbean. Many people coming this way are heading home to Europe after a circumnavigation, or heading for the Caribbean from Australia and New Zealand, getting help all the way up the South Atlantic. These winds create an equally useful South Equatorial Current, which flows westwards south of the Equator towards the shoulder of South America, then dividing with one leg heading north-westwards as the North Brazil Current, giving a free ride towards the Caribbean. The other arm is deflected southwards and becomes the Brazil Current, which flows as far south as Argentina before heading south-eastwards towards the Falkland Islands. It follows that a passage from the Canary Islands to Brazil and onwards is likely to have help from both wind and current.

Crossing the Equator

Crossing the line (as the Equator is often called) and moving from the influence of the north-east Trades to the south-east Trades can be tricky and involves a passage through the Doldrums.

Ocean Passages for the World gives advice on which point you should attempt to cross the Equator, warning that to go too far west, where the Doldrums are likely to be at their narrowest, might mean you are then unable to weather Cape San Roque, the easternmost point of Brazil. Remember, this advice was drafted with old sailing ships in mind and this becomes less pressing on a modern yacht with good windward ability and an auxiliary engine. However, the Equatorial Current runs strongly and if you did end up in a position where you had to fight it, you might find you had a struggle on your hands.

On emerging from the Doldrums, which usually occurs somewhere around 4° north (varying during the year), you will be lucky indeed to be met by south-east winds, but more likely southerlies from June to September. If there is a risk that going off on port tack will take you towards the north coast of Brazil, then you should make some southing on starboard before tacking. The best place to cross the line can be debated, but try anywhere between 25°W and 27°W. Once you have caught the south-east Trades, and the Brazilian Current, you should make a fine sail of it down the coast of South America.

Although an intriguing continent, South America presents some challenges. My experience of the crime in coastal cities was almost overwhelming and you will need nerves of steel in some Brazilian harbours. In contrast, I found tiny Uruguay to be as peaceful as they come outside of inner city areas – 'just like being back in Europe', say some. Argentina, although safer than Brazil, has paperwork problems; Chile, although still keen on its paperwork, tends to give you a warm welcome.

Many cruisers who venture into the South Atlantic are heading for higher latitudes. This means facing the Roaring Forties and the Furious Fifties if your ambition is to see Cape Horn, the Beagle Channel, the Falkland Islands and South Georgia. The truly intrepid will venture even further to Antarctica. These are all areas with their own, well-defined weather patterns and storm systems and you should consult local pilot books and become thoroughly familiar with how they work, and how to avoid the worst.

Kevin and Theresa Ruscoe took their Oyster 42, *Sapphire of London*, on a South Atlantic adventure that took them the length of the east coast of South America before peeling off for the Falkland Islands, after which they returned to the Beagle Channel and headed north through the remarkable Chilean channels, emerging into the Pacific Ocean. Their story shines a light on some of the gems of the region, as well as sharing some lessons about preparing for ocean sailing.

'We knew that we wanted to finish our voyage in Australia (Theresa is from Brisbane); other than that, by sailing the long way around the world we hoped to experience the greatest possible variety in scenery, culture and wildlife.

After competing in part of the first Clipper Round the World race, we got the sailing bug and decided that we wanted to do a long trip by ourselves. It then took us eight years to save up and prepare. We spent several of those years living on board in London. We didn't own a car (or a television) and replaced holidays with sailing courses.

As regards planning, there is a wealth of information in books such as Cornell's *World Cruising Routes* and the RCC *Atlantic Crossing Guide*, but we also did our own and referred to the British Admiralty *Ocean Passages for the World*. In particular, there is detailed guidance on how and where to cross the Doldrums, depending on the season. I followed that guidance to the letter and was rewarded with an excellent close reach in the south-east Trades. We also took advantage of various courses on offer to learn a wide range of practical skills (ranging from knotting and splicing to how to fix a head on board!) as well as knowledge about piracy and regulations. We also worked our way through a range of RYA (Royal Yachting Association UK) courses as, to all intents and purposes, we were both very much novices.

We set a departure date that was largely dictated by the need to make it down to the Antarctic Peninsula in time for the short cruising season. In the event, we were a little too late for that and contented ourselves with the Chilean channels. We had been steadily procuring spares/first aid equipment etc over the year prior to departure. We had a little bit of last minute work done on the boat (fitting a bracket on the transom for a water turbine), which held us up slightly. We eventually set off from Jersey and made sure that we had a few weeks there, just the two of us, to settle down before heading towards the Azores. We both found the first few days out of Jersey to be hard work as we were beating and tacking and not getting very much rest. I recall a point about four days in thinking that it had all been a hideous mistake and that there was no way I was going to be able to do this for another week, let alone the next few months/years. On day five the wind shifted, the sun came out, and life was wonderful. Suddenly everything was not only possible, it was exciting!

The Ruscoes off Cape Horn – privileged to spend time in some of the most breathtaking natural environments. (JACKSON)

One task I had not expected was to engage in some serious blind tasting of tea bags. We set off with a lot of tea bags (about a hammock-full!) and with that much tea I wanted to be happy with my choice. I eventually settled on Assam. One late addition to the to-do list was caused by our forgetting to refit the retaining pin to the liferaft cage after a round of metalwork polishing in Jersey. On our next shakedown sail, I was at the helm as, out of the corner of my eye, I saw the liferaft gracefully launch itself into the water. My despairing lunge failed to catch it, so we had to tow the liferaft behind us while we enjoyed the "helpful" comments from a fleet of French racing boats that happened to be passing. That little affair caused a delay of several weeks while we had the liferaft repacked and awaited a replacement canister lid.

With the benefit of hindsight, we should have had the boat lifted and re-antifouled in Brazil. We didn't as we were keen to keep going (we still thought we had a shot at Antarctica) and we thought the state of the bottom was OK. By the time we reached Buenos Aires we realised we needed fresh antifouling but discovered that soft antifouling is not permitted to be sold on the River Plate. So we opted for hard antifouling, which was not up to the job. We *should* then have had this rectified before crossing the Pacific, which we did not, the result being some very slow passages across the Pacific and a large number of jellyfish stings (incurred while scrubbing

Sapphire of London *clicks off the ocean miles heading for the Pacific.* (RUSCOE)

growth from the hull) and very high fees for antifouling in French Polynesia.

In the end, all the research matched up with the reality of it. We were privileged to spend time in some of the most breathtaking natural environments on the planet. We were also privileged to spend time with each other. One question that constantly surprised us after we stepped ashore again was "Didn't you get on each other's nerves, all that time cooped up in a small boat?" The reality was quite the opposite.

Our expectations of officialdom in Brazil had been set low – which was a good thing, as we found this to be impressively complicated. We did not expect much of Rio and that met expectations. For pretty much everywhere else we visited, our high expectations were exceeded. Argentina was a marvellous surprise, the scenery, the people and the food! The beauty of the Falklands blew us away, literally. The jewel in the crown, though, would have to be the Beagle Channel.

There were plenty of times when we thought all the hard work had been worth it. One that springs to mind was when we sailed around to Volunteer Point on East Falkland and spent an afternoon walking on the deserted beach with a thousand King and Gentoo penguins for company. Unforgettable.

The hardest passage we had weather-wise was probably coming back uphill from West Falkland to Isla de Los Estados – Staten Island. We had a favourable F8/9 all the way, then the wind died away before swinging around to head us at F10. Thankfully, we were close enough to the anchorage by then to stagger in. Our highest winds were F12 (twice) but on both occasions we were at anchor. The first time was very brief, during a truly spectacular squall in Golfo Nuevo. The second was more sustained and turned out to be the worst storm to hit the Falklands so far that year. We were anchored off Stanley while all of the cruise ship passengers were stranded ashore and had to be put up by locals.

Don't be daunted by the prospect of an ocean voyage. If you have a decent boat, have prepared her well, and sail only in the safe seasons, there is no reason why your first ocean voyage should not be a resounding success and an experience to remember.'

THE SOUTH PACIFIC

DISTANCES	
Panama to Galapagos	800nm
Galapagos to Marquesas	3,000nm
Marquesas to Society Islands	900nm
Society Islands to Tonga	1,300nm
Tonga to Vanuatu	1,200nm

The attractions of the Pacific Ocean are too many and too intense for most ocean voyagers to ignore. Of all the cruising routes in the world, the South Pacific 'Coconut Milk Run' must be one of the most travelled. Who could ignore the lure of the white sand beaches, the swaying palm trees, the vivid blue waters, the landscape and seascape like no other place on Earth. And also the variety of countries and communities that will give you a warm Pacific island welcome. Surely, to sail the Pacific must be like living an extended dream.

That is true, but it doesn't mean it is necessarily easy. A trans-Pacific crossing needs the greatest of planning given the distances involved and the need for self-reliance. Leaving aside the matter of the weather, there are administrative issues to surmount. At worst you can find yourself interrupted by the demands of complex and often incomprehensible paperwork at some islands, while others might be completely benign. A multitude of independent states may all have different rules and laws.

For this reason, if you want to capture the Pacific dream, meticulous planning will pay off as with any trans-ocean passage. Have a clear idea of where you want to go well in advance.

Your first point of reference should be the RCC *Pacific Crossing Guide*; also noonsite.com.

Remember, the Pacific is a big place and the passage distances can be huge and at times you might feel very alone. Galapagos to the Marquesas, for example, is 3,000 miles. The weather patterns of the Pacific Ocean have to be carefully considered. As in the North and South Atlantic, the pressure systems in the Pacific generally create a pattern of favourable Trade winds and currents. But in some years a complex interaction of pressure systems creates a complete change in sea temperature, currents and winds. These are known as El Niño years and can result in unexpected countercurrents and westerly winds. El Niño years are now reasonably well forecast and it pays to understand in advance what conditions are likely to be.

It is 9,000 miles from Panama to the point where many choose to dive north or south to avoid the cyclone season, and on such a lengthy passage there is plenty of opportunity for delay, either intentional or by accident. All these obstacles can be overcome, though, and many report the delights of the Pacific to be overwhelming at times. But the ones who enjoyed it the most were those who had attended to every detail in advance and were never taken by surprise.

Tom and Susie Partridge did the classic Coconut Milk Run in their Hylas 46, *Adina*, as part of their circumnavigation starting in 2013 and finishing four years later. They crossed from Panama to Galapagos, then Marquesas, Tuamotus, Society Islands, Niue, Tonga, Fiji, Vanuatu, the Solomon Islands and then to Papua New Guinea. Susie writes:

'The Panama Canal is an amazing feat of engineering and to see and experience it first-hand on your own yacht is very special. As you approach Cristóbal, the number of ships on your AIS increases, radio talk is frequent, and you quickly appreciate you're approaching one of the world's greatest waterways. It's exciting and intimidating in equal measure. In the marina on the Atlantic side there is a real sense of camaraderie as everyone is working hard to get their boats ready and source provisions, finding extra lines and tyres to protect the side of their hulls through the canal, recruiting line handlers for their transit and dealing with the officials as required to secure a transit. All the talk is about whether or not you have got your slot scheduled yet. Everyone is excited for the adventure that lies ahead.

We chose not to use agents and did all the paperwork and handling of officials for the transit ourselves. It proved to be easy and straightforward and saved us money.

Susie Partridge adjusting the main at the western end of their Pacific cruise. (PARTRIDGE)

(Check www.noonsite.com for the latest advice.)

After all the planning, our transit went well, and we enjoyed it. Coming down through the final lock and entering the Pacific Ocean was an emotional moment. You know you have made it and you just get so excited as you enter a new ocean full of adventure.

As far as our Pacific planning was concerned, Tom and I wanted a mixture of seeing the highlights, experiencing island life, meeting local people and exploring off the beaten track. We always said our priority was to visit places we couldn't visit easily by plane. We knew some of the Pacific would be expensive, but costs ebb and flow on a circumnavigation, balancing out over time. The attractions for us were exposure to different cultures, seeing unique wildlife and landscapes, meeting people (both locals and sailors), contributing where we could and, of course, the idealistic lifestyle of being at anchor surrounded by swaying palm trees and white beaches – seen at intervals between servicing the generator and cleaning the bilges!

We understood the remoteness of the Pacific and the resulting necessity to be self-reliant. We knew we had to be well-prepared to look after both ourselves and the boat. Key to this was having enough boat spares and tools, the right amount and balance of food, a good medical kit and confidence to use it, information about where we were going and detailed navigational information.

Downwind sailing for the Partridges on a well-planned Pacific crossing. (PARTRIDGE)

We spent a lot of time planning and researching in advance. Much time went into researching the areas we wanted to visit, the best times to go, what weather to expect, safe places to stay/anchor and what navigational information was available. We looked into the most likely boat spares we'd need, speaking to manufacturers of our major systems on what could go wrong to compile a list of spares to carry. We delved deep into provisioning, including what to take and how to make it last. Given the remoteness of some of the destinations we wanted to visit, health was a concern and we took a medical course tailored to our needs, as well as spending time with doctors to ensure we had a well-stocked medical kit that we would be confident in using. (See page 223 for their medical emergency experience.)

We used any pilot books we could find; blogs, articles, the internet. Jimmy Cornell's book *World Cruising Routes* helped us plan our high-level timings, while the Noonsite website was a useful source of information, particularly for entry and exit formalities. For navigation, we used our chart plotter with Navionics, plus backup software on our iPads and OpenCPN on our laptop. Satellite images were a great help in the Pacific as many areas were poorly charted.

One funny aspect was with our fishing kit. We enjoyed fishing but were novices when we set out, starting with a substantial fishing rod and associated kit as recommended by a professional. We ended up re-kitting to a much simpler set-up with just two hand reels and much smaller lures. This was a winning combination that saw us catching reliably and regularly.

Our route is called the "Coconut Milk Run". That implies it's easy and some did indeed have magnificent runs, but most agreed the stories of endless days of steady winds on easy seas were far from the truth. The seas are no different to other oceans in these latitudes. The equatorial waters could throw up days on end of rain and squalls, or days of light winds then strong winds. In some parts the seas were decidedly rough. In fact, we were surprised at how little we used our spinnaker crossing the entire Pacific as the Trade winds were more often than not above 20 knots and it was too risky to fly it. If anything, the storms and lightning in parts of the Pacific were worse than anywhere else we travelled on our circumnavigation.

Even so, the Pacific did meet all our expectations. It's an area of the world where you can still find remote communities with no telephone or television or, in today's world full of technology, no mobile phones or tablets. It's incredibly beautiful and the people are some of the most genuinely friendly people in the world. You'll find traditional values are still important, people respect each other, look after each other and want to be with each other. It was humbling to spend time with them. We knew if an islander came out to our boat, we would need to sit and spend time doing tok-tok (talking), no matter how great the differences in language. We often talk about our time in the Pacific Ocean as the jewel in the crown of our whole trip.

Personal safety was never a problem but we did think ahead and plan, and this applied more so in the remote areas where we travelled. We wanted to travel through north Vanuatu, the Solomon Islands and Papua New Guinea, areas very few yachts go, and indeed in six months travelling in this area we saw only one other yacht. The reason many don't go here seems to be due to security concerns. We did our research, stayed well away from main

The Partridges' Adina, *alone but safe in the Bay of Islands, Fiji.* (PARTRIDGE)

islands with known problem towns, devised and installed a security system on *Adina* and agreed some security principles, which we always adhered to.

Anchoring alone is a risk. We had a deck light and alarm system. If we felt in any way unsure about our safety we would have the deck light on at night time, though this happened very rarely. We never left things on deck to tempt people and only allowed people to come on board once we had got to know them and could trust them. If we had any doubts, we would lock all the hatches when we went to sleep. The number one trait we found in researching thefts/incidents on yachts was people leaving hatches open.

When we had to go to a city/town known for problems, for example to clear formalities, we prepared in advance and would get in and out as quickly as possible, preferring not to stay at night. That said, all the above are exceptions and in well-populated and popular areas in the Pacific we never felt unsafe.

When we arrived in remote places, we would go ashore and ask to meet the chief. We would ask for his permission to stay, then ask if there were any crocodiles (!) and finally asked if we would be safe. The last question would always surprise the chiefs, which in itself was reassuring. Many would ask us if we wanted them to keep children away from our boat and told us they would keep an eye open. Then we would make sure that whoever came to the boat first to trade got a little more so as to try to make a good impression with the village. We gave school kit (books, pens, pencils) or medicine freely to anyone who asked for it. Trading is a way of life in the more remote parts of the Pacific and it was something we really enjoyed as it drove engagement with the locals.

Here are some notes as a guide for others on how to trade in the Pacific Islands: yachtadina.co.uk/trading.

We found that sailing through the equatorial bands was never pleasant. We had to be on the constant lookout for squalls and storms, always reefing early. Winds could arrive fast and from any direction. For us it was the lightning that was the most unpleasant. We had one night sailing surrounded by 360 degrees of lightning, which is forever etched in our memories.

My advice would be to not over-provision in Panama. There are many scaremongering stories about the lack of provisions in the Pacific, but it's surprising what you can find. We bought Cadbury's chocolate, Worcester Sauce, and even Magnum ice creams! The one thing that was hard to find was gas, and we had to cut our usage right down towards the end.

The one thing I would advise cruisers in the Pacific is if you see it, buy it! I once saw eggs for sale in a shop in the Society Islands and thought I would buy them on my way back. Three hours later I returned to the shop and all the eggs were gone. Other cruisers had come through and stocked up, and the eggs would not be replenished for several days. We wish we had sourced a satellite phone in advance for weather; the SSB, while great for radio nets, was frustrating for weather and email.

Our lasting memory is of the local people; generous and caring people who would do anything for you and for whom life is simple and happy. We snorkelled with a bunch of children in the Solomon Islands as they dived down catching octopus, lobsters and clams, smiling with joy all the time. It struck us how we snorkelled for pleasure to see things, but for them it was a garden, a place that supplied food and gave life. Free of the modern trappings of life, people seemed happier. Our favourite stop was the Ninigo Islands in Papua New Guinea. People would stop by the yacht to talk, bring gifts and want nothing in exchange. We hosted people, took them sailing, ate with them, walked and talked with them. They relied on what the land and sea gave them, or anything that washed up on shore. The saying "One man's waste is another man's treasure" was so apt here. When we left, we gave away anything we did not need. The people here made such an impact on us, we left with tears rolling down our cheeks.'

NORTH PACIFIC TO ALASKA

DISTANCES	
Fiji to the Caroline Islands	2,200nm
Caroline Islands to Japan	2,000nm
Japan to Kodiak	3,000nm

This is one of the less travelled routes and there are three ways to tackle it. Starting from New Zealand, you can head more or less north, directly for the Aleutian Islands, which form the westward extending tail of Alaska. This virtually direct route goes via the Marshall Islands and through the heart of Micronesia, and should total less than 6,000nm. The weather patterns can make this a testing passage with the Intertropical Convergence Zone (known as the Doldrums in the Atlantic) having to be crossed, and from the Marshall Islands onwards you are likely to be hard on the wind. Cruisers using this route tend to leave in mid-April.

A more popular route leaves from New Zealand, again in mid-April, and heads north-east towards Tahiti, then roughly north-west to Hawaii, and onwards to Alaska, a total of 6,000nm, which is only a few hundred miles further than the direct route but can be broken down into three passages. The first leg can be rough where the north-east winds blowing off a central high pressure meet the east-going Southern Ocean swell.

For sheer variety, the route via Japan takes some beating, although because of weather considerations the 8,000-mile passage is unlikely to be achievable in one season. You must avoid the South Pacific cyclone season (by leaving by mid-April) but from the Caroline Islands northwards the Japan typhoons present a problem and these can occur at any time of year. July to October is the riskier time. An alternative route to Japan takes you up the western edge of the Pacific Rim, taking in the Solomon Islands, the Philippines and Taiwan. If you are approaching Japan from the Philippines, you can expect a tough beat against north-east winds.

Details of all these passages, including landfalls, can be found in the RCC *Pacific Crossing Guide* (Adlard Coles).

Mike and Hilde Gill (RCC) set sail from the UK for a classic Pacific cruise aboard *Quicksilver*, with the intention of spending as much time as possible in French Polynesia and points west. Their route took them across the Atlantic, through the Panama Canal (twice, as returned to the Atlantic via Panama), and westwards via the South Pacific islands eventually to New Zealand, from where the long haul home started via the Japan and Alaska route.

The true rewards of an ocean passage. Quicksilver *at anchor after a long passage.* (GILL)

'After the delights of the South Pacific, the key decision is which way to go once you get to Australia. Circumnavigation for its own sake holds attraction for some. Going north and east, as we did, we reckoned would provide the greatest variety of culture and geography. Indeed, the alternative routes back to Europe often come across as requiring lots of ocean passagemaking in either the Indian Ocean or the Southern Ocean, often in too much wind, and in the South Atlantic not enough. We had no desire to go through the Red Sea; Africa is a continent we feel best visited by land, and our route still left open the possibility of going down to Chile on our return, should we still be up for it. We had never been to Japan, the Aleutians are wonderfully remote, and we had heard lots of positive things about cruising in Alaska.

The narrowness of some of the seasonal weather windows, especially between Australia and the Aleutians, meant there were limited opportunities to fly home and remind the family of our existence and also meant we had to keep up the pace, sometimes at the expense of exploration. Even so, getting to the north of Japan before the typhoon season establishes, and being able to leave for the

Aleutians no later than early June, may mean going north through the Philippines before the north-east monsoon has calmed down.

This voyage had been more than just a gleam in our eye for some years. We began to make sensible modifications to *Quicksilver* over several years – twin topmast forestays with furlers, Webasto heater etc. One of us had previously done four transatlantic crossings, and the other had done two, so what might be needed was already reasonably familiar.

Planning did not stop the day we left England. It was a continuous process, enriched by the conversations with fellow cruisers, and modified in the light of experience.

The one thing we didn't plan for was condensation problems, and we seriously underestimated its severity. It was enough to dissuade us from going south to Chile.

Problems arose as soon as we left home. On passage down Channel the relatively new mainsail, just given a bill of health by its maker, started to show its age, the Aries self-steering blade kept auto-tripping, the chain-locker drainage got blocked by a shell, the forward-looking echo-sounder transducer stopped working, the heads seat split, and most unusually, Hilde was incapacitated by seasickness, so we made an unexpected stop at Guernsey to take stock. A little further on we lost the mainsail one night from an involuntary gybe when struck by a vicious gale south of Lisbon. Soon after, the main alternator stopped working, the wind generator pole fractured, leaks appeared in the saloon from the teak deck screw holes through the deck core, and several of the spinnaker boom track self-tapping screws fractured. Jubilee clips came loose halfway across the Atlantic, and we lost the contents of one of two water tanks in the bilge. By any standards this was a concentration of issues enough to make one of us almost despair!

Quicksilver *fully prepared for a North Pacific passage – note the awning and twin headsails.* (GILL)

All the effort of getting to the far side of the Pacific became worth it after a magical and fast Trade wind passage from Mopelia, the westernmost Society Island (one permanent resident) when we were surrounded by, it seemed, many hundreds of porpoises just before dusk while approaching Penrhyn, the most northerly and remote Cook Island. Here we spent an idyllic week getting to know the tiny community.

Generally speaking, the weather towards Alaska behaved as expected. The Aleutians were wetter and windier than in some years, as were Alaska and British Columbia, but we were sort of prepared for that possibility. The North Pacific High did not establish properly. The trip south from San Francisco as far as Mexico was much more windless than predicted.

There were just the two of us and we quickly got into a watch-keeping rhythm on passage, so we felt no need for anybody else. If you are thinking of taking crew, ask yourself if you are sure you really need anybody else. There's such value in living within the familiar bubble, where respective roles have become established, and each other's habits and foibles understood.

As Joseph Conrad said, peace of mind begins a thousand miles from land. Life is so much less complicated away from tides, rocks, and (mostly) other boats.

THE INDIAN OCEAN

DISTANCES	
Torres Strait to Mauritius	4,800nm
Torres Strait to Chagos	4,000nm
Mauritius to Madagascar (west side)	1,000nm
Madagascar (Morondava) to Durban, S Africa	850nm

The flow of the winds and currents in the southern Indian Ocean are similar to those of the South Atlantic, in that they revolve around a centre of high pressure in mid-ocean, although in the case of the Indian Ocean the high pressure may be less defined and instead consist of smaller areas of high pressure. Unlike the South Atlantic, the southern Indian Ocean has a typhoon season, which lasts from November to April.

To take advantage of easterly winds on the northern side of this high, it is worth noting that the area they cover is widest between July and September, at which time the south-east Trade winds in the Pacific are also blowing. It is therefore possible to sail relatively seamlessly from one ocean to the other, continuing on a downwind passage. This westward flow of wind again helps to create a favourable Equatorial Current.

As it approaches the African coast, it turns south as the Mozambique Current; this strengthens to become the south/south-west flowing Agulhas Current, which gives further help to yachts transiting to the Atlantic via the Cape of Good Hope. This is an increasingly used passage by circumnavigating yachts since the problem of piracy makes for troublesome passages via the Red Sea and Suez Canal.

For yachts coming via the Torres Strait, attention must be paid to the monsoon seasons to be found on the northern coast of Australia. The south-east monsoon from May to September is likely to give the best sailing weather, and the chances of a fair wind.

The trans Indian Ocean routes are numerous and offer a wide variety of stopovers, including Mauritius, Cocos Keeling, Chagos and Madagascar, and detailed advice on timings can be found in Cornell's *World Cruising Routes*.

Mike and Devala Robinson had taken the traditional route from the UK to the Caribbean. They describe their cruising experience as being '...a life where you're never sure exactly what's round the next corner (or headland). Slowly new friends become old friends and meeting several months or even a year later you slip into conversation as if it was only yesterday.'

They transited the Panama Canal and turned left for Easter Island before joining the Coconut Milk Run across the Pacific. But after eight years of cruising, a dilemma presented itself as a decision had to be made about how they were ever going to get home. It ended up with a crossing of what they describe as their 'least favourite ocean' – the Indian Ocean.

'For seven years we got stuck in the Pacific Eddy. This is the circuit that takes you up from New Zealand to the Pacific islands, then either back to NZ or on to Australia to avoid the cyclone season, then back to the islands, and on it goes. Eventually we broke free and went through the Torres Strait, across the top of Australia, and then across the Indian Ocean to South Africa where we rounded the Cape of Good Hope and came up through the South Atlantic to the Caribbean, then back across the North Atlantic to Europe.

We chose that route because it offered downwind sailing. Why fly in the face of all those years of experience from Captain Cook onwards? We are fair weather sailors at heart and had no desire to make the passages unnecessarily tough on us or our boat.

It all started when we asked ourselves, could we sail across the Atlantic? This thought

The Robinsons' Sea Rover *in splendid ocean sailing weather on the Coral Sea north of Sydney, Australia.* (ROBINSON)

slowly became a plan, then a reality, and that gradually grew into a circumnavigation.

We didn't own a boat so had the fun of deciding on which boat we would feel safe and enjoy living aboard. We gave a lot of thought to extras (from a large freezer to a washing machine) but didn't give enough consideration to solar power or our sail plan. With hindsight, we would have gone for a top down furling cruising chute and a cutter rig; the staysail would have been so much better than a heavily reefed genoa in heavy weather. We both did our Yacht Master as well as a rudimentary Boat Maintenance Course. Mike did an SSB course, though we made little use of the SSB and would suggest the money can be better spent. We didn't give much thought to power management but it became such an important part of our lives.

We foolishly thought the warnings in cruising guides, "morning for the boat, afternoon for yourself", wasn't going to be us, but far too much time was taken up doing boat jobs. We did find we had to actively carve out space to be able to enjoy our destinations. Breakages on passage were rare as we always sailed pretty conservatively, reefing early and trying not to push the boat; we weren't in a race and could afford to take our time. Once we arrived in port we'd have a daffy day doing essential maintenance etc and then get off the boat and begin to experience the place we had worked so hard to get to. The rest of the chores on the list could wait until later.

In the end, apart from things that had to be done for safety, we tried to prioritise the list of "to dos". We had the list of Essential Jobs that would stop us moving on; the Need Doing (but not necessarily immediately) list; and another list of jobs that we soon realised would probably only be done before selling the boat. As one friend said, when in your working life did you ever get to the bottom of the job list? Why should a boat be different?

For weather we used PredictWind, which allowed us to access both GFS and ECMWF GRIBs under way. And when all the models forecast similar conditions we had a fair degree of confidence in what to expect, even if not quite when to expect it. In our experience, margins of error in computer modelling often make it a difficult judgement call whether to detour around a large area where no wind is forecast or to gamble that there would be at least enough wind to bimble slowly through it. And yes, despite the improvements, occasionally forecasts can still become an entry for the Man Booker Prize for Fiction within hours, and lows can "bounce" or retrack back across your path. As we travelled from the Pacific back towards Europe we did ask local sailors and forecasters which model worked best in their areas. For instance, we found that the ECMWF model works well in the tropics but were advised that the GFS model was much more accurate when sailing from La Réunion towards and around South Africa.

Don't cut corners provisioning and preparing your boat; maintenance is so much easier when you are not bobbing around. And before you set off, test every system and every backup system. Be patient, you know your [own] and your boat's capabilities and as skipper, it's your choice when to leave. If waiting with other boats, don't just follow them lemming-like. Share information and learn from others' experiences – we did. But be wary of the "analysis paralysis" all too often seen in ports as everyone puts in their two pennyworths about the weather. Patiently waiting for a weather window is very often repaid by a more comfortable passage and fewer breakages. But don't wait for the perfect forecast. They rarely happen except in the cruising guides. We learned to leave with a forecast good enough for us and our boat.

The Indian Ocean is often described as an uncomfortable but offering a fast passage with winds F5 and above, and that was our experience. There is a danger of tropical storms forming north of the route, and you also need to be aware of large weather systems to the south, which can produce enhanced Trades and uncomfortable swell. Squalls (in our experience at dawn and during the first part of the night) can be vicious. And the crossing is tiring and tough on the boat and her crew. Overall the winds were often greater than forecast, which, combined with the squalls, meant we learned to go into the night with less sail than usual. The passages were wearing, and it was certainly the least favourite ocean of our circumnavigation. The seas seemed far more mixed as weather systems south of our position gave us periods of enhanced Trades and rogue waves, some uncomfortably large and totally unpredictable, that would suddenly wallop you side on. Our normally dry centre cockpit had one or two soakings.

As we approached the coast of South Africa we couldn't quite outrun a forecast southerly wind and we hove-to to the east of the Agulhas Current for 24 hours. While experienced local sailors may cross in some southerly conditions, the dangers should never be underestimated.

When it comes to the Cape of Good Hope, it's a question of watching the weather and planning "hops" down the coast to avoid southerly winds. Most involve an overnight sail and we had a not very long list of the ports of refuge that we could safely get into. As ever, patience is the watchword and being flexible and prepared to wait a week or more for good conditions.

We found locals in the yacht clubs along the way were very happy to share information and their experience on how best to approach the trip down to the Cape and getting round the Cape itself. Put simply, their advice was that you just don't want to be under way when the barometer is dropping! They were at pains to point out that one or two ports after Cape Agulhas would not be suitable refuges if the barometer starts to fall as they will be full of fishing boats.

Running repairs: Mike Robinson atop the mast midway between St Helena and the Caribbean. 'Far too much time was taken up doing boat jobs.' (ROBINSON)

Even if winds are good, you need to be prepared to motor sail if you are not making the miles. You do not want to be anywhere near the Agulhas Current when the wind changes. But if the weather does go southerly and you can't make your refuge, the advice we were given was to get out of the current, either by going further offshore or by trying to get between the current and the shore, which is not always easy. Neither option appealed!'

PASSAGES IN HIGH LATITUDES

High latitudes, meaning Arctic and Antarctic waters, have never been more accessible. Yacht construction over the past few decades has brought ever stronger boats into the reach of those who think of their ocean sailing more in terms of expeditions, and modern navigation aids, such as GPS, have removed a lot of the uncertainty that accompanied a voyage into these waters. Of all the passages described, these are the most challenging, for unlike the majority of ocean passages, which are carefully planned to take advantage of wind, current and weather, these ocean sailors must take it as it comes, battling it if need be. These are parts of the world where there are no reliable Trade winds to enjoy.

For good reason, some describe this kind of ocean sailing as banging your head against a brick wall. High-latitude sailing is for the hardy souls who like it cold but ultimately challenging. The satisfactions, on the other hand, are enormous. You will see parts of the world on which very few others have ever set eyes, you may drop your anchor where no anchor has ever landed before, you may step ashore from your dinghy in places where no human has trodden before. These thoughts alone are enough to keep these high-latitude sailors warm and cosy in their multiple layers of insulation.

Tom and Vicky Jackson's Sunstone *enjoys the rewards of high-latitude sailing.* (JACKSON)

DISTANCES	
(Approximate great circle distances to nearest landfall and given for guidance only)	
Scotland to Iceland	600nm
Dover to Svalbard	1,600nm
Land's End to Cape Farewell	1,600nm
Newfoundland to Cape Farewell	800nm
New York to Iceland	2,300nm
Falkland Islands to South Georgia	800nm
Falkland Islands to Antarctic Peninsula	600nm
Cape Horn to Antarctic Peninsula	450nm
Antarctic Peninsula to South Africa	3,000nm
New Zealand to Antarctic Peninsula, via Beagle Channel	4,800nm

Simon Currin, on top of the world. But crew needed to be 'resourceful and resilient.' (CURRIN)

When to go?

Because these passages are away from the traditional sailing ship routes, they are less influenced by prevailing winds and more by the need to be in each of these areas during the summer period, or at least the ice-free windows of opportunity. Remember, at high latitudes there can be very short periods of night darkness. Also note that in areas that are going to require ice navigation, the melting of the winter ice is a slow business and somewhat lags behind the seasons. For example, off the east coast of Greenland the ice may not be navigable till August, when it will be well past midsummer.

For Arctic weather patterns and advice, consult *Arctic and Northern Waters* (RCC Pilotage Foundation). For Antarctic weather patterns, consult *Cape Horn and Antarctic Waters* (RCC Pilotage Foundation).

Simon and Sally Currin sailed in the high latitudes of the North Atlantic, making a passage from Scotland to Iceland and onwards to Greenland in their 48ft *Shimshal II*, designed as their 'ultimate boat'. This is often known as the 'Viking Route', it being thought that the Vikings made early visits to the American continent by 'hopping' their way across the North Atlantic.

'We always intended to follow the Viking route to Newfoundland to start off our leisurely circumnavigation. We didn't intend to take three years over it and had not previously contemplated Scoresby Sound, believing it out of bounds for a plastic boat. We were made aware that it was possible to go there by an amazingly helpful Icelandic guy who looked after our boat when we overwintered it in Reykjavík and who has cruised these waters extensively. The appeal of this region was the challenge of cruising such a remote area with interest added by ice, spectacular scenery and the dangers of polar bears. It was a very pleasant surprise to find that the inner reaches of the fjord system enjoy an arid climate with long hours of sunlight during the Arctic summer.

Our greatest hope was that we would reach the deepest recesses of the Scoresby Fjord and survive a couple of crossings of the Denmark Strait as well as the ever present threats from ice, fog, weather, polar bears and vague charts. Of course, we hoped to find wilderness and solitude. Ice was our prime concern but the year we went was remarkable in that the sea ice cleared very early. There was, of course, plenty of ice calved off the glaciers and fog in the approaches to Scoresby Sound can make pilotage difficult as there are always grounded icebergs there. Protecting ourselves from polar bears and making sure that we had backup plans in place if our tender got trashed by a bear while we were ashore meant learning new skills and acquiring additional equipment in the form of a large gun and an inflatable kayak.

We have had high latitudes in mind for a decade and so had prepared our boat and ourselves over that period by cruising Norway and the Baltic and by undertaking a six-week skippered charter in the Antarctic Peninsula. Specific plans began 12 months before. Upon our arrival in Reykjavík, our first task was to seek crew that we knew would be resourceful and resilient. Most importantly we wanted crew who would appreciate the splendour of the objective but would also understand if the ice determined that we would not be going to Scoresby Sound after all. A lot of time was spent watching ice charts and satellite imagery and we had to make sure we had access to this information via satellite (Iridium) bandwidth. Securing that access kept us out of danger from both weather and ice.

Due to remoteness we needed to be completely self-sufficient so shipped additional medical supplies, scuba gear (which we had to use), spares and an inflatable kayak as a backup to our tender. Ice poles were a last-minute addition and were sourced from a wood yard in Isafjordur, Iceland. We also wanted to keep the boat warm and found new places on our boat to store an enormous amount of fuel. We upgraded our ground tackle to include a 45kg Manson and 100m of high-tensile chain as well as a plethora of polypropylene floating shorelines.

We had to set a date a year in advance in order to negotiate leave from work and co-ordinate flights as one of our crew came from New Zealand. Sally, being an accountant, keeps meticulous spreadsheets of provisions, expiry dates and where food is stored. All the victualling was perfectly executed. Written lists are not second nature to me but I have many mental lists, including where my tools and spares are stored on board. The latter caused our crew some concerns as they struggled to find things.

This trip really started from Isafjordur in NW Iceland. We had been watching weather and ice in the Denmark Strait very intensively and it was a relief to discover perfect conditions as soon as our provisioning was complete. The beauty, remoteness and the weather was better than we could ever have expected. Much of what we had read dated back to the early sealers who had originally mapped the area. Face-to-face meetings with two people that had sailed there were easily the most useful information sources. Both of these meetings were entirely serendipitous.

We knew it was all worth it when we saw dawn breaking as the fog cleared in the middle of the entrance to Scoresby Sound when we first glimpsed the icy mountains on either side of the Sound. That and the haunting sound of a Great Northern Diver in the Harefjord on a sun-drenched evening at anchor. And our evening cruise down the fjord, dodging gleaming icebergs, gazing up at the sheer, sunlit, 2,000-metre walls. Those walls, glowing in the evening light, were bedecked with glaciers dripping down from ice cap to the sea.

Things did go wrong. There was a sudden blast of a katabatic wind at a mellow anchorage, which ripped out our massive Manson anchor and left us motoring around for much of the night trying to get it set again while blasts of wind hurtled down the slopes above us. I well remember the "grunch" of keel on rock as we struggled to find a place to lay our anchor when at our most remote spot 180 miles from the open sea, where the tidal rise and fall was less than 20cm. We seldom left the boat for more than a few hours at a time. Icebergs and unpredictable katabatics can make a seemingly settled anchorage a dangerous place to be very quickly. Anchoring is challenging and in very deep water.

The only time we lost a perfect shore day to boat maintenance was when the inevitable heads problem happened. After cleaning out all the discharge pipes, we discovered the actual problem was in the intake. This was solved by a dive at 70 degrees north!

We invested a lot of time and effort in getting the best ice and weather intelligence we could. That investment paid off. We never got caught out by the weather.

Remarkable views are the reward of the high-latitude sailor.

We quite often take friends as crew on our voyages. This time we took two crew, neither of whom were sailors. We knew them both very well from our shared mountaineering backgrounds and knew that they would cope with the cold, with isolation and with adversity. One was very mechanically gifted and the other passionate about rocks, glaciers and mountains. The former didn't like my haphazard tool and spares storage and the latter was delighted by the whole experience. If going to high latitudes, make sure your crew have the right personal gear to keep them warm and dry. We have had friends join us with the most fashionable yachtie gear who have shivered their way through an Arctic fog. Find jobs and roles for your crew so that they have discrete responsibilities and don't feel like passengers on your boat. Involve them in the planning from the outset and get them watching the weather and the ice so that they know how precarious sailing to a timetable can be.

And make sure they come for the whole trip so that you don't have to divert to catch a plane connection.

Our advice would be: prepare well but don't overthink it. I think some get so preoccupied by risk awareness they never let go of the shore lines.'

Clive Woodman is a hugely accomplished high-latitudes sailor, having cruised in Arctic Norway, Svalbard, Greenland, South Georgia and the Antarctic Peninsula.

'When we first started to venture northwards in our own 38ft fibreglass yacht, ice was a primary consideration in selecting routes. Arctic Norway and the west coasts of both Greenland and Svalbard all come under the influence of branches of the Gulf Stream and consequently are far more ice free than other places in comparable latitudes. With care, it is perfectly possible for a well-found fibreglass yacht to cruise safely in these regions.

Contrary to popular perception, extreme cold and stormy weather are not the greatest challenges facing the high-latitude sailor. When cruising in high latitudes, for much of the time you will be under the influence of the polar high, enjoying brilliant blue skies, 24-hour sunshine and crisp, dry air, which, although cold, does not have the same chilling effect as the damper air of more temperate latitudes.

You will spend large amounts of time motoring in mirror calm conditions and running out of diesel is a more tangible risk than blowing out your storm sails.

Much is made of global warming and the breaking up of the polar ice cap. There is a misconception that this has made cruising in high latitudes easier than it has ever been before. In one sense it is indeed possible to get to places that may previously have been inaccessible, but in another sense the risks of doing so have never been higher. In summer the ice front is no longer a relatively stable and well-defined line on an ice chart. In its place is broken brash ice, subject to the vagaries of changing winds. What is a perfectly ice-free channel one day can quickly become an ice-choked death trap the following day as the wind changes and blows all the loose sea ice in.

This is nothing new and from time immemorial polar sailors have been aware of the risks of changing winds and drifting ice. What is new is a perception among some people that the risks have drastically reduced.

Planning for a high-latitude cruise is easier than one might expect, if for no other reason than there is a limit to how much prior planning you can do. The Tilman (HW Tilman – a high-latitude sailor and mountaineer from the 1950s and 60s) adage that "Any worthwhile expedition can be planned on the back of an envelope" is never truer than when making a plan for a high-latitude cruise.

Even in this day and age, relatively little is written about high latitudes and charts in many areas remain rudimentary. When planning our first Spitsbergen trip, we spent significant amounts of money purchasing the official Hydrographic charts for the north coast. Many of these were the most expensive blank sheets of paper we have ever purchased, containing nothing more than a large and long scale on its axes but not a single spot depth, contour or navigational feature in its centre. The satellite map for the area contained more usable navigational information than the charts.

A rigid itinerary and a detailed logistical plan have no place on a high-latitude cruise. Neither will survive contact with reality. Far more important than having a rigid itinerary and detailed logistical plan is having an open mindset and the willingness to adapt the plan as you go along, taking advantage of unforeseen opportunities that present themselves, while discarding those that no matter how desirable simply won't happen.

Likewise, a logistical plan needs to be based almost entirely on being self-reliant with enough redundancy in your fuel stores and spares to cope with any reasonably foreseeable eventuality, and a good measure of redundancy to cope with things you don't envisage but will nonetheless happen.

In short, as Eisenhower once said: "I've found that plans are useless but planning and preparation essential." On every long trip we've done, we've never started with the "to-do lists" completed. Inevitably you set sail with piles of "stuff" laying in the spare bunk, just waiting to be bolted on as you go along when time and weather permit.

Modern weather forecasts and satellite communications combine to make it relatively unlikely that you will be caught by surprise by a weather system. However, once you close land it becomes a very different story and in high latitudes weather systems become just one small piece of a much more complex weather picture. Weather systems, while not completely irrelevant, seem to play a relatively minor part. Far more important are geographical considerations and thermal effects. In terrain where glaciers and ice caps often reach the water, katabatic and fall winds can be extreme. During the height of the day it is not uncommon to experience mirror calm conditions in many bays and anchorages. However, as the sun gets lower in the sky and the ice starts to cool the air immediately above it, fierce katabatic winds quickly develop, and it is not unknown for the wind to go from 0 to 40 knots in almost as many seconds.

We did take crew but in retrospect we wished we had stuck to our tried and tested routine of sailing two-handed. In reality, the presence of additional crew caused as many difficulties as it solved. Ask yourself the question: "Do I really need to take extra crew for this trip or could I do it in the way I would normally sail?" If taking crew on a high-latitude trip, they need to be people you have known and sailed with for an awful long time, and even then you will discover things about your crew that you never knew before.

My advice is to just get out there and do it!! Making the decision "Do I or don't I go for this?" is always a lot more difficult than anything you will encounter once you are out there.'

THE CIRCUMNAVIGATORS

DISTANCES	
Land's End (UK) to Canary Islands	1,400nm
Canary Islands to Panama	4,000nm
Panama to the Torres Strait	8,300nm
Torres Strait to Cape Town	6,400nm
Cape Town to Canary Islands	4,600nm

How far do you have to sail to circumnavigate the globe? No real answer for, clearly, it depends where you start from. But as a ball-park figure let's call it 25,000 miles. And how long will it take? Again, tricky question. In 1969, Robin Knox-Johnston sailed solo around the world in 313 days, Francis Chichester in 226 (not non-stop). Then in 2017, the Frenchman Francis Joyon and crew sailed their trimaran all the way round in just under 41 days. By the time you are reading this, they may well have got it down to under a fortnight! By contrast, you will meet many cruising sailors who have spent years getting round; some might have started 20 years ago and are yet to set their bows homeward. A circumnavigation seems to be a simple thing to define, but there are so many variables leading to a wide variety of experience.

If planning for an ocean crossing is demanding, coming up with a workable plan for a circumnavigation multiplies the effort needed. You will now be looking at not one pilot chart for one ocean, but a full set of them for every ocean of the world. You will need a grasp of not just one hemisphere's weather systems, but both. You need to know the hurricane and typhoon seasons, the flows of all the oceans' currents. This alone can provide months of work before you even set off. And don't forget the international politics. Get a sense of where the danger spots are, think piracy and conflict, and devise ways of keeping up to date on these ever-changing issues.

And because you are going to be spending more time on your boat than ever before, you are going to have to start thinking of it as less of a sailing vessel, and look more closely at how comfortable it might be to live on. A few degrees of improved windward performance is worth nothing compared with the ability to be able to rest, sleep and eat in comfort.

Be very careful of unrealistic timetables; things will go wrong, weather will not always go by the book, places you thought you would enjoy you won't be able to wait to get away from, countries you hadn't given a thought to might reveal a charm that tempts you to stay. Have a broad outline, but keep your options wide open.

Chris and Lorraine Marchant made their first ocean passages in the early 1980s, completing an Atlantic circuit in a 27-footer. Now with a Beneteau Oceanis 423, *Gryphon II*, they undertook what they call a 'classic circumnavigation', taking them from the UK, across the North Atlantic to the Caribbean, onwards to the Pacific via the Panama Canal. From Indonesia they returned via the Cape of Good Hope and the South Atlantic islands, eventually to the Azores, southern Ireland, and home.

'We started out with the ambition of sailing to New Zealand where we have relatives but made plans for continuing should that be decided. In the end we became fully committed to keeping going and doing a complete circumnavigation.

We chose this specific route as it felt relatively safe and straightforward both from the point of view of piracy and weather. There was plenty of supportive information from pilot books and other publications as well as the blogs and websites of other voyagers. We felt that this was a route a number of other circumnavigators would follow and this would give the potential for good communications while on passage and on shore. This definitely proved to be the case.

High on our list was sheer pleasure. We wanted to make the most of Europe as well as faraway and more exotic places. Some of the European harbours we planned were places we had been in the past and thoroughly enjoyed, so some nostalgia could be satisfied as well as investigating new harbours. Exploration and challenging sailing were also very important so we decided that we would attempt the unusual when we could.

We loved the experience and challenge of crossing vast oceans by virtue of our own resources and those of our boat; and the joy of deep sea sailing, working with wind, weather and currents on a grand scale, and honing our sailing skills.

We expected there would be some difficult sailing, such as the crossing from Tonga to New Zealand with unpredictable conditions. The Indian Ocean has its reputation for lumpy seas and strong Trade winds. This was a big concern for many cruisers we met who had permanently hauled out their boats or put them up for sale in Malaysia and Thailand rather than do that crossing. We met a lot of sailing wives who decided to fly to South Africa while their partners took on crew for the crossing. Some who could afford it shipped their yachts to the Mediterranean. Crossing from Réunion to South Africa and negotiating the infamous Agulhas Current and unpredictable weather patterns concentrates the mind. We were glad we had a relatively large fast boat to get us through. The possibility

Lorraine Marchant steers Gryphon II *mid-ocean on their classic circumnavigation' – 'High on our list was sheer pleasure.'* (MARCHANT)

of piracy from Venezuela and around Trinidad & Tobago was increasing. In fact, on our outward leg we met a traumatised German family in Grenada whose boat had been stripped by armed pirates while en route from Trinidad. This was unsettling.

When it came to planning, the first consideration was financial. I had to work out if I could afford to retire early; Lorraine had already retired and had her pensions. We also had to work out how we could release some capital so we could have a better boat and also generate more income to cover all possible expenses including items such as health insurance, flights home and contingencies that might arise with the boat, ourselves, our family. This entailed sorting out the downsizing of our property, an aspect that we did not enjoy having to do.

We also had to think about our elderly mothers. Our two young adult children were settled and supported, and investigating the best kit to maintain good communications with them at all times was important. A satellite phone was the answer.

We also had to decide on, and find, a suitable boat that would be a good ocean passagemaker as well as providing us with a comfortable home for several years. We had undertaken several long passages to familiarise ourselves with the new boat and this helped us prioritise our spend on equipment, how best to organise the boat, and make decisions on best storage and stowage options especially for emergency gear.

There were several things we didn't give enough thought to, such as personal alarms in the event of falling overboard. We bought them but we're not sure how much use they would be at night in a rough sea, which seems the most likely time this might happen. These days they can be co-ordinated into the AIS system, which could be much more helpful. Our AIS received but did not transmit.

Protecting ourselves from UV was a big issue. Fortunately, our boat came with a first-class bimini, which proved to be one of our most essential pieces of equipment. However, we quickly realised that a bimini was not enough and ended up with extra side panels to add shade to the cockpit, and a huge awning that stretched forward to the mast for use in harbour.

We started off with a water maker that produced 5 litres an hour, which as time went on we found very restricting. We managed to sell that one and had a second shipped from Germany, which produced 32 litres an hour, perfect for passagemaking unless there is Sargasso weed about.

We just hadn't appreciated the weight of fishing line and lures we would need for the Pacific, Indian Ocean and South Atlantic. Most of the fish we caught were whoppers but we weren't really geared up for this until we spent time sorting it out in the Caribbean and Panama. Fish was plentiful and formed a really important part of our diet when at sea.

We made lots of lists: paperwork, vaccinations and medications required, stowage inventories, updating contact lists, insurances, banks and bank cards, establishing a blog site, emergency procedures etc, etc.

The most difficult thing was the decision to go. Once decided, the rest fell into place little by little. Because we had a year living on the boat we were well organised to leave. It is certainly a relief once you are under way, but still with a feeling that something was bound to go wrong early on and put paid to the whole adventure. That being said, there was excitement and a sense of euphoria that – yes, we're finally off! The most unpleasant incident we had early on was when one of our new and expensive jerrycans split, sending a slick of spare diesel fuel through the boat. We were on our knees, and in some most awkward places, cleaning for two days and most unhappy.

Almost everywhere we went during our six years of sailing made us realise what a great decision we had made. When we spilled out of the Panama Canal into the Pacific it was thrilling, and several landfalls particularly wonderful. However, there are some occasions that made all the planning, spending and persistence feel very worthwhile. For example, meeting our children in Grenada for our first Christmas away. They had never been to the Caribbean and were overjoyed with the climate, the scenery, the fabulous swimming and snorkelling, seeing turtles and coral reefs for the first time. It just felt wonderful being there and them calling the boat "home" for a few weeks.

Arriving in the Marquesas was such a good landfall as it happened on Lorraine's birthday, one of the best birthday presents ever after 21 days at sea. Staggering scenery, rock stacks towering above and plunging down to the harbour, it felt like paradise and the harbour gave us a great anchorage. We met friends we had made elsewhere and spent time meeting all the other yachties whom we had only met over the radio on the way across. There was a great sense of achievement and camaraderie. This is when we all started to feel part of a cruising community.

We visited the most westerly and most isolated of the inhabited Society Islands. The highlight was meeting the only family that lived there, getting involved with them and being given a gigantic coconut crab. Sailing around Sulawesi and the Togean Islands we didn't see another yacht for two months, and this was certainly worth every scrap of effort we put into our trip.

In Sandakan, in Borneo, I went ashore to get good Wi-Fi to send birthday greetings to our daughter and while ashore a squall came through with 50+ knots of wind. By the time I realised what was happening it was near impossible, and certainly dangerous, for me to get in the dinghy and return to the boat. Lorraine was left to manage while we and all the boats dragged their anchors. On her own she was unable to retrieve the anchor and resorted to motoring into the wind to minimise the dragging while boats careered about. She spent a very fraught two hours before I was finally able to help.

In harbour, we divided our time between boat jobs and tourism, probably about 50/50. Shopping, getting diesel, water and gas, dealing with the sometimes overwhelming bureaucracy of customs all takes a lot of time, but these are definitely part of the joy of cruising. You do have to be prepared for shopping to take all day, but visiting local markets and meeting the locals is very much part of the fun.

We didn't take on extra crew and were never really tempted. We have seen and heard of too many problems with crew. We met people further on in the Pacific who had picked up crew in Panama at the Canal Basin and had regretted it. Some boats we met who had crew were having social/communication issues on board. If you are taking on crew, make sure it is someone you know really well and have preferably sailed with before. Do not pick up crew ashore unless you have absolute confidence in references from other yachties. Good crew can be an asset but a bad crew can seriously damage your enjoyment and possibly your boat. Also remember that you are then responsible for them in a way you would never normally be, and some countries require that you can show return tickets for flights home for crew when you land.

I would say to anyone daunted by the prospect of a circumnavigation, don't be. The year we crossed the Pacific a friend circumnavigated the UK – this is a far more demanding passage with rocks, storms, fog, ships etc, all determined to stop your enjoyment. In contrast, the Pacific was like a rather sedate marathon. I think the most difficult thing with a long voyage is to make the decision in the first place, and to do it for the right reasons. Some people think that it will solve all their problems. It certainly will not.'

Some Pacific destinations bring out surprise visitors.

David and Annette Ridout were accidental circumnavigators, given that a full trip round the world was simply not part of the original plan. However, they did plan to spend a few years living on their boat, *Nordlys*, and had arranged to let their house and tidy up their affairs so that they could be managed from a distance. They strongly believe in the idea of your boat being your main home, but still having the opportunity to return to land if you need to. The route they chose started with an Atlantic crossing to the Caribbean.

'We felt this would be a comparatively easy ocean passage, our first, and it would lead to warm weather and waters. We had lists, and a starting date, but this went by the board when we got to the end of the Lymington river in mid-September to find that the boatyard had made a mistake when installing a rope cutter and the stern gland was leaking. This took over a week to put right and was a mental strain! We crept out quietly once that was fixed. Perhaps this was the start of the learning curve – always be flexible and relaxed about your leaving date, which can be difficult as invariably you get somewhat wound up beforehand.'

Annette took charge of the galley.

'I had sufficient food and drink and other household needs for three months away from shops. Dry stores such as rice and pasta, plus plenty of tins. Cereals would be muesli, and we had powdered milk, which needed less storage space. To avoid weevils, all corn-based products such as cereals, pasta, plus of course flour, should be stored in plastic containers. Once in a warm or tropical environment, no cardboard packaging was allowed on board to avoid cockroaches. Our doctor son provided a list of essential medical kit and gave us a few lessons in sewing and half cast plastering (a plaster cast to contain a fracture that does not encompass the whole limb).'

David writes:

'Having been a guest on a yacht where the dinghy got damaged and getting ashore became a nightmare, we decided to go with the two soft-floored type dinghies we had been using in home waters since we began cruising, with 3.5hp and 5hp outboards. This was the wrong choice. Life in the Caribbean showed us that a small RIB combined with a 10 or 15hp motor was needed to carry two people and lots of stores. Why? Because you often have a long distance to go and often over choppy, windswept water. In a small, soft-floored, non-planing dinghy, you will get soaked every time. Hard bottom for dragging up beaches of coral, and for planing, and ability to take a bigger outboard to achieve this plus

The Ridouts' Nordlys *thunders westwards in mid-Pacific where the weather proved less reliable. (RIDOUT)*

larger tubes gives a fast, comfortable, dry ride. Almost without exception, this is what most cruisers end up with. We sold our two English type dinghies and bought a small hard-floored Carib with a 15hp Yamaha and did many many happy miles in it and it added a lot to our cruising experience and comfort. We found that with a small crane at the stern and a harness on the big outboard, getting it on and off the boat was almost easier than lifting a small outboard by hand.

It is important to get refrigeration right. We set off with two refrigeration boxes, each with a small freezing compartment. In New Zealand we changed this to one bigger compartment that was very well and expensively insulated and had no side next to the hull. We had an external sealed water cooler for the fridge compressor. This resulted in small electricity consumption and over ten years' reliability. The cost of this was worth every penny. We elected not to go down the freezer route as power consumption goes up, and if it breaks down you are really stuck.

As we entered the warmer, sunnier climates, we improved our awning arrangement and later fitted a "tap" in the middle to take advantage of tropical downpours and fill our tanks as water maker water, we gather, lacks certain minerals.

We never had a chafed halyard nor any serious rigging problems although we had a failure of a comparatively new block where the sheave cracked due to becoming brittle in the sun. This happened near the San Blas Islands. Use metal sheaves in masthead blocks. If it had happened three weeks later, I would have had to have gone aloft mid-ocean. In the end, I never had to go up the mast at sea on the whole trip. By the time we got to NZ, the old lady had clocked up nearly 28,000 miles since leaving the UK with no serious problems of either the vessel or its equipment.

If you are preparing for a circumnavigation rather than just an ocean passage, your anchoring equipment has to be at a different level. You also have to be able to carry on with various levels of equipment breakdown, and not to reckon on getting a boatyard to help. In reality you can get equipment flown into almost every inhabited place that has a commercial runway in under a week, certainly in under two weeks. But you have to be able to install such equipment yourself.

We found the weather in the North Atlantic to behave pretty much as it should. In the Pacific it was a lot less reliable and on the eastern sides of Southern Hemisphere land masses, eg Australia and South Africa, the sudden changes were a big shock for those of us used to the depression belts of NW Europe. From north-east 30 knots to south-west 70 knots in 15 minutes takes a bit of getting used to! In fact, the storms at sea were easier but the storms at anchor were much worse. Work hard at talking to experienced sailors/locals in each area you go to.

I would recommend taking plenty of diesel if there are likely to be prolonged calms. The worst for us was 8 knots of wind from astern. If you tried to sail, the ocean swell caused horrible wear on the endlessly slamming sails and we did not have enough diesel to motor. Since few of us have the patience of 19th-century sailors, I strongly recommend having the ability to store at least 1,000nm worth of diesel.

There were five of us on board at one stage, and we had a lot of fun, but we never wanted to do it again. Logistics, both in daily life and stores, are hard work. There were just three of us for the Pacific crossing and this was a great success. I had the kudos of being known as the man with two women among the fellow cruisers, but more importantly we never got tired even on the 3,000nm passage. Three is a great number with the right person. A good crew must be capable, or at least a good learner. We would be very wary of taking any extra hand just to make the numbers up. If you do have crew, don't get yourselves trapped into times, dates and places. You can say to friends where you will try to be, but if they are the sort of friends who cannot cope with change, either financially or mentally, then avoid. We met so many cruisers who were having things ruined by inelastic dates.

David Ridout: 'Always be prepared for the big one that doesn't get away.' (RIDOUT)

There is something especially satisfying about a circumnavigation, although we did not realise this till after we had done it. Only as time has gone on and we have seen friends who for one reason or other never actually completed the circle, do we realise this. The unsaid slight disappointment comes through.

Try and join, or set up, a radio schedule with fellow travellers if this is possible. The 0800 and 1800 hour chat is a great morale booster. When I asked a well-known ocean sailor what was the worst thing about passages, the answer was, "the second night at sea". How right he was. When we set off, I had never done more than three consecutive nights at sea. After two you are tired, not yet used to the motion etc. Things get better and after a few days you are in a great state of contentment with your surroundings. A friend who did a similar voyage a few years ahead of us wisely said, "You will find after a few months that you feel you are on a holiday, but strangely you are not allowed to go home." A kind of homesickness. The answer is to make the boat your main home and you will find these thoughts go.'

3 It's Time to Buy

Is there a perfect boat for ocean sailing?

Let us imagine that we have taken the decision and we are going to sail the oceans of the world. The excitement starts to build, reaching its peak when it's time to go shopping for a boat. This is the moment when you take the most crucial decision of your voyage. Choose the wrong boat and you could be embarking on what might be an avoidable miserable experience.

Let us assume you've decided which oceans, and when, and where you would like to end up. You know how much money you have in your pocket and you are satisfied that your sailing skills are up to the job. All that remains is to find the perfect boat for the job.

Remember, this may be the most difficult aspect of ocean sailing that you will encounter.

The choices before you are simply vast, especially if you are taking a broad view and are willing to travel far and wide to find a boat – the numbers of boats for sale in the world must be in the hundreds of thousands. But there's only one boat that's right for you, and the secret is recognising it. You will meet plenty of brokers along the way who will happily tell you that what they have to sell just happens to be the perfect boat for the voyage you are planning – beware the seller who listens first to your plan and then tells you how lucky you are to have met them. Instead, ask him/her what has been achieved in the boat they have for sale, and you'll get a better snapshot of what the boat might be capable of. I'm afraid the words 'world girdler' and 'blue water capable' slip so easily off the tongue that they have been used to death and should be politely ignored. In the end you are going to have to make up your own mind and ensure you don't become the victim of misplaced persuasion.

But I've never been ocean sailing before, you plead. How am I expected to know the right boat when I see it? To try and answer this, we are going to imagine ourselves standing amid a vast boatyard filled with tempting craft. One of them has caught your eye. But is it the right boat for you?

Don't just imagine her in a tropical anchorage. Try and get a feel of what she will be like when the weather turns against you. (JACKSON)

Jack and Zdenka Griswold's Kite *– what most would consider a 'proper' boat for an ocean crossing.* (KENNEDY MCLEOD)

It is worth looking at the idea of the perfect boat through the eyes of one of the world's most accomplished ocean sailors, Annie Hill, who has been voyaging since 1975 and is famous for her 'stripped down' attitude to ocean sailing, which embraces economy and simplicity. She has criss-crossed the oceans of the world, including the Arctic and the Antarctic, and holds the CCA's Blue Water Medal and the RCC's Goldsmith Exploration Award. It is not the purpose of this book to persuade anyone that they should not spend a lot of money if they are able to do so. Rather, it is to underline the fact that ocean sailing need not be for a wealthy elite, and is within the grasp of more of us than you might think.

Annie Hill says:

'Keep it simple, and tread lightly on the planet. To me one of the great joys of sailing is one's proximity to nature, which is why I prefer a smaller boat. I like the boat to look after me in return for a minimal input. Simplicity makes this easier to achieve. When I arrive somewhere new after a few weeks at sea, I want to go ashore and explore; I don't want to have to attend to the "job list". If your boat has "systems" it's too complex, but I'm very happy to make use of modern technology to keep the boat from leaking and having sails and ropes that last longer. If you have a sound, simple boat, you should easily be able to voyage on less than a hundred pounds a week. With practice on less, and if you are really motivated perhaps fifty pounds a week. If you don't think you can afford a large enough boat, buy a smaller one. People have circumnavigated in boats of under 20ft and thoroughly enjoyed themselves.

The most important things are low maintenance, seaworthiness, comfort, and handy under sail.

I rate comfort very highly, but first of all we have to define comfort, which far too many people confuse with luxury. I would sum it up by saying that in a comfortable boat everything works at sea; things stay in place, you can

Annie Hill has sailed the oceans of the world – and simplicity is the key to her success. Note the uncluttered layout of her junk-rigged boat.

Annie Hill's Badger *– 'The most comfortable boat I ever had.'*

always cook, you can always lie down safely and comfortably in your bunk, you can sit and relax at all times, minimal water comes below, you don't have to work on deck, condensation isn't an issue, and things stay dry. You arrive at your destination rested and eager to see what the place has to offer.

The most comfortable boat I ever had was *Badger*, a 34ft, home-built, plywood dory with a junk schooner rig and for many miles she had no inboard engine. She fulfilled all the above criteria. The least comfortable was *Stormalong*, a 28ft Wharram 'Tane' catamaran. The "double bunk" was 18 inches (0.5m) wide at the head, to sit below we had to sit in tandem with about 3 feet (1m) of headroom. You slept in one hull and cooked in the other. She fulfilled very few of the above criteria, but for all that, two of us sailed across the Atlantic and back in her.

In the time that I've been sailing, boats have changed tremendously. They are much bigger, most of them are plastic, and they are ludicrously sophisticated. Anchoring is considered an evil one tries to avoid, marinas are almost a necessity, advanced communications are essential so that spare parts can be ordered to keep all the "systems" running, and they are too complex for the owner/skipper to maintain. The boats couldn't be more different from the yachts that surrounded me when I first crossed an ocean.'

Annie Hill believes there are certain parameters that, for her, make up an ideal boat. Not all of them might suit you, but finding the right boat is about engaging with the experience of others and adapting those thoughts to your needs.

Annie's perfect boat, mindful of her desire for her much sought-after blend of economy, comfort and seaworthiness, is the boat she is building now and looks like this:

DESIGN

- The boat has to be simple to build and inexpensive
- About 3 ton(ne)s displacement
- Hull: 26ft (8m) or less, wood of some sort
- Offshore capable
- Genuine windward ability
- Maximum 2ft (610mm) draft
- Single-mast junk rig
- Full-width cabin
- Rudder on stern
- Outboard engine
- Windvane self-steering
- Room for 120w solar panel on deck
- Watertight chain locker
- Room for 5ft 1in (155cm) dinghy
- Sufficiently robust to dry out regularly on oyster shells
- If flat-bottomed, no slapping of waves at anchor
- At least 5ft 1in (155cm) headroom, preferably about 5ft 6in (168cm) for my guests
- Good-looking – at least to my eyes!

Not a world-girdling, go-anywhere ocean voyager – but certainly a trade wind passagemaker.

ACCOMMODATION

Essential

- Double berth
- Screened-off heads with composting toilet (but a separate compartment is not necessary)
- Good galley (with opening port over the side)
- Spare berth for guest
- Solid fuel heater
- No sliding hatch
- No lift-out washboards
- Comfortable cockpit
- Storage for paint, spare rope, etc
- Bookshelves
- Storage in lockers
- Decent table for eating and writing
- Room for plywood sheet as half-size chart table (it can be stowed when not required)
- At least 2 galley drawers

Would be nice

- Raised saloon so that I can see out
- Avoid quarter berths
- Pram hood
- Water in 4-litre jerrycans
- Athwartships cooker
- Vegetable locker
- Mast in a tabernacle

Have a good look at the rig. Is it going to be too heavy for you to handle? Is it well laid out, like this? Or will you have to spend more money to get a rig that suits you? (JACKSON)

And to prove she practises what she preaches, her new boat is currently under construction, having built it herself. It fulfils all of the above.

But first, do you need a new boat at all?

Let's take as our starting point the old wisdom that states, somewhat unhelpfully I admit, that the best boat for setting off across the oceans is the one you own already. You might disagree. You might know only too well that, somehow, your boat is lacking – and it's sensible to admit that. Knowing the limits of both you and your boat must surely be one of the secrets of successful ocean sailing. But a boat that already fits you like a glove, a boat whose ways you already know, whose internal workings you can find your way round in the dark, is an enormous asset. Remember the learning curve when you first bought this boat, and how long it took you to be able to reef without thinking about it, and how long before you came to know every creak and rattle. Try to remember all the things you instinctively know about the boat you already have, and consider how long it might take to learn them afresh with a new boat.

So before you dismiss this idea of hanging on to what you've got, you need to be able to put your finger on exactly what your boat doesn't have that you think it needs for ocean cruising. Once you've drawn up that list, you might well come to the conclusion that your present boat isn't the right one, but at least you'll have gone through the thought processes. It is worth remembering, as Annie Hill points out, that some people have set off in the most unsuitable boats and had the experience of a lifetime. Those pioneering circumnavigations by Eric and Susan Hiscock in the 1950s and 60s, which inspired a later generation of ocean sailors, were achieved on crude yachts compared to even a modestly equipped modern one: their early trans-ocean passages were done with no self-steering because it hadn't been invented! Sails were made of canvas, prone to tearing and being attacked by mildew. Fridges afloat were unheard of.

Sailing literature is littered with accounts of hugely successful cruises in the most unlikely boats, and the accounts are worth reading. John Guzzwell sailed round the world in a 20-footer. At the age of 16, Robin Lee Graham became the youngest person to sail round the world in his 24-footer, *Dove*. Webb Chiles' adventures got him around the globe in his 18-foot open lugger. Let's not forget that ocean sailing pioneer Joshua Slocum, who made the first ever solo circumnavigation, setting off from Boston, Massachusetts, in 1895 and returning to Newport, RI, 46,000 miles later. His boat, *Spray*, was hardly a handy craft, but it was the one he had and it did him proud. He sailed without a chronometer, fixing his longitude by dead reckoning and his latitude by noon sight, doing this *all the way round the world.* His craft was certainly crude by modern standards, but it was all he had – a good example of the boat you have and know being the best boat for the job. Of course, few will deliberately suffer the privations of some of the above navigators, but it is worth remembering that if you are sufficiently driven to sail across oceans, ambition can overcome many difficulties.

But back to our boatyard and the fine boat that the broker is proudly describing to us. It is standing proud on its legs, revealing everything about its hull. Linger for a moment and admire it, then look closer and start to think.

Love at first sight

The first question you ought to be able to answer is: 'Could I love her?' As we know, love comes not only from appearance but from character as well, and you can have no clue to her true character yet. But you'll know straight away if there's something about her that catches your eye. If there is, that's a good start. You are going to be spending hefty chunks of your life with this boat and if there's something about the sight of her that puts you off, it doesn't bode well. A better question to ask yourself might be: 'If I saw this boat in a dream anchorage, would the place be better or worse for her being there?' You are going to have to row ashore from this boat, gaze at her from the shore and want to feel proud that you own her, and even prouder as you paddle back. If she catches your eye straight away, that's a pretty good start. If you get the slightest sense that you might not get on, walk away. There are lots of other boats for sale in the world and the boat you eventually choose is going to determine how much you enjoy your voyaging. A bit of love at first sight does no harm, providing you remember that love can sometimes be blind – so be careful.

Don't be beguiled by a sporty look. You should be able to tell an out-and-out racing boat a mile off and instantly strike it off your list. Pointing ability is of little matter in ocean sailing, where you use the wind patterns to your advantage whenever you can. The salesman might talk of reduced passage times, which might be attractive at first glance. But aren't you there to enjoy your time at sea, not want to rush back to land as fast as you can? And you want comfort – not only physical comfort but peace of mind, too, to know that you have not only a strong boat but a stable one, which will look after you when the weather turns against you. And don't fall for that old expression 'cruiser-racer'. It will either cruise well or race well, and it is true that for inshore work it might make a decent job of both cruising and racing. But on the ocean and wider seas there are racing boats and there are cruising boats, and the two are not close relations.

Don't get beguiled by size, either. There is reckoned to be a 'sweet spot' for a cruising couple of average strength and ability, and that falls between 35 and 45 feet (10.5–14m). A bigger boat will be heavier to handle and trickier to bring alongside when lightly crewed. Much smaller and a couple will be falling over the mass of gear that has to be stowed. It is also worth remembering that if you are cruising as a couple, then for much of the time the boat will effectively be managed singlehanded while one person sleeps, and a deck/cockpit layout that makes singlehanding easier is a huge asset. If you think these figures are too modest, I suggest you pop aboard a 50-footer and try swinging its spinnaker pole, then consider how you might do that at sea in worsening weather while your partner is asleep.

The hull and rudder

It's time to get personal and start looking at her underside. Of all the things now staring you in the face, her underwater shape determines just how good a boat she is going to be for ocean sailing.

Does she look anything like this (opposite)? If you know the displacement and the length and divide the two, and the answer is 360 or above, then it is a heavy displacement hull and this is how they commonly look. In extreme forms, these can fall into the ultra-heavy category of weighty boats, yet they have done generations of ocean sailors proud. They have a lot going for them, although fashions change and these days they are less popular. You will find many, however, on the second-hand market, for these boats were built to last and there is no reason why an example built back in the 1980s, and looked after since, shouldn't make a capable cruiser for a very reasonable price.

Let's get the downside over with first.

Heavy boats like these will sail more slowly, not only because of their weight but also an increased surface area, which has to be dragged through the water. That is why you hear owners of these boats saying 'she doesn't really get into her stride much below 20 knots of wind'. To try to compensate, you can add more sail area (longer mast equals more weight, though), but to keep her reasonably upright, that requires more ballast – yet more weight. Do not expect her to sail in light airs.

They are poor to manoeuvre under engine and their inability to go backwards in a straight line is legendary. Many an owner has gone grey prematurely when trying to move these long-keeled boats around tight marinas in strong tide and wind.

The plus side, however, is very persuasive.

These boats have excellent direction stability. A lightweight boat will spin like a top the moment you let go of the tiller/wheel, but not one of these. If you have a particularly good example, with sails balanced and in a constant wind, it is not beyond the realms of possibility that you could leave her alone while you make the tea and still find her plodding, on course, when you get back to the cockpit. Mid-ocean with a self-steering failure, this is a useful talent for a boat to have.

You also have to consider what happens when the boat heels in changing wind. These boats should remain well balanced, but the sloping arrangement of the rudder

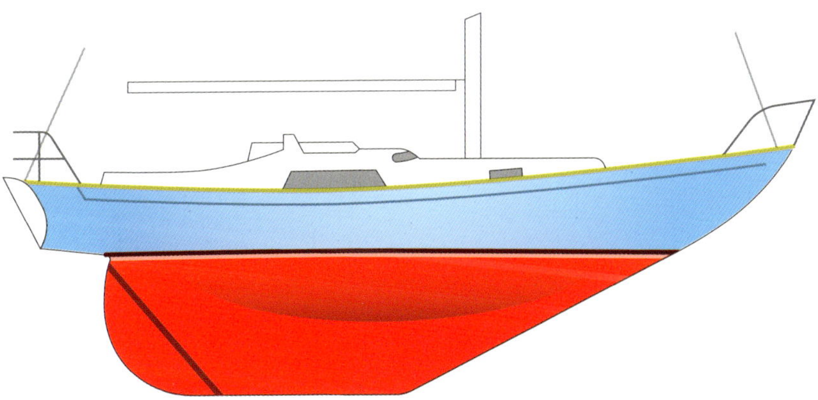

The long-keeled yacht will heave-to with ease but is slower than some modern underwater profiles. (MARK SILVER)

can make them heavy on the helm. But at least the rudder is not going to snag nets or floating ropes.

Hull shape ultimately determines how comfortable a boat is going to be at sea, and the V-shaped nature of the bow, or forward sections, means that she will tend to cut through the water rather than bounce across it. Boats like these rarely slam when sailing through a steep sea where a flatter-bottomed boat would, but some will tend to bury the bow and send considerable amounts of water aft along the deck. These things would be of little importance on a day sail but after weeks at sea such things make a difference to the quality of life on board.

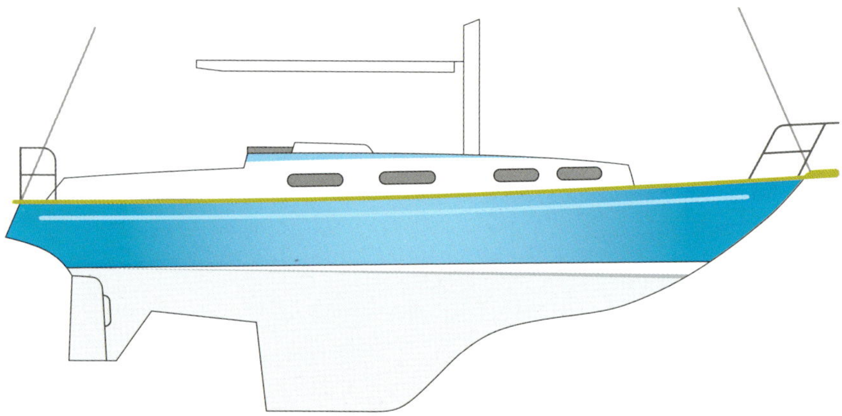

The 'long' short keel. This improves on the full keel design and can give greater speed. Make sure the rudder is well protected, as here. (MARK SILVER)

If she looks like this (above), and if you have done the displacement/length division and come up with an answer at 300 or below, then you are looking at a moderate displacement hull. Clearly the keel is shorter, so to support the rudder a separate skeg is needed. Boats like these, although a compromise between the more stately heavy boats and the skittish racers, do seem to work. They can make good ocean sailing boats. If well designed, these boats can sail with the same degree of directional stability as a long-keeled boat – but check the pedigree before buying by researching the designer's history, his successes and failures. There is real skill in getting these designs right.

If the boat looks like this (opposite), you must think very carefully. In fact, you might want to save yourself the effort of thinking at all and just walk away. I know many long voyages have been made in boats like these, but here we are talking about finding the *ideal* boat for the job.

The keel is short and all the ballast is confined to the 'torpedo' at the bottom, the size of which is limited, and so in order to provide stability the designer increases the beam. This makes for a roomy boat, without doubt. But the pay-off is that the more they heel, the harder they can become on the helm, and the flatness, particularly of the bow sections, means that she will be slapping down hard on to the trailing face over every wave that goes through. At times it can sound as though you've fallen from a height on to concrete, which is very tiring on a long passage.

It is worth examining the way in which the keel is attached to the boat. Keels can be bolted directly to the hull or they can be 'encapsulated'. This means that the keel becomes an integral part of the hull structure and not literally a bolt-on. There have been high-profile cases where substantial yachts have lost their keels. While it would be wrong to discard a boat with a bolt-on keel, it might be worth wider research to discover the true extent of the problem, possibly having discussions with existing owners – who always seem keen to help. You might want to ask your surveyor to specifically examine the hull/keel connection.

The rudder installation needs to be of the highest order because it is unsupported and very exposed. The weight of these boats can be quite low, 5 tons for example. If you are going to load it with a ton of spares, equipment, diesel and water that you

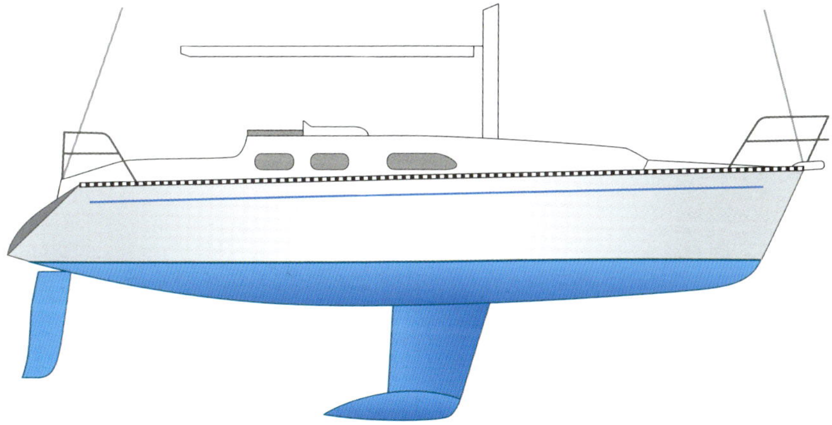

These are built to race and not to cruise. Directional stability will be poor and you could be in for a wild ride. The rudder is very exposed and poorly supported. (MARK SILVER)

need for a long passage, you are increasing her weight by a fifth, which will have repercussions for speed and stability. A heavier boat of, say, 12 to 15 tons would hardly notice the difference.

It's your choice, but for me these are not ocean sailing boats. Many such designs have been built with huge success for the charter market, usually sailed in warmer waters. That is probably the place for them, where their space, accommodation and speed are all advantages.

Centre-boarders

No apparent keel? Or at least a very shallow stub? Then you are probably looking at a centre-boarder.

These come in two configurations in which the keel is lowered around a pivot point, rather like a pendulum, or as a dagger board, which drops through a casing in the hull and is locked in position. Some are simply plates and provide no real ballast; their job is to provide lateral 'grip' on the water. Most boats with plates have the ballast built into the bilges. Heavier lifting keels employ hydraulics, which can make for one more thing to go wrong. It wouldn't be a total disaster to be left with a keel you couldn't raise (in the right circumstances), but one that won't drop when you need it would be a severe handicap.

They tend not to be the closest-winded boats, but off the wind they can be fast, stable and easy to sail. Raising the plate when sailing downwind can add speed. The French-built OVNI range have some creditable world cruising to their name. But the centre-boarder's greatest asset is when you eventually arrive and suddenly find that with a minimal draft, all manner of small harbours and anchorages become available to which the deep-keelers will have no access. You can even go a step further and provide your boat with legs and enjoy drying out on sandy beaches and in coves. These would be the keel of choice for real explorers who like to poke their noses where none have gone before. It also makes for cheap and pleasurable hull scrubbing while your monohull mates might be sailing some distance to find a boatyard to lift them out.

But consider that the centre board has to go somewhere when it's raised and that is certain to be into the cabin. The centre board casing can use up valuable below-deck space.

An ocean-going catamaran, mid-Atlantic, and going like a train. (RUSSELL)

Multihulls

You only have to look around some of the world's more popular anchorages to see that multihulls are on the rise. Whereas a multihull would have been a rarity in a Caribbean anchorage a couple of decades back, they are now commonplace and their numbers rapidly increasing.

One reason for this may be that sailors are recognising that a multihull gives them some of the comforts of home. They are roomy, can be fast in the right conditions and, most importantly, you live life on the level for much more of the time. They also have an advantage in rolling anchorages where monohulls might be dipping their rails under while the multihull merely rises and falls and those aboard hardly notice. There is also considerably more stowage space for the same length when compared with a monohull.

Look at the clearance between the bridge deck and the surface of the water – it needs to be as high as possible. If not, you will get the slapping and banging as the seas go through, and that doesn't make for restful sleep. It also slows the boat.

A multihull designed for coastal cruising might not make the best ocean sailer. Although lightness, and hence speed, is one of the great advantages, if that is the result of less robust building methods then you might want to be cautious. Also, multihulls are great favourites in the charter business and if you are buying second-hand, the specification you require for open water sailing needs to be more robust than that required for day sailing with a secure berth at the end of every day.

Some multihulls are built for sport and their owners enjoy both the speed and the ability to accelerate. These are not necessarily advantages on the ocean. Far more important is a modest loss of performance in exchange for ease of sail handling.

Also, that vast expanse of sun deck, the broad decks and the spacious saloon are undoubted luxuries in harbour. But how will they feel on passage? Can you imagine yourself at the steering position for long periods of time?

People tend to divide quite clearly between multihull and monohull types. If you are a mono sailor and you are tempted, be sure to take someone of experience and spend some time at sea in a multihull before doing any kind of deal. Also make sure you get the feel of the boat in heavy weather as well as light. And be reassured that those who have taken to multihull sailing hardly ever go back to their old mono ways.

While you're there...

Since you are standing in the boatyard and everything below the waterline is clearly visible, it might be worth taking a glance at the propeller. Is it two-bladed or three? Two blades cause less drag than three but might be less efficient when motoring. If it is feathering or folding, this is useful, for even a 10 per cent drop in drag will make an observable difference in light airs over a long distance. Bronze props should be looked at for pink discolouration and possible pitting – a sign of electrolysis problems. If you tap it, it should sing. If it sounds dead, it probably is. These are, strictly speaking, jobs for a qualified surveyor who you will doubtless consult but a quick, if uninformed, glance is always worth the time taken.

Don't start looking for moisture problems, rust in steel boats, or electrolysis in aluminium hulls, or even rot in wood. Leave those to a surveyor. And unless you are a real expert, let him offer an opinion on the state of the engine and electrics.

Is it seaworthy?

A boat for ocean sailing needs to be both stable and blessed with endurance. Stable in the sense that when you are on it you feel safe from capsize, and endurance in that it is simply capable of keeping going and taking the punishment when needed.

In the most extreme case, a truly stable boat is going to survive a capsize (meaning the mast ends up parallel to the water) and come up, if not smiling, then certainly ready for some more. But stability, although it can be mathematically measured and predicted, is often overtaken by the multiplicity of events that occur in heavy weather. For example, the steepness of the seas, the heights of the crests, the ever-changing wind direction – all these influences are difficult to predict and a boat that might be highly stable in easy going finds it can be tripped up in storm conditions.

If you can – especially if yours is a newish production boat – you should be able to obtain from the designer/manufacturer a graph like the one below, which is called a 'stability curve'.

As the angle of heel of the boat starts to increase and the boat becomes less stable, if yet more force is applied to her she eventually arrives at a state where it is easier for

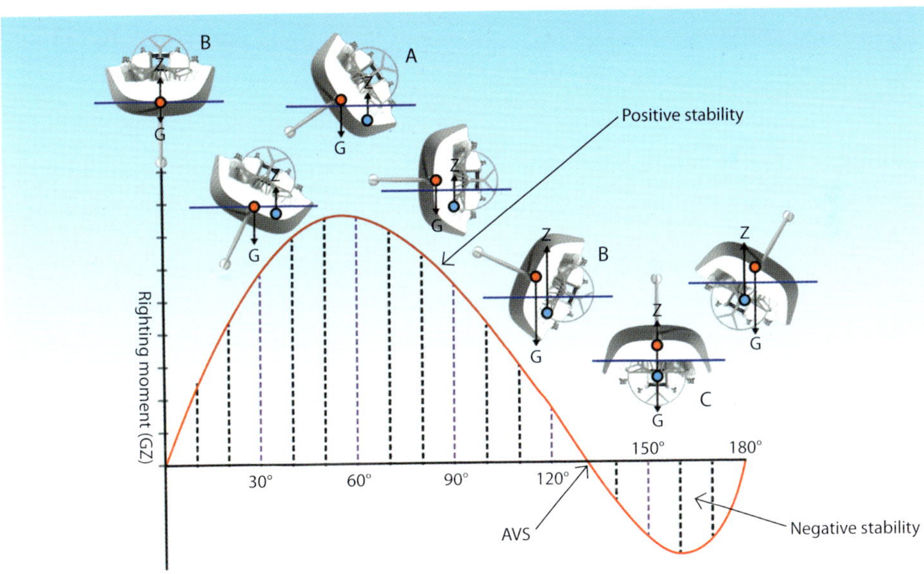

If your intended boat comes with a set of stability curves, compare the areas above and below the line. For a good cruising boat, make sure the area above the line is much greater than that below. The higher the angle of positive stability, the better. (GREG FILIP/PPL)

her to continue rolling than it is to come upright. This is the point where the curve dives down to meet the lower axis of the graph and is called the Angle of Vanishing Stability (AVS), or the resistance to capsize. What the rest of the graph tells you is her tendency to stay that way. If she has a deep keel that provides a strong pendulum effect, then she might come upright quite readily. If she was extremely broad-beamed with a lighter keel, she might take longer to right herself, if at all.

These graphs can be the stuff of nightmares but you needn't lose sleep over this. If the AVS is around 130 degrees for your 40ft boat, this would be in accord with a common requirement of racing authorities. This means that your mast can be 30 degrees below the waterline and she would still spring upright. As a rule of thumb, you can work out the AVS for traditional-shaped boats by taking 160 degrees minus the waterline length of the boat in feet.

If you want another rule of thumb, look at the graph for your boat and ensure that the area contained by the graph before the AVS is large, and the area after very small – then you've got a stable boat.

None of this applies to multihulls, of course, for once they are upside down they are going to stay that way.

How you stow a boat can make a difference. It requires no mathematician to tell you that the higher you stow heavier items, the less stable your boat would be. That's why diesel and water tanks are best sited as low as possible in the boat, as these can carry considerable weights.

Stability is not to be confused with stiffness, which might be described as the initial stability of the boat, or more technically the force required to heel her the first degree. The easiest way to assess, if not measure, this is to wait till she's launched, stand on the pontoon, place one foot on the toerail and pull yourself aboard by the shrouds. How much did she dip? Hardly at all? A good, stiff boat, then. Did she bend like a straw in the wind, and did the person struggling in the galley tell you to tread more carefully? Then it's probably a more tender boat than you need for ocean cruising. Leave that one to the racing boys.

Let's go on deck

There's no point trying to second-guess what a surveyor might say about cracks or corrosion or other obvious deficiencies that could set alarm bells ringing. Serious-looking blemishes can be trivial and easily remedied, while microscopic spots of corrosion can be hiding major failures. Determining which is which is a job for professionals. Your job is to sit in the cockpit, behind the wheel or at the tiller, and imagine yourself sitting there in all the conditions you expect to be facing in this boat.

If you are bound for the tropics, is there shade from the sun or an easy way of providing it? If you're set on high latitudes, is there protection from cold winters and chillier seas? What's the visibility like from where you are sitting? Does everything come to hand as you would like it, such as instruments and winches? If you were to shout to someone down below, would they hear you or would you have to get up and move? In other words, do you get the feeling that the cockpit of this boat fits you like a glove, or is it more like a squeaky pair of shoes that will forever irritate? You are going to be spending a lot of time sitting here, in good times and in bad. If you feel uncomfortable about any aspect of it that can't be easily and economically changed, then you might want to look elsewhere.

Two other things to look at while you're strolling the deck. We will come to rigs later, but glance quickly up at the mast and see how far back the spreaders are swept. Swept-back spreaders have been described as a modern curse and the result of a fashion for fractional rig where the forestay is not attached to the masthead but some distance below it. To provide full support over the entire length of the mast requires some backward pull by the shrouds, achieved by allowing the spreaders to come aft. It doesn't make for a weaker rig, but in ocean sailing where more time is spent off the wind than on it, you can end up sailing several thousand miles with the mainsail rubbing hard up against the spreaders. If you haul the mainsail in, you are spoiling the balance of the boat, which doesn't help your sailing either.

While you are near the mast, grab the main halyard and feel it in your hand to get an idea of how heavy the gear might be. Does it feel as though this boat could be managed by the number of people you intend to sail with? If it's just a couple, could the two of you work this boat in all weathers? Have a look at the size of the winches and give them a swing to satisfy yourself.

And take a look at the anchoring arrangements. Do they look well thought out and could the anchor/s be easily deployed and retrieved? Does the anchor chain stow of its own accord below decks? Ocean sailing often ends up with destination anchoring and anchors need to be able to be dropped and lifted with the minimum of fuss and energy. There's a lot to be said for simple systems on long-distance boats. If this boat appears to have unnecessary complexity, you might find it makes life difficult for you.

Let's go below. And here, again, simplicity is a great virtue. This is especially so when it comes to systems such as engines and electrics. Boatbuilders, like software designers, love to cram as many 'features' as they can into a boat, but many of them are nothing more than distractions. A simple switchboard should not imply a crudely built boat – quite the reverse; it might mean more care than usual has been given to the planning of it. Likewise the engine space, which should not look as though it is an intricate working model of a lunar landing module. Everything should be clearly visible and easily accessible. Here, particularly, look for redundancy, which is a useful ingredient in a boat, especially in the fuel department. In the event of a filter blockage or airlock, could you quickly and easily fix it? Perhaps not, and it might only be a few hours' work for an engineer to rearrange things, so consider it.

On the subject of engines, ask about the tankage. You may set off with the intention of sailing all the way there but sooner or later you are going to burn some diesel and, eventually, need to refuel. The refuelling interval is determined by the size of the tankage. If you have a rough idea of the engine's fuel consumption you can easily work out how long a full tank will last. For a decent-sized ocean-going boat it is not excessive to be able to carry enough fuel to motor for a thousand miles. If you're looking at the tank, see if there is a convenient inspection hatch and a means of draining water from the sump. Most diesel engine problems are due to contaminated fuel, which often calls for tanks to be cleaned. The easier the access, the better you are going to be able to do that.

Equally, check the water tankage. Even if you plan to carry a water maker, the bigger the water tanks the better. The average size tank across a recent transatlantic fleet was 500 litres, although most yachts carried extra supplies in bottles – upwards of 150 litres on some boats – despite being fitted with water makers, which can be temperamental.

Now look around the cabin of this boat. Did you have to switch all the lights on before you could see a thing? Dark interiors, more common on older wooden boats where varnished mahogany was the fashion, can easily become claustrophobic if not enough light gets below.

There can never be too many grab handles. The current fashion is for boats to provide enough open space in their cabins to hold a dance – yacht cabin meets Manhattan apartment seems to be the aim of a lot of current designers, which is desirable in a charter boat where much time will be spent alongside, and less time at sea. But the ocean sailor is, sooner or later, going to have to cling on for dear life and needs good grabs to be able to do that. Cabin steps need to be designed and installed in such a way that they can be scaled when the boat is leaning at crazy angles. If you don't see enough grabs, budget to have more fixed. It is worth seeing how the cook can be made safe in the galley. We will come to galleys later.

Stowage is vital for long-term sailing. Some designers provide cavernous lockers, others will divide them into smaller units. There are pros and cons for each. If you want to bring a rubber dinghy below decks while on passage, then a cave locker is a blessing. But if you want a dry little corner for the sextant, a neat little cupboard easily reached is what you want. A decent boat will have lockers large and small. By now you should have an idea of the amount of kit you'll want to be bringing with you – make sure it fits. That applies to cockpit lockers as well. These are the places where things get chucked when you've nowhere else to put them – fenders, warps, boathooks, buckets and all the other bits and pieces that you 'will need one day'.

Boats need air through them. It doesn't matter if you are in the tropics or the ice, a passage of air through a boat keeps it sweet and dry and dispels that 'bottled-up' feeling that some boats have, so count the hatches, how they open, how they secure in heavy weather, and will they give you ventilation in the Trade winds even when green water is coming down the deck?

While on deck, have a good look at the hatches. In tropical waters, you can't have too much ventilation. (RUSSELL)

After all that, it's time to lie down. Probably the most important of all the below-deck examinations you need to carry out requires you to go to bed. Kick your shoes off and lie down on each and every bunk, including forward and stern cabin, if there is one. Of all the risks that can overtake the ocean sailor, tiredness comes at the top of the list. It can be exhausting at times and if you are not able to get proper rest when you need it then you are putting yourself, your crew and your boat in danger. The bunks should be long enough for the tallest person in the crew to be able to stretch out full length, and be broad enough to be comfortable so that you don't feel precariously balanced. Then look at the arrangements for keeping you in your bunk in bad weather. A boat that is not equipped with lee cloths or lee boards has never crossed oceans, no matter what the enthusiastic seller might tell you.

And now we must return to where we began, with the question: do you think you can love this boat? Boat owning is a true relationship, and like all relationships it has its ups and downs. But even after you've been through a boat with a fine-tooth comb and found everything in order, but for some reason you still feel uneasy, then it's probably because it's not the boat for you. You can go into a boat with a cool head but keeping the heart and the instinct under control is just as important.

Boat owning is a true relationship – you know when you have found the one for you. (CHARNLEY)

Have these thoughts in mind:

- Pointing ability is not so important. Ocean sailors choose their routes to maximise downwind sailing.
- Don't get hung up on passage times – comfort matters more.
- Long-keeled traditional boats have a narrower beam, and don't have the space of the flat-floored boat. But the motion at sea is much easier. They have more grip on the water and less chance of broach. They don't slam upwind, and can heave-to well.
- Short-keeled boats are an attempt to blend racing with cruising yachts, and both suffer.
- Spade rudders, which hang independently with nothing to protect their leading edge, can be vulnerable. But the vertical trailing edge makes them an asset when moving under engine in harbours and marinas as they give better control when going astern.
- Keels that are bolted on are more vulnerable and you should check after every grounding. Check the bilges to see if the keel bolts are easily accessible. Bulb keels, where the majority of the weight is concentrated in a torpedo-shaped structure at the bottom of the keel to create the maximum amount of leverage, are more prone to picking up lines and nets.
- Don't buy a boat that you don't think will heave-to.
- Does the deck have good handholds, and how easy will it be to work at the mast?
- You need strong deck cleats and plenty of them.
- The bow roller needs to be able to carry two anchors.
- Below, check for handholds and imagine yourself trying to walk the length of the cabin safely in a gale.
- How is the storage organised? Lockers need to be in many shapes and sizes, and plenty of them.
- How comfortable is the watch-keeping position? Imagine it in all weathers. Also, is the chart table workable in all conditions and at all angles of heel?
- Are there enough hatches to provide a good airflow in good weather, and can they be quickly and easily secured in bad?
- Check that the chain will stow easily and the anchor can be retrieved by one person.
- If you have any doubts about the anchor windlass, buy a new one and never regret it.
- Go for the largest diesel and water tankage you can – the water maker will break down.
- Be able to afford to buy it, maintain it, and pay the inevitable maintenance bills along the way.

And now leave the rest to the surveyor to poke around the hidden corners and let him assess the amount of wear and tear, and how much needs to be renewed or upgraded – it will be far more than you imagined. Then read his report carefully. Always be prepared to walk away – there are plenty of good boats in the world and the next one you look at might be perfect.

4 The Boats They Chose

There are any number of craft in which you can go offshore sailing

You can cross an ocean on a basic boat, an ordinary boat, a luxury yacht or a multihull. You might choose a steel yacht, a traditional gaff rig, a boat with unstayed masts, or a motorboat. There are any number of craft in which you can go offshore sailing.

Let me guess – you're still bewildered by the vast number of boats out there and uncertain which of them has your name on it. But there's the added complication of the rig and what kind of sail plan works best for ocean cruising. The more you look into it, the more rigs you might come across that you have no experience of. There are as many ways to sail the oceans of the world as there are days in the year and the secret is finding the one that suits you. But within the three great cruising clubs, the RCC, OCC and CCA, you will find just about every rig under the sun and every possible combination of masts and sails that have wafted its members around the globe.

There are few people more supportive of others than the cruising community and you only have to come alongside another boat or sit next to a sailor in a bar and raise the question of anchors/batteries/rudders/ self-steering – the list is endless – and several hours later you'll be coming away with enough opinions to keep you awake for the rest of the night. Some of it, of course, might be best ignored, and the knack lies in deciding what to cast aside and what to cling on to. The opinions expressed here you can rely on, even when they differ, because often there are no rights and wrongs.

I've broken down the choice into nine categories. You could split it further but my guess is that the boat you are looking for is going to fall into one of these on account of either style, cost or simply desire.

The basic boat

This is the one for those who, through lack of cash or a wish to shun material obsessions, choose a modest boat and make the best of it. It might be small and affordable, or an elderly boat requiring work and going cheap. Beware, though, of the trap fallen into by many, which is to buy a wreck thinking it will take a couple of years to sort out, only to find that a decade later you still haven't even started on caulking the seams. Ocean sailing has to begin on the water and it's not sailing if you're still in the boatyard.

The ones who choose this style of budget-conscious ocean sailing will not require a fridge, air conditioning, water makers, or any of the trappings that those further up the scale aspire to. In fact, some might sail without any kind of electrics, relying on non-rechargeable batteries to power a pocket GPS, for even the hardiest will not sail without one of those these days. I know of an adventurer who set off for Cape Horn and back with only a pocket GPS. He switched it on once every day at noon and fixed his position on the chart, having no need to know where he was every minute of the day. As a result, he got from the Falkland Islands to the UK on one set of batteries.

Max Campbell prepares his basic boat for an ocean crossing – it's a no-frills adventure.

Self-steering will be driven by the no-cost wind. Engines might be shunned. Fresh food will have to be fished for. This is the most pared-down ocean experience you can have and, some would argue, the most intense.

Those who like it this way can often be at the far ends of the age spectrum, although not exclusively. Youthful ambition will overcome all minor obstacles, such as comfort, in favour of the satisfaction of the adventure. At the other end of the scale, towards the end of a working life when new freedoms appear, then that might be the time you choose to cast off. If funds are limited, the cut-down approach suits them perfectly. The world is littered with harbours that, for one reason or another, seem to be at the crossroads of the world's great cruising routes. And in each of them you will find someone who fits into these categories, and most likely they will become the best of friends because their philosophy is the same. The love for the ocean comes first and makes up for any discomfort they might suffer along the way. You might argue that this makes their achievement all the greater, and there is some force in this.

Here's an example of a simple, low-budget approach to getting across the Atlantic. A youthful Max Campbell set off from Europe to the Caribbean in his elderly wooden sloop, *Flying Cloud*, together with his mate, Harry. In his account of his voyage, he writes:

'We had loaded my 22ft sloop *Flying Cloud* with surfboards, a foldaway bicycle, two pasties each and a pint of milk, and set sail for Brittany looking for nothing more than an adventure. This was our gap year. For the first time we had no commitments to work or education, and the freedom was overwhelming. And what better way to travel than a small sailing boat? We were transient, able to make a home wherever we dropped our anchor, and always had the reassurance of a warm bed and a hot meal. For me, as a means of travel, it made sense.

In Portugal, Harry succumbed to a girl with a van. It was an emotional goodbye, and initially I felt lonely and slightly dispirited at the thought of no longer having my best friend around to share conversation and boost morale. However, the feeling quickly passed as I became distracted by my new offbeat clique of fellow singlehanders. Harry was replaced with a bungee attached to the tiller – the ultimate short-term self-steering system.

While on the Cape Verde islands off the African coast, and after filling my lockers with provisions, I lubed up my self-steering gear, scrubbed below the waterline, and sailed out of Mindelo harbour. The wind howled in the rigging and I flew only my small jib. I

Flying Cloud *leaves home, bound for an Atlantic crossing – everything Max Campbell needs, but no more. Ocean sailing at its most basic level.*

was confident and felt no feelings of fear or nervousness, just happiness, and excitement. I wanted adventure, I wanted challenge, and I wanted to push myself. This was the trip that I had been planning for so long. It felt so good to make it happen.

In the first week, I developed a daily routine. In the mornings, the sun would rise through the companionway on to my squinting face. I always woke in a positive mood with my entire world contained in this tiny space. I got out of bed and scanned the horizon but changes in conditions were rare. Occasionally I had to climb on to the foredeck to change the headsails. Back in the cabin, I played music while boiling water on the paraffin stove, then drank tea in the cockpit under the morning sun.

With just 200 miles to go, while priming the paraffin stove, a flaming bottle of methylated spirit exploded in my hand with a squeaky pop. Barely clothed and covered in flames, an overwhelming sensation of searing pain ravaged my face and torso. Without a moment of thought, I held on to a stanchion and flipped myself over the side. Extinguished, I climbed back on board and assessed the damage. My duvet and other items of clothing had caught fire so I threw a bucket of water down the companionway to douse the flames. It was obvious that the worst of the damage had been inflicted on my body. Charred pieces of skin fell off my arms, chest and torso, my face felt stiff, and several big blisters had already formed. My days of working with the RNLI (the UK lifeboat service) had prepared me well for this situation but I never foresaw having to treat myself. I used dressings, creams, antibiotics and painkillers, making myself look more like an Arabian nomad than a sailor. After eighteen days of heaven I had to endure two final days of hell. On 1st March I spotted a faint etching of a mountainous terrain conflicting with the shades of blue I had become so familiar with; it was Grenada.

Of all the advantages that a small yacht has over a large one, there is one that towers above all the rest – cost. *Flying Cloud*, my 22ft mahogany sloop, cost me less than what your average skipper would pay for a new headsail. She was beautifully simple and could be maintained on a shoestring. I embraced Larry Pardy's creed – "*Go smaller, go simpler, go now.*" For a 20-year-old, with a normal 20-year-old's budget, a small boat appears to be the only way to go.

I don't think size has too much to do with seaworthiness; more important is buoyancy, stability and water shedding ability. These are the ingredients for a seaworthy boat. A decked-over cockpit removes the worry of getting pooped, and any solid water rolling over the deck is gone in seconds. Inflated tenders, fenders, empty tanks and polystyrene can all be used as buoyancy in the empty cockpit space and forepeak.

Self-steering doesn't need to be expensive. *Flying Cloud* had a transom-hung rudder, so a vertical windvane to trim tab was the obvious choice. With 200 euros, a rummage around the boatyard and some "fag packet" sketches from someone who knew what they were talking about, I had a simple and robust self-steering gear. Some "perfectionist" sailors I met consider even self-steering gears unnecessary. They will choose to cross oceans singlehanded – relying purely on sheet to tiller and using a speargun cord as a bungee. I'll never forget Kiwi Jon, the paraplegic who crossed the Pacific singlehanded in a modern fin keeled without any self-steering. He presented his bungee to me with the words, "I bought this baby for 5 bucks and she's already taken me 7,000 miles."

In terms of electronics, I had both a handheld and DSC VHF, both of which could provide a GPS fix. I had another handheld GPS, a sextant and a folder of paper charts, although you only really need one for the crossing (Imray C100). A Garmin satellite tracker allowed me to send the occasional message to my family, and EPIRBs were located both in the lifejackets and above the chart table in case of disaster.

As it turned out, *Flying Cloud* was more than capable. She rode out some strong weather and consistently ticked off daily runs that impressed me. I completely agree that small boats are uncomfortable – not everyone has the willpower to squat over a bucket every morning, to walk around the cabin on their knees, and to go weeks without properly washing. The rare moments of perfection, though, always manage to make any anguish worthwhile; in a small boat, they just appear that much more real.

For me, she is my first rung on the ladder of owning an ocean-going yacht, a ladder I would like to climb higher. She has allowed me to gather so much knowledge of ocean sailing at a young age, knowledge that I simply wouldn't possess if I had chosen to wait until I could afford a bigger boat.

Max Campbell's self-steering is home-made, but it worked – 'do it yourself' is the secret of stripped-down ocean sailing.

And I do think that anyone can afford to undertake a similar trip. A small boat just makes the whole process that much more attainable. Take a trip down any creek or river and you will see dozens of small but capable yachts just longing for an enthusiastic owner. Small project yachts are often free, and the process of restoring a boat doesn't have to be costly. Go to boat jumbles, take a peek in the bins and substitute marine paint for some oil-based domestic paint. Keep electronics simple, and remember that an engine is useful but by no means essential. The cruising community is unique. People are always willing to help someone who is willing to help themselves. I'm always humbled by the generosity I receive from others who share the same passion.'

The ordinary boat

I would claim to own what I call an 'ordinary' boat – a Victoria 38, designed by Chuck Paine, with a shortish keel and a skeg-hung rudder. But design was not the only thing about this boat that appealed to me. She was built like a nuclear bunker. Everything spoke of strength, including the keel-stepped mast. The surveyor gasped when he saw the strengthening around the keel area, which gave reassurance.

Despite all that, she is typical of many of the boats you would find in any of the marinas of the world. She is a middle-of-the-road boat to look at, being neither long- nor short-keeled, and neither heavy nor light displacement. Her Bermudan cutter rig is neither extreme nor old-fashioned. She has enough room below to be able to lead a civilised life; she's not too small but neither would you call her voluminous. However, within my ownership, she has taken me to Cape Horn and back, to Europe, and enjoyed Arctic Circle sailing in the last few years. So for an ordinary boat I would say she has done some quite extraordinary things. The other thing she had was the falling-in-love-factor; to our eyes, she's a gorgeous boat.

Why did we choose her? Because there was nothing about her that was too extreme. She easily passed the first test, which is that she should be easy on the eye. The designer gave her a graceful look. The builders also gave us a strong hull and a robust fit-out, for which they had a reputation. She was not mass-produced, but the interior was created by carpenters going below with a pile of wood and some tools. This does not make for a cheap boat but it's one that fills you with confidence.

But there's often a price to pay if you have an attractive boat, and in our case it comes at the price of low topsides, which can restrict headroom below. The payback, though, comes when you have to jump down on to a dock with lines, or climb the topside from a tossing dinghy – you don't have to attempt a cliff-face of fibreglass. She is 38ft LOA (11.6m), which means that she will find a space in most harbours, the mainsail remains easy to hoist and the anchor and chain are far less daunting than on a larger boat. At the back of our minds is always the thought that we could manage this boat if all the electricity failed and all the winch handles had been lost over the side. For us, this boat is just about on the limits of what we have decided is our desirable sweet spot.

So we've got an average boat that average people can easily manage. The downsides? They are the same as with any boat, no matter how large or small. We'd like a bit more stowage for larger items, but I dare say that some big-yacht owners grumble that

The author's 'ordinary boat' – a standard production boat that proved herself Cape Horn capable. (WILKIE)

there's nowhere to stow the motorbike. We'd like bigger fuel tanks to increase range, and bigger water tanks to allow us to sail that bit further without anxiety. So should we have bought a bigger boat? Not if we valued the ease of handling, the sea-kindly design and all the other things that made her the perfect boat for us. Don't dismiss the 'average boat' option. It's tempting to go for the biggest boat you can just about afford and only later discover that she's too much of a handful. If you get the sense that the boat you're looking at will fit you like a glove, then comfortable sailing awaits you.

The luxury boat

There's much to be said for choosing a big boat if you can afford it – and we're talking 50 feet (15m) and upwards – and that's apart from the wow factor. You get speed, security and stability and all the comforts of home, even if you end up with a considerable black hole in your bank balance. But if you have not carefully thought through anchoring, sail handling and all the other demands on your personal strength, then you might find that crew becomes necessary and with them come management issues. It has often been said that big boat handling is more about brains than brawn; and while that is probably true, such instinctive big boat handling also takes time to acquire. Since the cost of big boats requires sums of money that take time to gather, those who choose the big boat option will probably have worked their way upwards through a cruising career in which every change of boat has meant something bigger. This is a great advantage as older and more experienced sea dogs often find it easier to learn new tricks.

This book is not here to teach big boat handling, but there is one secret that Rachael Sprot discovered as her charter business developed to include 60ft expedition boats sailing to demanding parts of the world and taking in pretty much everywhere between Greenland, Morocco, the Caribbean and Central America.

'When I first started skippering larger yachts, I found it daunting. I spent nights worrying how I was going to get a steel sloop weighing 40 tons out of her berth. The difference with a big boat is that you have to get it right. You can't solve your problems by getting a crew member to jump ashore because the topsides are too high and the boat so heavy that you can't manhandle it either. The best advice is to choose your berth carefully and don't be pressured into taking one you're not happy with.

Once you've got a boat moving she will carry her way for a long time so go as slowly as possible while keeping steerage way. Because of the momentum of a big boat, when changing from forward to reverse can be tricky – that's why your motto should always be "slow is pro". Apart from that, choosing the right rope for the job is the key to coming alongside. I nearly always use a midships line and motor gently ahead against it with the wheel over. Then she will sit there and we can get the other lines on.'

Clearly, big boat handling can be daunting, and should be considered before buying on length alone. It might also be worth having the words 'Slow is Pro' carved somewhere where the skipper can always see it.

Mike and Donna Hill did a circumnavigation in their Oyster 56 *Baccalieu III*, built in 2004 – a substantial and comfortable craft. They took time off the Pacific run to head south to explore the waters and harbours of New Zealand. So how did they plan their voyage, and what led them to choose a lengthy 56ft boat that comes with a hefty price tag? Donna writes:

'There are several advantages to owning a large boat. Clearly, the waterline results in more speed. Our 115hp Perkins turbo-charged engine was capable of punching through steep seas. A heavier boat offers a better ride with less motion, and a deep keel results in better tracking.

More storage is available: a utility room for tools, spare parts, water maker, pilot berth, work bench etc. Living space included three sleeping cabins and head, plus an owner's cabin with en suite. Davits held a 12ft RIB. It was convenient and ready to use.

When offshore, we were glad to have fuel tanks that held 1,000 litres, and water tanks the same size. We had a water maker capable of producing 100 litres per hour. This allowed us to make enough water to supply five to six crew members with drinking water and daily showers. A generator – Westerbeke 7.5 kWh – supplied batteries with enough charge to run the refrigerator, freezer, fans, lights and navigation instruments. I used a bread-maker not only for baking bread, but for roasting meals on the "bake only" cycle. This allowed us to save propane. The washing machine could only be used in flat sea conditions. The galley was spacious and included a large freezer and a separate pantry.

With regard to boat handling, powerful systems can create challenges. The electric winches are an example. These mighty tools don't give the same feel when hauling-in sheets that manual winches do. We took careful measures to control the speed at which we pulled sheets so as not to wind them too tightly and damage the sails. Furling the mainsail with an in-mast electric furling system required diligent handling to avoid jamming the mainsail within the mast. Releasing sheets from manual clutches, while using electric winches to pull other lines, was a delicate task of coordination. I incurred a severe rope burn on the palm of my hand while letting off the mainsail sheet from a clutch. It took time to get accustomed to the boat's super powerful mechanics and consequently, there are several opportunities to be injured. Everything is bigger, heavier and bulkier.

The Hills chose a big boat offering big comfort for their circumnavigation – Oyster 56 Baccalieu III.

It was our first boat with a bow thruster. Thrusters are miracle workers when docking. But it takes time to learn how to use them. The electric windlass was another powerful tool that could be mishandled. Occasionally, we would get the anchor jammed in the bow roller. When dropping it, we let the anchor drop freely rather than using the electric windlass to lower it. This avoided overheating the fuse when repeatedly raising and lowering the anchor in areas it wouldn't dig in. When we had visitors aboard, we supervised almost everything because they would not be accustomed to handling such powerful hardware.

To make sail handling easier, hydraulic furling on both mainsail and headsail, enabled easy letting out and reducing sail in variable winds. The staysail had manual furling and I had to use a good amount of upper body strength to furl it. Manually raising the mainsail was a task I didn't have the strength for. However, with in-mast furling, it only needed hoisting after lowering it for inspection or to take it off the boat for the sailmaker. They were bulky and heavy, but we managed. We used a halyard to swing them off the boat to the dock.

When choosing places to go, we were aware that an expensive boat might attract criminals. We chose areas that were noted "safe". For instance, we avoided the Red Sea and chose instead to travel around the Cape of Good Hope. The boat was sturdy and sound. She could handle heavy weather and steep seas. Besides, we knew nothing about combat, but we knew something about sailing. If anchored in an area known for theft, we would stay on board. Before retiring, we locked the companionway and overhead hatches. When docked, we raised the passarelle like a draw bridge. A switch controlling the spreader lights, located beside the bed in the master cabin, enabled us to floodlight the deck without going outside. We did not carry weapons. If you choose to carry weapons you may need to shoot first. We didn't possess that mentality.

Despite the size of the boat, it was hardly ever a problem when choosing spaces to moor. We sailed 50,000 miles and we can count on one hand the number of times size prevented us from entering a marina or an anchorage. However, in Vanuatu, we couldn't reach a dock due to a mast height of 75 feet (23m) that wouldn't fit underneath an overhead wire. Fuel had to be delivered by barge. But we never had to turn away from an anchorage due to lack of a suitable mooring. Planning is key.

To summarise, a large boat offers more comfort, and a powerful engine allows for driving against strong, adverse tides and currents. Power can be a form of insurance. The downsides: the initial cost and the upkeep of sails, rigging, hull and decks. Bigger boats have more and bigger systems which demand more maintenance time and cost to keep in working order. There are more winches to take apart and clean. Dockage and insurance are also costlier. But we loved all of it.

Big boat sailing gives you speed and an easier ride, but at the expense of bigger sails and the effort needed to handle them.

The multihull

There are more multihulls, usually catamarans, making ocean passages than ever before. It can be the expensive option as, at its most basic, you are paying for two hulls instead of one. But the bonus comes in the sheer amount of space that becomes available, which is always attractive to long-term cruisers, and the comfort you get from spending most of your sailing time pretty much close to upright. There's also the speedy nature, particularly off the wind; but other factors can reduce that advantage, such as loading, which can soon knock back their speedy nature. Anecdotal evidence suggests that taken over a long period of time, and taking into account windward and downwind conditions as well as adverse weather, catamarans do not always outpace monohulls of the same size. But without doubt, for harbour work, and in anchorages, the spaciousness of the multihull starts to make sense.

Capsize is the dread word that springs to the mind of those contemplating a multihull. It is true that catamarans are very stable and have great natural buoyancy, but when they're over they're over and there's nothing you can do that will put that right. In contrast, a monohull will right herself, even if she does come up a little the worse for wear, and possibly minus a mast. But at least the multihull will remain floating when she's inverted, which is a small comfort, whereas the monohull can fill and sink. But capsize on a well-managed and planned voyage is extreme and rare, and multihull owners appreciate that moving around the flat deck with minimal angle of heel is often far safer than the scrabble along the sloping coach roof of the monohull.

Of the other plus points, the most common are that seasickness seems to be much rarer in catamarans, and the easily driven nature of the hulls, combined with a much reduced wetted area, means you are using far less diesel to drive them along. And if you have twin engines, as many do, you are going to be able to spin completely round on the spot, which makes harbour work much easier despite the often daunting beam. Their shallow draft can be a great advantage for those who like nosing up close to the shore in coves and anchorages too shallow for deep-draft monohulls. Being able to dry out upright on warm sand can also be attractive. Also, in anchorages prone to swell, as some Caribbean ones famously are, a catamaran will give you a far easier ride at anchor than a monohull.

Richard Woods is a catamaran designer and builder who worked for a time with the multihull legends James Wharram and Derek Kelsall. Over 30 years he has sold 3,000 of his hundred or so multihull designs. His personal preferences are for building and sailing smaller boats, but he understands the ways of the catamaran inside out.

Multihull sailing – where the living is easier and more horizontal. Richard Woods at sea on Eclipse *off Panama.* (JETTI WOODS)

'An ocean cruising boat is much harder to design than a day sailing or racing boat because it must meet many more requirements. Not only has it got to sail easily with a small crew, it has to be ultimately seaworthy and more important, it is also a live-aboard home. Indeed, probably 90 per cent of the time an ocean cruiser is at anchor or in port, not sailing.

So the features must include a comfortable cockpit and deck because when you are anchored in a tropical lagoon you will want to enjoy the view, not sit below in the dark. No one buys a penthouse basement! The best houses always come with a view.

I am writing this on our 28ft Skoota Powercat. OK, it's not sail but similar space/load carrying to a sailing boat. We have basic food for three months, water for four weeks, fuel for 250 miles. Bicycle, sewing machine, lots of books and DVDs, kayak, rigid sailing dinghy, three computers, BBQ, cabin heater, good fridge. We have two wardrobes of tropical and warm weather clothes. Yet the boat floats just about on its marks. More important, it is all stored away below decks in lockers. Nothing is visible, which is why people think we are living a spartan, stripped out existence. Many ocean cruisers don't have storage space so keep bikes on deck with spare fuel cans lashed to stanchions. Some even tow their dinghies while ours is in davits.

Probably the most important feature for an ocean cruising catamaran is good bridge deck clearance. Higher is always better, but there is a compromise. More clearance means more freeboard adding weight and windage, so lower is faster and lighter. My simple rule of thumb is that you should always be able to get a normal (ie not a RIB) inflatable dinghy under the bridge deck between the hulls.

The shallow draft is a great asset. Although much of the Caribbean is deep water, I have managed to run aground there on deep-keeled monohulls. But many places, like the Bahamas, Belize and most of the east and Gulf coasts of the USA, are very shallow, less than three metres for much of the time. Deep-drafted boats forego a lot of great cruising areas and in bad weather are very limited in the places they can hide. Traditional cargo sailing ships were always designed to be beached, even warships would be careened. So modern keel boat sailors are unusual in fearing beaching, considering it a stranding.

When it comes to living aboard, everyone gets lots more privacy. We used to own a 34ft Romany catamaran, which we cruised to the Bahamas for a couple of years and it has since made several more cruises there. One time we invited a couple of builders to sail back with us. We had never met them before. They were on board for about two weeks but we never had any problems – we had our own hull and they had theirs.

A catamaran is a different kind of craft to sail. They don't heel and you are well above the water so don't get the same sensation of speed. In general you sail a monohull as fast as you can, a multihull as fast as you want to go. We once spent three days sailing along the north coast of Cuba in north-east Trades. Day one we did 60 miles in six hours under spinnaker with hatches closed and hand steering. Day two we took seven hours for the next 60 miles, no spinnaker, hatches open and autopilot on. Day three I reefed the main, took another extra hour for the 60 miles but it was very relaxing, in fact I don't think we went on deck. So you need to control speed for comfort.

If people are planning to ocean cruise a multihull, it is worth going to a sailing school that specialises in multihull training and understands the techniques.

From a safety point of view they are certainly better as the deck is essentially level and flat with no pointed ends. You can reach the outer end of the boom safely, you don't have a genoa blind spot and you can safely walk along the lee sidedeck even when sailing to windward. Although the boat is upright and doesn't roll, it still moves around. I liken it to being on a bus. It stays upright but you have to hold on to seats as you move down the aisle. Which is why I don't like big open floor plans in the saloon and no handholds. I also don't like the modern, sharp-cornered interiors which you get on both multi and monohulled boats.

The increased area of the boat can make for more expensive mooring but you can often go in areas deep monohulls cannot, and of course you can go on drying moorings. And you have to compare like with like. A multihull has more interior and deck space, so a 40ft cat will have more room than a 50ft monohull so moorings can be cheaper. Certainly I have never paid extra for being a cat. In the past it might have been a problem but now there are so many multihulls no marina can afford to turn them away because of overcharging. Of course there is less need to go into a marina if you don't roll at anchor!

If they have twin engines (inboard or outboard) then manoeuvrability is superb, certainly you can turn on the spot, rather than turn in your own length. And with no prop kick effect you can get into any berth in either direction. If you have a dagger-boarded boat it is best to manoeuvre with the boards down. But one big problem is haul-outs. There are very few travel lifts that can lift a 7m+ beam so you are reliant on the few multihull-specific yards, which have the equipment to lift pretty much any beam. It is certainly a major problem in the US where people have reported going 1,000 miles just to haul out to antifoul.

I believe the average monohull built now is 47ft. I read a report where the author called a 40ft catamaran a "starter boat". I always tell people that the first catamaran to sail round Cape Horn was the 30ft Oceanic with Colin and Rosie Swale and their two young children on board. The distances between ports, the seas and weather, haven't changed in 40 years.'

John Charnley gave up life as a pilot for British Airways back in the 70s and as the only two things he knew anything about were boats and planes, he launched a highly successful career that led to the UK charter business Sunsail, and more recently the establishment of Discovery Yachts with the ambition 'to produce the perfect boat for a couple to sail round the world'. His current boat, taken from his own stable, is the Bill Dixon designed Discovery Bluewater 50, a catamaran at the luxury and expensive end of the market. It's a 50-footer with the beam almost half that.

John Charnley

'We bought this boat with the idea of heading to the Pacific. We'd sailed something similar over to the US in 2010 and cruised the eastern seaboard extensively down as far as Panama and back to Florida. We love the space and stability of a catamaran, in particular when you end up in a rolling anchorage. We also love the comfort at sea, especially in quartering seas when monohulls can be less comfortable. We had no reservations about a catamaran for the kind of sailing we were going to do, but if we were going to Antarctica we'd choose a mono.

For long-term cruising, the space, stability and privacy means that cats have great advantages, although with monos you get more pure sailing pleasure as the boat responds to the wind. In a cat you just sit there and watch the dials go up!

We have aircon, a water maker, a large fridge and two freezers, and a small generator. The beds are large and comfortable, we have a fuel capacity of 1,500 litres which is a lot, and two good sized water tanks with 750 litres. We want to be independent for many weeks if we want to.

One thing we do carry, and I recommend this, is a second small dinghy and outboard in case the first gets lost or stolen.

As far as heavy weather goes, I've never been in a situation where I feared capsize, but my upper limit of experience has been force nine. I feel more confident in heavy weather because it's much easier to move around the deck and you're not hanging on for dear life. We sail this boat just as a couple with no problems but we do have hydraulic in-mast reefing and twin headsail reefing. We can set all sails singlehanded and reef on any point of sailing without disturbing the off-watch crew.

When it comes to working under engine, like any boat it can be tricky in a very tight space with a strong cross wind blowing. Also, remember that you have twin rudders. We damaged one when we hit something and it jammed. All we had to do was disconnect it and sail on using just the other rudder.

My advice? Get your rig set up for easily handling. Don't overload her as performance drops off more quickly than with a mono. Make sure the cat you choose has good bridge-deck clearance otherwise the banging of passing waves can be annoying.

I am writing this from St Lucia and we were last here in 2012. Back then, 50 per cent of the boats in this anchorage were cats, now it's 85 per cent. Quite amazing.'

Metal boats

Choosing a steel yacht implies a tough sort of sailor, heading for violent waters, dicing with ice and rocks and ready to face the worst weather on the planet. They build battle tanks out of steel, don't they? So why else would you want a steel boat if not for survival in ultimate situations?

But steel boats are not just for rufty-tufty sailors. They have many advantages that all ocean cruisers can enjoy.

Steel does not make for a compact cruiser. The sheer weight of the stuff, compared to fibreglass, means that a smallish boat would never be able to carry a rig substantial enough to give it the power to get moving at anything like a decent speed, except in strong winds. But if you're looking at a boat longer than 35 feet (11m), steel has a lot going for it.

Its greatest quality is probably its inherent strength. If a steel yacht meets a GRP yacht, there's no doubt which of them is going to come off worse. If you make a grounding on rocks, you are more likely to remain in one piece than if you were in a GRP craft. And if you do need a repair, you are only looking for a yard who employs a half-decent welder, whereas the GRP yacht will need someone who can master the chemistry of GRP. When considering strength in hulls, you have to consider how far the hull material is going to bend before it breaks. Steel goes further than any other common hull material. It is also worth considering fire resistance. It doesn't take much to turn a GRP hull into a smouldering wreck, but while a fire in a steel yacht might well destroy the interior fittings, the hull itself will remain intact.

Maintenance is the key, though, to running a steel yacht. The demon rust is ever waiting to emerge and if you don't get on top of it the instant it's spotted, then your boat will surely turn into one of those rust buckets down the far end of the marina that nobody wants to look at. That's why, if inspecting a steel yacht with a view to purchase, the bilges should be your first port of call. Filthy, rusty bilges (or suspiciously freshly painted ones) sound alarm bells on steel boats and you can save yourself the rest of the day if a poke in the bilges reveals corrosion on anything but a minor scale. Remember the old saying – steel boats rust from the inside out.

Rust on the outside is less of a problem as sand blasting is comparatively easy, and modern paints have a long and durable life. Nor is the painting of steel boats as technical or precise as trying to get a new coat on to GRP. Anyone who can wield a brush can make a decent job of it. If you spot a small outbreak of rust, possibly the result of a scratch, slap a length of PVC tape over it to discourage it from spreading, and also to make it easier to find it again when the time comes to get the brushes out. However, on a long passage, which involves any amount of sea sweeping the decks, expect your eventual joy on arrival to be slightly marred by the sight of weeping rust, which will have appeared as if by magic – someone called them his boat's 'tears'.

If you plan a cruise where you might get 'knocked about', particularly in fishing or commercial harbours, a steel boat is a handy thing to have since you are, sooner or later, going to end up in a sandwich between working boats, which would remove the shine from a GRP hull without noticing.

A steel hull might also provide a better radar reflection, which is comforting, and you will have no problems providing a decent ground for your SSB radio.

But they're not perfect. Apart from the weight/size ratio meaning that only larger yachts benefit from steel construction in colder, damper climes an uninsulated steel hull will be running in condensation. Anecdotal evidence suggests steel yachts are hotter than others in warm climes, and colder than others in chillier places, but this depends on the insulation and colour of hull and decks – off-white colours will result in blisteringly hot decks in the tropics.

A typical underwater profile of a steel yacht – for any ocean. (RUSSELL)

Insulation is vital on a steel boat or condensation problems will make your life miserable. Typically, foam is applied with a sprayer. (RUSSELL)

The metal yacht owner's greatest fear must be electrolysis – that insidious effect that produces stray electrical currents, causing metals to, apparently, dissolve in sea water. It occurs when you get a combination of dissimilar metals together in a saline environment, which is inevitable on all yachts, but the consequences are most severe with aluminium and, to a lesser extent, steel yachts. With steel and aluminium yachts fittings such as sea cocks and cleats must be chosen and fitted with care. Even the wrong choice of screws or bolts will eventually catch up with you.

On a positive note, if you get struck by lightning you are safer on a steel boat than any other – providing you're not holding on to the shrouds at the time. The Faraday cage effect means that the electrical charge travels to earth via the outside of the boat and not the inside. If you stay below, you'll probably get away with it. Although you might end up with a magnetised boat, but that's another story.

Aluminium is a popular choice for long-range cruising yachts and there are many fine examples. Like steel, it has great strength in impact situations, which is why they are the boat of choice for Arctic and Antarctic sailors, where some collision with ice is inevitable. But the lightness of aluminium – 30 per cent less than steel –

removes all the weighty issues that steel brings with it and gives you a more easily driven hull. If you've ever wondered why most aluminium hulls don't carry a scrap of paint, it is simply because, although aluminium is relatively corrosion resistant, if it is painted and then scratched, corrosion in the form of bubbles can quickly form. Aluminium is best left unpainted above the waterline to allow a protective coating of aluminium oxide to form. Paint, or a similar barrier, is needed between opposing metals, such as cleats and decks, where electrolysis problems could arise. Welding is more problematical, requiring specialised equipment and technique, although if having a boat built from scratch, aluminium is quicker and easier than steel to shape and work with and reckoned to be three times faster than working in steel. However, tonne for tonne, aluminium is far more expensive than steel. Some have compromised by having a steel hull and aluminium superstructure; this moves the centre of gravity some way towards the waterline, which is desirable.

David and Jane Russell have had two steel boats: *Tinfish*, a 37ft Piet Hein on which they completed a five-year circumnavigation, and *Tinfish II*, a 39ft Mike Pocock design on which, with their two children, Peter and Jennie, they completed a Mediterranean circuit.

'We inherited the name *Tinfish* with our first steel boat. All the way round the world the name raised a smile. Friends still called us the Tinfishes.

We chose steel over all the other materials because she looked up to the job of crossing oceans and we could afford her. There seem to be two schools of thought: choose a light fast boat to minimise time at sea and reduce risk, or minimise risk by having the strongest boat you can. We went for steel as it's more resilient than aluminium. We also like the fact that maintenance and repair was possible worldwide without specialist knowledge.

If you've never owned a steel boat before and are looking around, peer in the bilges and be suspicious if they're freshly painted. *Tinfish I* had lead ballast overlaid with concrete with fresh layers added each time she'd been sold. Check for rust in damp areas such as under the heads, mast base and anchor locker. Also check under the engine, round non-integral tanks, battery boxes and the bilge sump. Check for bimetallic corrosion at mast step, particularly for keel-stepped masts and anywhere else aluminium is used. A gasket or some form of insulating material will protect against this.

Make sure paint coatings are well adhered; pay particular attention to cracked filler, which

Tinfish II *survives a grounding. One of the advantages of a steel yacht is the sheer strength of the hull in situations like this.* (RUSSELL)

usually hides problem areas. If steel decks are covered in anything other than paint, look for telltale signs of rust weeping around the edges.

Ideally the chain plates are stainless steel and stanchions should be welded to the deck rather than through bolted. Any damage to paintwork is an issue and special care should be taken to avoid chafe from running rigging.

What surprised us most about having a steel yacht was how resilient they are, and only a marginal drop in performance compared to other long-distance cruising boats. Also, the excellent value for money they are if bought on the second-hand market.

They are noisier than other boats if they are empty and uninsulated. A well-insulated hull that has full lockers is not a noisy boat at all. One upside is to be able to hear the coral, dolphin clicks, and other sea life from the comfort of your bunk.

Tinfish I was 36 years old when we sold her and had been tested in extreme conditions that would have wrecked most other boats, but she came away bruised but not broken and is still sailing 18 years later. You don't pull the cleats out of the deck or bend your anchor roller. She survived a lightning strike, or very near strike, in an intense storm in The Flats anchorage in Colon near Panama, popping the fibreglass sheath around her masthead VHF aerial and the mast lights, but otherwise no damage or problems.

The problems come with rust on older, less well-built models (and the lack of a Wi-Fi signal below decks can be a real pain). *Tinfish I* was 30 years old and treated with conventional rather than epoxy paint, with teak decks laid on to the steel. It was pretty much a constant programme of rust treatment. *Tinfish II* with epoxy paint has a much lower maintenance burden. Apart from mechanical damage to the coatings, there is no real issue other than where fittings were incorrectly fitted. Touching up the paint is a lot easier than gel repairs or scarfing in timbers.

You do need insulation and if it's done as part of the original build, so much the better. Spray foam is ideal, but retrofitting Celotex-style insulation on to well-painted steel is also viable.

Steel suffers much less than aluminium from electrolysis problems, and far less than fixings in wood. All boats are vulnerable; most commonly, any electrolysis takes place between stainless steel propeller shafts, bronze propellers and skin fittings. A much bigger risk is stray current corrosion. Thorough maintenance of electrical systems, particularly shore power systems, is vital. Steel boats tend to use more anodes to mitigate the risks.

Whether a steel boat gives you more security depends on what you are most afraid of. In a collision situation or grounding, you will have a relatively good chance in a steel yacht. We've been dragged down on to by a big fishing boat while on our mooring, resulting only in a couple of bent stanchions. We've grounded, we've been set on to a dock wall by surge, but any damage was just cosmetic and easy to fix. When we crossed Biscay, there was another steel yacht heading south. A few weeks later we were in Cascais, Portugal, and she limped into the anchorage with her rig heaped up across her deck. She had had a collision with a container ship, bounced along the side of the ship until the rig caught the bridge side balcony and was brought down, but she got herself to harbour under engine. We found a guy with his steel yacht on legs on the beach in Darwin after he'd spent several days lifting and grounding over the top of a reef. He was damaged, but not sunk, and it was all easily fixable.

The community of fellow steel yacht ocean cruisers is sometimes eccentric, but seems to share a bond worldwide and you'll make friends of complete strangers. Buy a steel boat – you won't regret it.'

The gaff rig

Isn't gaff rig a relic of a vanished age? Isn't it a throwback to the days before we understood the sheer efficiency of the modern masthead rig? What can gaff rig have that might appeal to the modern ocean sailor? Before we write it off, it is worth remembering that it has been a faithful servant of fishermen and traders for centuries and should not be dismissed lightly.

It remains a low-tech kind of rig that can be repaired without sophisticated tools or the need for precise spare parts. Look at the number of fittings on a Bermudan mast, any of which could break and put the whole rig at risk. Count the number of fittings on a gaff rig and you'll find them to be far fewer, and most of them under less stress. Because the centre of effort of gaff sails tends to be lower, there can be less pressure on the hull of the boat transmitted through the shrouds. Less stress is also felt in sheets and halyards, meaning the gaff rigged boat does not have to be festooned with heavy handling machinery, such as massive winches. However, the weight of a mainsail and a gaff combined can cause the fittest to sweat when they are hoisted.

Gaff enthusiasts will also tell you that the mainsail can be raised or lowered whatever the direction of the wind – often not possible with a conventional rig. Do they go to windward, though? We've cautioned before about the emphasis on windward ability

One of the most widely travelled gaffers in the world – Trevor Robertson's Iron Bark *emerging from the mist in Nova Scotia.* (FLANDERS)

when it comes to ocean sailing, where lengthy beating tends to be the result of poor planning. But sooner or later you will have to beat and the gaff rig might not give you confidence. In situations like these, the topsail is the gaff sailor's secret weapon. This extra length of luff hoisted above the gaff mainsail makes the difference, and removal of the topsail provides a handy first reef.

The gaff rig probably needs more care and attention, if less tuning, than the masthead rig. Chafe can be a problem, especially on a long passage, and that lengthy bowsprit can cause the heart to flutter in tight harbours.

Andrew and Máire Wilkes sail *Annabel J*, a 66ft modern replica of a Bristol Channel pilot cutter, and they have owned gaff rigged yachts before that. Their cruising under gaff rig has been extensive, including Arctic waters, and in particular the North-West Passage. Andrew writes:

'I cannot deny that element of hopeless romance about gaff rig. However, romance is part of the decision-making process when buying any boat. Bermudan rig yacht owners should admit that they too are romantics and stop settling for second best.

On a more practical note, the straight keels mean they are difficult to spin around the cans in confined waters, but they sail in a straight line beautifully on an ocean passage. With the sails trimmed on *Annabel J*, I can leave the helm, wander up to the foredeck for a chat with Máire, and return with barely a touch on the helm. Being low-tech is good because things always break on a boat, whether it be a new production cruiser, a racing machine or an old gaffer. However, the low-tech nature of traditional boats normally means that they can be fixed by the crew. This is cheaper and more satisfying. Also, if sailing offshore or cruising in remote places, it is often just not possible to find a technician to fix high-tech equipment.

While Máire and I were sailing through the North-West Passage in 2010, we broke the wooden gaff. We motored to a sheltered anchorage and made a new gaff from a spare wooden spinnaker pole we had on board. When crossing the Atlantic in 2012, an accidental gybe broke the boom (not much wind but too much swell). We completed the passage with our two headsails and the mizzen. On our arrival in Ireland, we got some Douglas fir delivered to a friend's workshop and made ourselves a new boom. It would not be possible for us to repair or make a new boom from extruded aluminium. The rig uses simple materials and relies on human ingenuity to make it work, I find this satisfying. The low-tech rig feels more at one with nature and feels right.

Annabel J – *the near perfect gaffer for ocean sailing. Undeniably romantic.*

On the plus side, with gaff it is easier to reduce sail power quickly by tricing, or scandalising, the mainsail, perhaps in a quick squall or when manoeuvring in confined waters. An unexpected benefit is that whenever you berth or anchor in a new harbour, people call by to ask about the boat and to say hello. Traditional boats come with a ready-made social life. It's true that they are generally slower than Bermudan rigged boats, and do not point to windward as well and there is also more work maintaining a traditionally rigged boat: wooden spars have to be varnished, blocks removed to the garage every winter for varnishing or oiling.

When it comes to sailing, there is more flexibility to tweak things and get the best out of the rig. The running rigging looks complicated initially but any sailor would get to understand it quite quickly. Some traditionally rigged boats do not have winches. It takes a knack to handle lines and tackles efficiently. *Annabel J* has winches for sheets but not for halyards. These are traditionally rigged: for example, the staysail has a block at the head of the sail through which a double-ended

Andrew and Máire Wilkes choose gaff rig for its low-tech nature.

halyard is passed – this gives it a 2:1 purchase. One end of the halyard fall is led to a belaying pin to port. The other halyard fall is led to the starboard side and ends in a 4:1 tackle. To hoist the sail, haul away on the port halyard fall. When the sail is almost hoisted and the work gets harder, belay the port halyard fall and transfer your efforts to the 4:1 purchase which will be comparatively easy. It sounds complicated when written down but it is easy and has an elegant simplicity.

Sail trim principles are the same as for Bermudan rig: flatter sails for going upwind and in strong winds, more shape and camber in light airs and when sailing downwind. The gaff mainsail has four corners so there is a bit more scope for playing with sail shape. Topsails tend to be fuller and cannot be sheeted in hard but the wind up there is normally freer than lower down. It pays to take things a bit slower when sailing a heavy gaffer: don't sheet in too hard, ease into a tack and use the boat's momentum.

Reefing systems vary but are generally simple. This makes them less likely to go wrong than some modern systems. Some gaff cutters – *Annabel J* is one – have a lot of their sail area in the mainsail. If the mainsail is not reefed early there will be weather helm in heavy weather and steering will be difficult. To make it easier to steer, "relieving tackles" on the tiller can be used.

In light airs, heavier displacement boats need more wind to make them sail; however, once they are going, they have more momentum. When tacking upwind, sheets should be eased a little more than would be normal on a Bermudan rig and you should not try to point too high. Once the boat is sailing well, you can afford to experiment by trying to sail a little closer to the wind. When I teach this to teenagers on sail training boats, I compare it to winding up a teacher in the classroom: you can push it so far but, overstep the mark, and you are in big trouble.

If you are thinking of gaff rig but are nervous about it, there are several companies who offer traditional gaff rig charters. If you have not sailed a gaff rig before, try it and see.

Or take me to a pub and ply me with ale, and I'll tell you what it's like.'

The unstayed rig

A boat that has a mast with nothing holding it up! Wouldn't only a fool face the ocean in such a vessel? I mean, surely masts bend and sway and if there's no rigging, sooner or later they are going to snap! No, ridiculous idea.

Far from it. Unstayed rigs, which range from the traditional, oriental junk rig to the modern sophisticated Aero and Freedom rigs, have served ocean sailors well and their advocates see many advantages in them. Be warned, though; the arguments can go to and fro with not much headway. 'The masts are expensive to make with a huge cross-section causing windage,' says one. Yes, but add up all the wires in a fully rigged boat and then see how much windage you've got. And each of those lengths of rigging wire has to remain attached to the mast. How many fittings does that add up to, remembering it can take only one to fail and bring down the whole lot.

The historian will tell you that unstayed masts have survived since man first hoisted sails to move him along, so a rig can't be all that fragile. 'But they bend in the wind!' someone screams. 'But so do skyscrapers, but they don't blow over.'

Junk rig – no stays and no rigging but ready for any weather. Annie Hill's Badger *hard on the wind and well reefed.* (HILL)

A cat-ketch with unstayed masts. Nick Charman's choice – 'A trusted family member.'

These arguments pass across yacht club bars every time a boat with an unstayed mast sails into view. Probably the person who says 'you don't see many unstayed masts because cruising sailors are quite a conservative bunch' is pretty much close to the truth.

Nick Charman was introduced to sailing in his mid-twenties on *Robertson's Golly*, the famous Ohlson 38 originally sailed in the OSTAR by Clare Francis. In return for helping maintain the cantankerous diesel and the strange gas and sewage systems on that boat, he sailed as crew many miles in all weathers in the Channel and Irish Sea, learning navigation and pilotage. He was introduced to the cat-ketch rig by Sir John Oakley, the famous Olympic sailor, and bought *Fera*, a Tanton 43, in Florida USA. *Fera* is a 43ft cat-ketch with unstayed carbon-fibre masts and wishbone booms. She has been a strong trusted family member for some 60,000 miles. Since the transatlantic delivery passage from Florida in 1987, these miles have been in European waters.

Nick Charman writes:

'For a start, you get a quieter and softer ride in an awkward sea. It's a bit like having a softer suspension on a car. And it's quieter because there's no rigging for the wind to howl in. They're also better to handle in gusty winds because the bendy mast allows wind to spill from the sail when the gust hits. In a stayed rig, gusts are more difficult to deal with; if you reef you're under-canvassed when the gust has gone through, but the unstayed rig just spills the wind when it needs to. I simply like the fact that they're much safer. You don't have the crew going forward across a rolling deck to hoist spinnakers or put up poles. Everything can be reefed from the cockpit so there's no need to be on deck when it gets rough.

It's very easy to set up a downwind rig, especially if you have a two-masted boat. You just let the sheets out as you turn. If you've got a ketch rig you can set them wing and wing, which moves the effort equally to each side of the boat so there's no tendency to keep rounding up. If the boat does start to roll, you just sheet in the mizzen till it stops – easy peasy!

You need a slightly different frame of mind to sail an unstayed rig. For example, the lack of rigging means you can set sails at all manner of unlikely angles. You can allow a sail to set forward of the beam, which might appear odd, or even set a sail to weather. But these are all valid ways of getting the best out of an unstayed rig.

You can have wishbone booms on unstayed masts, which you can't have with a conventionally rigged boat. Wishbones are a very efficient way of setting an aerofoil shape and it's very easy to change the draft of the sail – use a fuller draft off the wind or in light airs, a flatter sail for upwind work or heavier weather, and all with just one rope led back to the cockpit.

My boat is a 43ft two-masted cat-ketch and I find that to windward in light airs, a genoa-driven sloop will be faster and sail closer than my ketch. This is because the mizzen sail is working in the downwind turbulence of the forward sail, which is a disadvantage in lighter winds. When the wind is stronger, I will out-point the other boat if it has a roller reefing genoa. On a single-masted cat-rigged boat, in light airs, the performance would be similar to that of a sloop.

When it comes to heavy weather, it's a great comfort when setting out knowing that the rig is easier to handle, and the reefing can be done from the cockpit. And the relative quietness of the rig is comforting too, especially as there seems to be less tendency for the hull to pound, perhaps because the flexible rig is more forgiving. But it's not the rig, it's the shape and design of the hull that determines long-term comfort at sea.

Most conventional mast failures happen because of rigging or fitting failure. It's possible for a stayed mast to have well over a hundred components if you include all the split pins and swages. An unstayed mast, if it's securely attached to the keel and clamped at the deck you end up with a simpler and more reliable rig. Unstayed masts can fail, of course, but it's very rare and it's usually a design or manufacturing fault, as in any boat. But once you've been out in strong winds in excess of 40 knots and all has gone well, then you soon learn to trust your rig. I have the comfort of knowing that my masts have been designed and built to a bending force ten times the righting moment of the boat. You don't suspect an aeroplane's wing is likely to fall off, do you? So why should a properly designed unstayed mast?

Boat buyers are conservative people and they buy boats they know and boats they were taught to sail on, and you can't blame builders for selling the kind of boats that people want to buy. And I doubt a lot of the sailing hardware manufacturers are all that keen on them either. All those complex and expensive engineering systems, such as in-mast reefing and so on, have no place on unstayed rigs. So who are they going to sell them to if everyone went over to a simpler rig?'

A cat-ketch – easy and relaxing to sail – 'A softer ride in heavy seas.'

The motorboat

The motorboat is a rare choice for ocean cruising because the requirements are, essentially, the same as for a small ship. You need fuel-carrying capacity, and engines powerful enough to transport it in all weather. Also, small powerboats are not designed for the oceans of the world. Marinas might be full of them, and while they're great for a two-week cruise along the coast, or as swimming and fishing platforms, the idea that you might make an Atlantic crossing in one, or even brave the Southern Ocean, is a step few would wish to take. So if you're thinking of the motorboat option, you need a stout vessel and a deep pocket because in motorboats, strength seems strongly linked to size.

Scott and Mary Flanders chose a Nordhavn 46, *Egret*, for their circumnavigation, in which they proved that a motor vessel, if carefully chosen and managed, can take you across the oceans of the world. Not that their original idea was to cross oceans at all. Nevertheless, they successfully completed a west-about circumnavigation that took in all the five great capes of the world and in doing so took the record for the first motor yacht to achieve that. They were full-time live-aboards for 14 years.

They write:

'Before you can even begin to think about plans and preparations, you must start with a first step – a realisation that adventure by water is a dream you'd like to achieve. Once you've "caught the bug" you simply need to get yourself on a boat and start accumulating hours.

So many people set their goals high in the beginning and if they attempt reaching their goals without the requisite skills it soon becomes tedious, and could even border on dangerous. In many cases, their boating dreams are dashed and the boat goes up for sale. In our case, all we wanted was to make it to Chesapeake Bay from our former home in South Florida and winter in the Bahamas. This we did. The following year we lengthened our stride and did our first offshore trip from South Florida to Nantucket, a distance of 1,000nm, then on a direct shot to Nova Scotia. And so it began, we kept learning and ultimately spent quite a few years at sea.

We spent four years planning our voyage. Our original plan was to sell the family home and keep a small Florida Keys weekend home and buy a semi-displacement coastal trawler and follow the sun north and south. Once we got the long-distance bug, we realigned our thoughts. In the end we went

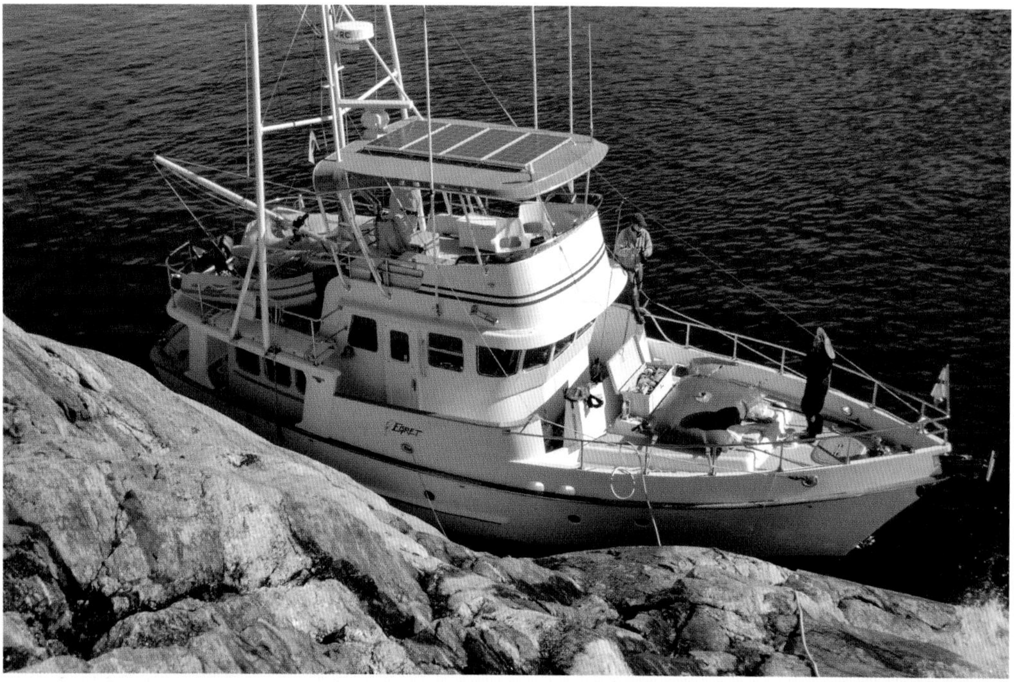

The Flanders chose a motor yacht for their circumnavigation – strength meets comfort – seen here taking on glacier meltwater in Greenland.

to a local boat show and toured an early Nordhavn 57. The boat was well out of our price range but it was Mary who said "let's sell everything and order a *new* Nordhavn 46". So we did and never looked back. She was super seaworthy, simple enough I could do my own maintenance, and comfortable enough to be a full-time home. For us, we couldn't ask for anything more. There are many pluses and we have zero regrets.

Nordhavns are actually built to cross oceans. In *Egret*'s case there was three tons of lead in the keel, the laminate schedule was bulletproof, and every detail that would compromise her safety was attended to. Traditional production builders build for different markets and price points. Sales people trying to sell less capable boats occasionally try and sell sizzle but when you are "out there", steak is more important. That said, I once figured only about 5 per cent of ocean-capable powerboats actually go somewhere besides coastal cruising.

I spent my working life in the boat business and had a reasonable handle on the difference between want and need. We outfitted *Egret* simply, but what we did buy was necessary and we didn't compromise on safety. Like every long-distance cruiser, power or sail, it is easy to look back and see what we did right or wrong. We went overboard on spares once we made the decision to head out, and I would do it

With enough diesel, the Nordhavn 46 is a go-anywhere kind of boat.

again even though the majority of spares were used to help other cruisers.

Our luxury was a giant water maker – 25 gallons per hour. And a Dickinson diesel heater when in cold countries. In clean water we used the water maker to load the generator while charging batteries at anchor. If we made too much water we would wash salt off the boat before daybreak before the anchorage came to life. I can't think of anything more pretentious than wasting water in front of our cruising peers, but we were never caught.

Mary refuels while crossing the Indian Ocean. They carried 1,360 US gallons and arrived with a 255-gallon reserve.

Only five times did weather make us change direction at sea when it was so severe we had to round up and face the seas, matching the throttle to the conditions and basically hold position. It's like heaving-to with very little drift. We followed the time of year rules and in all the miles spent very little time in bad weather.

Fuel is our sails and it's pretty important not to run out. We *never-never-never* took a slight chance on running out. I can't remember ever completing a passage with less than a 20 per cent reserve. For big pushes, like the 3,365 miles from Fremantle to Mauritius, we filled three aircraft-quality fuel bladders and assorted jerrycans. Getting fuel was not an issue anywhere in *Egret*'s travels, except once. On arrival in Mauritius after more than a few days at sea, the local fuel dock wouldn't sell us fuel. We were invited to carry jerrycans from the local gas station – no thanks. We had 255 gallons of fuel aboard and the next stop was La Réunion, a French island an overnight away with duty-free fuel no less. We figured *Egret*'s fuel burn at 50 gallons per day, although it was less in reality. Fuel mileage in a powerboat is in your right hand – the one on the throttle.

Boat insurance was expensive in out-of-the-way places. During years of big pushes, the fuel costs were higher but with little wintering costs. In the Med, fuel costs were down but wintering costs were up. We seldom ate out, rarely visited marinas during the cruising season, so we controlled our costs like anyone. Plus we didn't have to replace strings and rags like our sailing first cousins.

All that matters is you are happy in your travels. Cruising is not a competition; it is a lifestyle that pushes your comfort level, makes you learn, and most of all makes you happy. World cruising in itself is not dangerous. As I write these words, *Egret* is well over 1,600nm offshore from Brazil and 1,300nm from Angola, yet we feel perfectly safe. You are at greater risk driving to work tomorrow. Learn the skills and if you want to cruise a thousand nautical miles from shore on a grand adventure, good for you. If you want to coastal cruise, good for you. It doesn't get any better than happy.'

A final thought, from a yacht broker

Most boats that you will be considering will most likely fall into one of the above categories and, with luck, you will now have formed a rough idea of what you're looking for. You looked at the underwater configurations, the hull shapes and the variety of rigs. What do you do next? Probably ring a yacht broker to ask what's around?

The broker's telephone probably takes more calls from would-be dreamers than a sleep clinic. And experienced brokers learn to differentiate the serious sailors from the ones who have only a vague idea of what ocean sailing involves, or what kind of boat they are looking for.

John Rodriguez is a UK-based yacht broker and he and his wife, Nicola, are experienced ocean sailors, having cruised extensively with their four children. This is 'finding the perfect boat' from the broker's point of view. Many a caller arrives at his office seeking the perfect boat for ocean sailing.

John Rodriguez, the yacht broker who knows what does and doesn't work when it comes to ocean sailing.

'The first thing I ask callers is where do you want to go, for how long, how experienced are you, are you going Trade wind sailing or are you going off the beaten track? Some come to me having no idea of what they would like, so I listen very carefully to their plans then we will go to the boatyards and narrow down a shortlist.

I find it is becoming more common for people with little experience to head off on a "gap year" with something like the ARC. For the inexperienced we really do advocate going on the rallies and doing the courses, and suggest they attend as many of the lectures and talks given by the organisations and cruising clubs. We also encourage them to read and learn as much as possible from every available source, and to consider taking an experienced skipper for the run, say, from UK to Gibraltar, and to allow plenty of time for that first leg – several months if you can. A lot can be learned on a slow cruise over three or four months before embarking on something like a long Atlantic crossing.

There are several questions that come up over and over again: how much does it cost per month to cruise, how common is piracy, how much bad weather will there be!

The biggest mistake a lot of people make is to come up with unrealistic time frames. That sets alarm bells ringing. Also cruising plans that are too rigid. And they don't always appreciate that things will fail, and that this is normal. Some don't have any appreciation at all of fitting-out costs. We try to help as much as we can by drawing on our own personal experience.

The boat that most people are looking for at the moment is 45ft plus, well built with a deck saloon, and three cabins below. Comfort tends to come before performance.

As far as our own cruising was concerned, I think we got it just about right. We crossed the

Atlantic in a Westerly Corsair (36ft sloop) and cruised the Med, Caribbean and East Coast USA on a mid-90s' Bill Dixon Moody 38. By then we had two children and the Moody was pretty much perfect for us, although we should have fitted a bimini before we left.

Some people come looking for a bargain boat that they can "do up". This can be done, and with the right quality of base boat can be a cost-effective way to have a boat that may otherwise have been out of budget. I have done it myself and refitting can be very rewarding. But it's not for the beginner or faint-hearted. If you are on a limited budget, my best advice is to look for a high-quality marque with no major structural issues. Replacing rigs, sails, engines, electronics and interiors can be done. But de-lamination and rotten cores quickly become expensive to fix. Having said that, a boat with osmosis can be a real bargain and can be fixed.'

An afterthought – even the most carefully chosen boat might prove not to be the best boat for you in the end. The variety of boats available, the mass of data that is now at our fingertips, the amount of opinion now widely published, rather than making the choice easier can make it far more difficult.

Andrew and Máire Wilkes, now devotees of gaff rig (see page 112), made an ambitious passage from the Pacific to the Atlantic via the Chilean channels. Their destinations included Panama, Galapagos, Chile, Argentina, Brazil and the Azores. The total distance was 22,000nm and it took a year and a month. The boat they chose was a Swan 44, an admirable and highly respected craft. But to prove that no boat is perfect…

'*King of Hearts*, our Swan 44, had many admirable characteristics but not everything was ideal. It would have been better if the rudder had not fallen off! I bought her two years before this cruise, thinking a boat with a higher displacement and a greater LWL would be more comfortable and faster at sea. I wanted a strong and seaworthy boat. Many very accomplished cruising people advocate small boats for long cruises, but I do not totally agree. I think a boat with more displacement and a greater LWL is faster and more comfortable when making long passages. A bigger boat also gives more room, comfort and privacy if sailing with several people. Heavier displacement boats are more likely to have larger fuel and water tanks.

However, bigger boats have heavier rigs, which require more muscle power. We used extra blocks to create a mechanical advantage (for example, a block on the head of a mainsail for the halyard can give a simple 2:1 advantage), we minimised friction by lubricating sail slides, and used Dyneema halyards to reduce weight. The smaller rope diameters needed if using Dyneema mean that they will run with less friction through existing blocks. At the time, I thought a well-designed and rigged boat of about 45ft would be about right.

King of Hearts was a great all-rounder. She was great fun to sail but was a little too "high aspect" for long ocean voyages and cruising in harsh conditions. The sail from Galapagos to Chile was a tough one: we were sailing hard on the wind for many miles during which the (new) inner forestay broke. It was also pretty uncomfortable. The Swan 44 is a "cruiser/ racer" and I now think a heavier displacement, more conservatively designed boat would have been better. In comparison to boats I have owned since *King of Hearts*, she was too light to be bouncing around in big Pacific swells and hammering into the strong winds there. The balanced rudder was vulnerable and the keel could have been too. We don't know the reason why the rudder fell off. It could have been damaged in a grounding before we bought the boat or we might have hit something in the South Atlantic just before it fell off.'

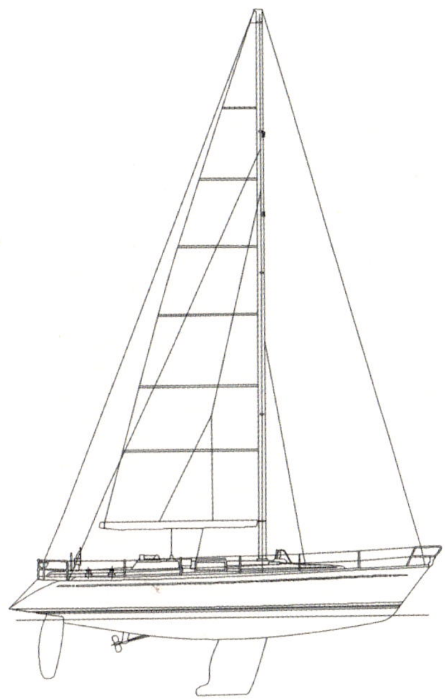

The lines of a Swan 44 – a strong and seaworthy boat but 'too light for bouncing around in Pacific Ocean swells.'

What this story proves is that choosing a boat for ocean sailing is probably the most difficult of all the decisions you will have to make. The multiplicity of choice can turn it into an impossible process. Even when what you think is the right boat sails into view, many months and many sea miles down the line you might be changing your mind.

There is no perfect boat that perfectly fits your needs, your pocket and your ambitions. But if you even so much as get close to it, you will have done well in your choice.

5 How Much to go Ocean Sailing?

'All of what you have, plus a little bit more'

The most frequently asked question, without doubt, is how much does ocean sailing cost? How much do I need, how little can I get away with? Note that the question is *not* what are the storms like, or did the pirates come and get you, but rather how did you afford to cast off and sail away? 'You look so tanned and relaxed, but how did you pay your taxes?' they will ask. Talk to anyone who has had an ocean adventure and they'll tell you that if this isn't the first topic of conversation when they meet other potential cruisers, then you can bet that within the first 15 minutes of a dockside conversation, the subject of money will rise to the surface.

Here's a decent bit of advice – don't consider if you have enough money to go, ask yourself if you can afford not to. Or as was once wisely said, 'Twenty years from now you'll be more disappointed by the things you didn't do than the ones you did do.' So throw off the lines, sail away from that familiar harbour and catch the Trade winds in your sails. Explore. Dream. Discover.

That philosophy is OK as far as it goes, but you need some money in your pocket, and you also need some courage. If financial considerations were the ruling factor in any sailing adventure, a large proportion of people who have gone on to have the most profound experiences of their lifetimes would otherwise be spending their time at home, counting their pennies, and feeling thoroughly miserable about it. It is, I suggest, not a question of asking if you can afford it, but making sailing plans that fit into the money you already have. Circumnavigations have been accomplished by people without the money to scratch their topsides with, so make your plans fit what you have to spend, and not the other way round.

There are, of course, those who have substantial sums to spend, want washing machines, a tumble dryer, gimballed wine rack and, for all I know, a billiard table. Most of us do not fall into that category, and we can think ourselves lucky. I know of one owner of a substantial craft where the systems were so complex and interconnected that he remarked, 'The Caribbean? Yes, I think we went there. Perhaps I missed it. I spent most of my time below decks chasing amps.' Nothing about sailing pays any respect to bank balances; you can't throw currency at a storm and ask it to go away. Those who think they can buy their way across the oceans are likely to be disappointed.

So don't be despondent if the boat you have may be a good metre or so shorter than you would like, and don't be afraid if the step you are about to take is a dauntingly large financial one. You can still go! Ocean sailing should be the making of dreams come true, and dreams have never been very good at spreadsheets. No one who sits down and does detailed calculations on the increase/decrease in the value of their boat, who forecasts detailed rental income from properties ashore, who watches the world currency fluctuations and decides where to head on the basis of getting the best value for the cash in their pocket, is ever going to live anything approaching a dream. Indeed, it's the certain way to turn a voyage into a nightmare. Leaving the shore under sail is going to mean a lot of letting go, and top of that list has to be the cutting of most of the financial strings that tie all our lives in knots.

That might sound like a thumbs-up to the financially reckless, but only if you approach it in that way. The ones who budget carefully and wisely, and not in a foolhardy way, are the ones who will be able to move money away from the forefront of their minds, and allow space in their heads to be filled with the uplift that ocean cruising provides. In other words, by all means consider money and how you are going to pay for your adventure, but be master of it and don't let it scare you. Your sailing should be driven by the wind, and not by the huffing and puffing of your bank balance. Remember, no matter how little money you think you have, there will be countless people who have set off round the world with far less than you.

People's idea of how much they need depends on the standard of living that they expect while they're sailing – that much is obvious. Some will not consider setting off for the tropics without a fully air-conditioned boat, others will be happy to sweat a little and live off pulses and tinned fish till they get to the other side. It's easy to draw up long lists of essentials, but few of them are vital when it comes down to it.

It's not a bad idea to draw a baseline, putting above it all the things that you really, really would like to have – generator, satphone, freezer, electric winches, hydraulic windlass, RIB and high-speed outboard – and then below the line note the things that you really can't do without such as compass, GPS, liferaft, safety equipment, decent cooker, blow-up dinghy, spare anchor, good sails. When you've done that, you might want to shift the line up or down. For example, to the list of basics you might want to add a generator. That's fine, but somewhere you have to draw that line. By doing so, you are admitting to yourself what are the basics and what you would like to have on top of that. Once you've got that straight in your head – and there might have to be a lot of negotiation between couples on exactly where that line is drawn – you can come up with a pretty accurate figure for the absolute minimum amount of capital expenditure before you set off. This figure is always useful to know. If it turns out to be ridiculously high, and you don't think you can throw anything off the list, perhaps you are thinking of a boat that's too big. On a smaller boat, for example, a generator is never going to be on the wish list because there isn't going to be room for it – simple as that.

But there's another problem. What about the unexpected, the big surprises, the disasters that demand instant money to provide instant solutions? In that list might be sudden flights home to elderly relatives, taking children to medical facilities better than the ones to hand, or simply having enough spare cash to come home for a few weeks when homesickness strikes and only setting foot in your own country can cure it. And don't forget repairs. Add those costs in to the essentials, and then ask how you are going to live. Is it going to be a meal ashore every night in every harbour, or are you going to buy sacks of beans wholesale and live off those for a year? – plenty have done just that. Are you going to hire cars and bikes and explore inland? – something cruisers are not always very good at, preferring to be on their boats. What about marina bills, though? In the cruising hotspots they can really kick a deathly hole into the best of budgets. The alternative is to anchor off, of course, but if you do that then perhaps that RIB and hydraulic windlass for anchor handling are going to have to move from the luxury to the essential list. Then there are the things that are very difficult to predict, particularly in the more remote destinations where advance information is difficult to get hold of. I'm thinking of that perfect Pacific island of which you have dreamed, which turns out to have a $500 landing fee nobody told you about, and another $500 to depart. It doesn't take many of those to set a budget back.

You can play for hours like this, and it's a good and enjoyable exercise for you will question every aspect of the voyage you want to undertake and, with luck, emerge with a much clearer idea of the cruise you are going to undertake.

But keep your eye all the time on that imaginary line that you have drawn through your budget – luxury above and essential below. Think of it as a Plimsoll line. This was invented to prevent unscrupulous owners overloading their ships with cargo at the expense of the crew's safety. A similar line can do the same for your budget. When you see the line sinking ever further, it's time to start some unloading.

Let's get down to some figures.

Terysa Vanderloo and Nick Fabbri rented out a three-bedroom flat in London in order to sail the world in their yacht, *Ruby Rose*, a Southerly 38 chosen for its build quality, its proper double bed, and the fact that it could be easily handled by a couple. They were in a position to have a new one built for them. So far they have ticked off the coast of NW Europe down to Morocco, the Canary Islands, and across the Atlantic to the Windward Islands and up to the Bahamas. They have only two quibbles with the boat: Terysa doesn't like the top-loading fridge, and a shower that wasn't part of the heads would have been better. Despite those minor niggles, they declare, 'Life thus far has been so much more than we dreamt. We are ridiculously happy with it.'

When it came to their cruising budget, in their first year they spent $3,000 a month (2017), which works out at $100 a day. But behind that figure lies *everything*: repairs, insurance, 'what ifs', spares, boat storage, groceries, the occasional big purchase such as outboard and dinghy – not just everyday expenses. Reassuringly, they have met people who claim to live happily at anchor off $10 to $20 a day, which proves that there is more than one way to conduct an ocean adventure.

Terysa Vanderloo budgeted carefully to take Ruby Rose *across the Atlantic. Their budget? $3,000 a month.*

Careful budgeting is one of the secrets of relaxed ocean sailing. Nick Fabbri hoists the Parasailor on their way across the Atlantic.

'We never realised how expensive repairs would be. Have a slush fund and make it a big one. We like to have at least $5,000 in savings and that will deal with everything unforeseen. Remember, when repairs have to be done, they must be done. We never realised how much repairs would cost, even though our boat is only five years old. Try and imagine all the "what ifs" and budget for those. It also helps if you learn to do as much as you can yourselves, saving on labour costs, which are the most expensive part of boat maintenance. We have friends who employ varnishers, for example. We do all that ourselves.

Where do we get our money from? Some people do it from savings, some get jobs along the way, and some work six months on and then six months off. But if you're thinking of working off the boat and you have the kind of job you can do remotely, it can be stressful always chasing the internet and mobile phone signals – data and connection costs can be high. Costs, of course, will be determined by where you go, so choose destinations to suit your budget. So we pay for it from the rent on our flat. We were nervous of living on savings. We've written a few articles for sailing magazines and been paid for them.

It was very important for both of us to be able to go home once a year, and that has to be part of the budget. It costs a lot. And, of course, if we are away for three months we have to spend money on storage. That's a big cost. We pay for medical insurance. Our aim is to cover all the "what ifs?"

We eat out now and again, and don't often go into marinas. We eat locally, buy local produce. It was all part of wanting to get away from consumerism.

As far as buying a boat is concerned, of the people we've met, the minimum you're going to spend on an ocean cruising boat is about $40,000, unless you're very lucky. That would be a 40ft boat about 30 years old. Expect to pay quite a bit on top of that for fitting out and repairs. Our strong advice is to buy a boat with a pedigree, that's already done some ocean sailing and has got some gear on board.'

They have condensed all this into a mission statement, which it would be wise for all ocean sailors to consider:

'Make a lifestyle for yourselves with as little stress as possible. And remember that money is the biggest stress of all. We looked at all the things that kept us awake at night, and tried to remove them.'

Chris Cromey and Suzanne Hills decided to retire early when they were in their late thirties with the intention of sailing from Scotland to New Zealand, Suzanne's home country. They searched for a boat by establishing a top limit of £65K and looked at every boat in the UK below that figure and longer than 35ft. They didn't find a boat that spoke to their hearts so widened the search into Europe. Not wanting to buy a boat that was a major restoration project, they found several good boats for sale in Europe, the selling prices helped no end by the financial crash of 2007. The result was *Whanake* (a Maori word), a Chris Robertson designed 42ft cutter, which was in such good shape that a mere two weeks after purchasing her in Gibraltar, they set off for Scotland. They advise against buying a 'wreck' with a view to restoration as costs are impossible to predict. Nor do they recommend buying new, based on conversations with fellow cruisers who have done that and suffered endless 'new boat niggles'.

Their shakedown cruise was to Norway, where they overwintered in the coldest winter there for 93 years, suffering temperatures not rising above -15°C (5 °F) for three months. Mindful of the budget, they always anchored and never spent more than seven nights alongside. Given the price of drink in Scandinavia, once the Scottish supplies ran out they stopped drinking. They lived on oats, bread, potatoes, carrots and Norwegian prawns, supplemented by caught fish and foraged fruits and mushrooms (with great care). They were impressed by the fact that in a traditionally expensive country like Norway, the ski lifts were half the price of European ones.

They left Europe in 2009, reaching Brazil six months later, then cruising south. North of Rio, and at anchor, they suffered considerable damage when a substantial yacht left on an inadequate mooring dragged down on them and scraped its substantial bowsprit the length of their boat. This being Brazil – cruisers be warned – getting compensation for the £5,000 of damage proved troublesome. Five months after the incident, the Brazilian navy had become involved but had not yet filed a report. They were warned that it might be a further two years before any action was taken. Chris and Suzanne later reported to have breathed a sigh of relief at leaving Brazil.

Early retirement, careful budgeting and a ship's cat helped Whanake *sail home to New Zealand.*

Cruising the Falkland Islands and the Chilean channels before heading into the Pacific, they became skilled at sailing both on and off the anchor. This was not only done for the satisfaction of it, but as they said, 'Eliminating thirty minutes of engine use every time we anchor really adds up in terms of diesel over a cruise as long as ours.' En route to Easter Island, they celebrated the catching of a 25lb tuna, and took in all the evocative Pacific destinations: Robinson Crusoe Island, Easter Island and Pitcairn. It was a remarkable cruise, but the budgeting had been as carefully planned as the sailing.

'We had a period of two and a half years between making the decision to go cruising and actually casting off and used this period for not only saving (we were both full-time working then) but also ruthlessly selling on eBay everything that we wouldn't be taking on the boat with us. We also lived aboard during this time to minimise living costs and accelerate the selling process. We didn't want to end up in the situation of having to stop somewhere part way through cruising and fly home to work, so we were committed to saving as much as possible and ending the dual living costs of a land life and a boat life.

The decision to go cruising came before the boat. We were both savers anyway, and the bank balance was healthy. Not being big spenders, we had spent the years from university to our late thirties working in professional jobs, but still living largely on a student budget, from making our own lunch to buying second-hand goods etc.

Whanake was in excellent shape. We did not want to do an extensive refit of an older boat. A refit is a big commitment in both time and money and we wouldn't advise anyone to go down this path unless they have a lot of both and a real passion for the vessel. Given the amount of ongoing maintenance that's needed for any boat, we thought it better to purchase a sound vessel to begin with and keep her that way.

Part of the great pleasure of cruising for us is the back-to-basics, simple lifestyle. Add all the latest and greatest boat equipment and cruising life can easily become as complicated as land life. So we've kept the old equipment the boat came with in working order, and we keep things as simple as possible.

Apart from a basic GPS chart plotter, we use the essential navigation equipment – log, compass and depth sounder. We do also have a basic stand-alone radar. The boat came with a 1980s' era water maker and we kept this maintained, but used for emergencies only. We use windvane self-steering and believe this is a far superior system over modern autopilot systems. Windvane steering is reliable, requires no power, is easy and simple to maintain, and it lasts (ours is 1980s' era). We've heard discussions among cruisers go on for hours about the problems with their integrated autopilot and navigation systems. We only operated a fridge, not a freezer.

Our advice would be to keep everything as simple as possible. There's an endless array of boat equipment out there; but so much of it is superfluous. Make sure you've checked off the essential navigation and safety equipment for ocean cruising, have the spare parts needed for the boat and a good set of tools. Beyond that it's simply filling the boat with food, water, gas and diesel supplies. We would often take several weeks to victual the boat before a long passage, making regular visits to supermarkets to buy up special offers, discounts and impending out-of-date stock.

For the first two years while we cruised in Europe we did still have a house and rented it out with an agency, but then they started talking about the property needing a new kitchen etc and we sold it. Selling up completely was very liberating. Casting off the lines with the knowledge that our life was now contained in our boat gave us a great sense of freedom. It was partly driven by the fact that we were on a one-way trip to New Zealand and had no plans to return to a life in the UK. It gave us a real sense of adventure to cut all the land ties and greatly simplifies everything. We didn't want to operate a dual life with land costs.

We kept up full comprehensive boat insurance for the first two years in Europe. But on leaving Europe, insurance premiums greatly increase and with the added annoyance of insurance companies trying to insist on three people for ocean passages we gave it up. We had nothing until arrival in NZ, where we took up third party only insurance. Given the premiums once outside of Europe, the cost/benefit of insurance (short of total loss) seems marginal. Also, the greatest risk of damage to the boat seems to be among marinas and crowded mooring fields, both of which we avoided as much as possible, so we felt perfectly comfortable not having insurance. We also did not have medical insurance because at the time no travel insurance would cover sailing outside of incidental sailing as part of a holiday. Risky, but we got away with it. But we did not cruise in areas like the US. We only had one medical incident in Chile where we visited the hospital, waited in the queue with the locals, and paid for the services at the reasonable non-insurance claim rate.

We used a prepaid currency card as we cruised. If you go with Mastercard or VISA, it works virtually everywhere. You can withdraw local cash from cashpoints and use for purchases. Preloaded at a set currency rate, it incurs no other charges at most cashpoints. And if stolen, it only contains the preloaded balance, which you can keep at a low level. We also kept a few hundred US dollars as

Knowing your financial position as well as your precise position was the key to Whanake's *ocean crossing success.*

cash hidden in the boat for emergencies but we only took currency cards on to land, and a minimal amount in cash, and left everything else hidden in a fake electrical box on board – which is no longer there, incidentally. Otherwise we took all the usual recommended precautions when on land. We also tended to cycle and used folding bikes rather than walk when in dodgy areas.

Two main things helped us to reduce our expenditure. We avoided marinas, and we undertook everything that we possibly could to fix and maintain the boat. Avoiding marinas means choosing cruising grounds where there's plenty of natural shelter for anchoring. In Europe we chose to cruise Scotland, Ireland, Norway, Sweden, Finland and Galicia – all with good natural shelter – and then later sailed right past the entrance to the Mediterranean. We always invested in cruising guides for the area and always found them invaluable with the anchoring options. Needless to say, having good ground tackle and anchoring skills makes it possible. We would often anchor in a bay just a few kilometres outside a city and use our folding bikes to get into the centre rather than use a marina.

Only very occasionally did we allow ourselves treats. We can count on one hand the number of evening meals out in seven years. We got greater pleasure from fresh fruit and vegetables on making a landfall, and just enjoying buying and cooking local food.

We didn't give ourselves a monthly allowance but we were always mindful of keeping costs down. We loosely tried to live within the rental income of 400 GBP/ month for the first two years, but monthly expenditure was highly variable depending on boat maintenance, victualling for remote areas etc. For example, we had a period from Boxing Day to Easter in the Falkland Islands when we didn't even open the wallet.

We always had about GBP 10K readily available at the bank. We probably would have got a bit anxious if it went below about 5K, but it never did. 10K seems about the right figure to sort out some major job on the boat such as rigging replacement. Also, with elderly parents it was inevitable we would have to fly home at least once. In the end, it all worked out as planned as long as we kept it simple, avoided marinas, and did all the work ourselves. It's a low-cost way of living, and a way of having an adventure at the same time.

The bottom line is that, on average over seven years of cruising, we spent about GBP 11K per year. That's for two people and includes everything – boat and personal.

Cruising, like any sort of life, can create financial stress if you let it. It's all about working with what you've got. There are plenty of cruisers out there doing it in much smaller boats and smaller budgets than ours.'

Keeping costs down – less easy than you think

Mike and Windy Robertson set sail in 2012 with their two young daughters, Eleanor and Frances, aged seven and five, with the ambition of being able to live at the US government's official poverty level for four people. At the time they set off, that figure was $23,000 a year. As Mike says, 'I thought our lifestyle could be had for less than that. I was wrong – so far.' Mike gave up a career in IT, Windy was a map-maker. Mike said, 'I will miss good, hot showers and internet access and everything that a good, land-based kitchen brings. Windy will miss her cats, and all the above.'

Eleanor said, 'I will miss the animals, friends, and a Christmas tree.' Frances merely adds, 'Yeah, same as Eleanor.'

If you exclude the refit costs of *Del Viento*, a heavy displacement 39ft Sparkman & Stephens Fuji 40 built in the late 70s, then Mike estimates that their annual expenditure is around $36,000 a year (2013 prices). The largest part of their monthly costs come from purchases of food, which includes coffee at Starbucks when available, dining out, alcohol, groceries. Eating out depended on where they were: in Mexico they ate out often and spent about $800 per month on food. In Victoria, Canada, that figure rose to over $1,000 and so they reined in their onshore appetites. However, Victoria offered other expensive attractions, such as gym classes and activities for the two girls.

Mike is clear that those expenditure figures could come down by making less use of marinas, and possibly fewer visits to Starbucks. 'In Mexico, we spent much more time in marinas than we wanted simply because of the work we were doing to the boat. Slip (marina) fees in the US and Canada are high. In the US, we chose to visit friends and family in places where anchoring out wasn't an option. In Canada, we chose to stay over in a slip in an expensive city.'

Also, insurance costs can knock a substantial hole through many budgets (see below). For example, their October figure for total expenditure was $2,400, rising sharply to nearly $6,000 when a family health insurance premium came due, also liability insurance, which was required in Mexico, and to an even greater extent in Canada.

Refit costs, however, far eclipse monthly living costs. Although a lot of money had been spent on the boat before moving aboard, further major expenditure totalled $40,000 and included (new) outboard, chain plates, water tanks, holding tank, instruments, turbo rebuild, mainsail, code zero, interior lights, hatches, mattresses, radar and mainsail cover. They are wise enough to realise that this will not be the end of the list. Those engaged in long-term cruising reckon on a major refit every five or so years. In the case of the Robertsons, an expenditure of $3,000 in April 2012 jumped dramatically to $22,000 when they realised they needed a new anchor windlass, mattresses, new instruments and radar, an electric outboard, and a versatile Portland Pudgy (www.portlandpudgy.com), an inflatable rowing dinghy, sailing dinghy and liferaft in one. There were also the inevitable surprises: 'We had to spend $800 on medical care for an eye problem.'

To supplement their budget, Mike became the author of several books (see bibliography) including *Selling your Writing to the Boating Magazines* and co-authoring *Voyaging with Kids*.

Very small budget sailing

When it comes to fitting out, there are less expensive routes than buying new. Although you need to be cautious with things like electric autopilots, outboard motors, and items that may have had a lengthy previous life, second-hand kit can provide a lot of bargains. Boatyards can be good places to start – one boat's throw-outs can be just the thing you are looking for. One cruiser reported having found davits, roller furler, stainless steel boarding ladder, pumps and light fittings for the cost of a few beers. Even better than that, some advocate following in the wake of the great cruising rallies, such as the ARC, which leaves from Las Palmas in the Canaries. The trick, according to one source, is to wait till the fleet has left and then go quickly round the marina skips. Great bargains have been unearthed that way.

Clearly, mooring costs can suck up a lot of cash and around the world the price of marina berths is ever on the increase. To avoid them you need to be able to anchor safely and securely, and you also need a safe and reliable means of getting ashore. Budget to make sure you have a sufficiently heavy anchor. An anchor that is good in kelp might not work so well in mud. And once you've chosen a main anchor, budget for more than enough chain – no one has ever had a sleepless night because they had too much chain out. If of good manufacture with no signs of stress or rusting, there is no reason not to buy a second-hand anchor.

To make getting ashore as safe and comfortable as possible, spend money on a good tender, which can again be safely bought second-hand. Stability is the key here. You might be anchored in a chop and you don't want to be ejected from it the first time you board it. RIBs are popular, but can be heavy. The cheapest way to get around is to row, and some dinghies row better than others, so make sure it is equipped with good, strong oars of a decent length and row whenever you can to save on petrol costs. You will probably want an outboard too, but think of it as your reserve and not premier form of propulsion. The best type of dinghy for rowing will be solid, probably made of wood, with sweeps built for the job. But you need substantial deck space to be able to carry one of those.

The more maintenance work you can do yourself, the more comfortable your budget will be. Acquiring electrical and mechanical skills before you leave are as good as having money in the bank. If you can tackle all routine engine tasks you can save a small fortune in ever-increasing engineer costs. Handiness at basic carpentry will avoid the cost of repairs, and even the ability to wield a brush of antifouling paint will avoid a steep bill. With these skills, of course, comes the need for tools, often specialist ones, and if you apply the principle of careful second-hand shopping there are big savings to be made when putting a toolkit together.

If you want to be really cautious about your budgetary control, at the end of every day make a note of every last penny you have spent, so you know where the money's going and can spot the unexpected.

Here are some thoughts gleaned from successful ocean sailors:

- Don't sail away with any debts. Pay off everything you can because that is what gives you freedom.
- Don't budget for a miserable time. You will need to see movies and buy books and DVDs so don't pretend you can do without them.
- Think carefully about credit/debit cards and how you access your money in the bank. There's little fun in arriving in a new country and the ATMs spit back your card in disgust. Know how you can quickly access money, particularly emergency money, anywhere in the world.
- When sailing from country to country, ask around how food prices at your destination compare with what you are already paying. Lots of cruisers arrive in a new country wishing they'd stocked up with staples at their last port of call. Food prices can vary dramatically from country to country. Learn what has a long shelf life and if you see it cheap, buy as much as you can stow. Some countries charge for water. It has been reported that basics such as soap, shampoo and toilet paper can be very expensive on some Pacific islands.
- Think carefully about sailing off having sold everything behind you. Even the best planned cruises can go wrong and you might wish you could quickly get back to somewhere called home.
- Beware some of the budgets revealed by cruisers on the internet. Although they might not be trying to deceive you, they may not be painting the full picture. If a crew seems to be spending a lavish $3,000 a month per person and you are feeling nervous that you can't spend the same, ask yourself if they might not have some private income that they aren't mentioning. Work out a budget that fits your lifestyle, and be aware that comparisons with others might not be helpful.
- Going home might be the last thing on your mind, but at some stage you will want to, if only briefly. Tuck away the money for this so it comes as no shock if an elderly relative, for example, needs an urgent visit.
- Think about costs ashore, which is not just meals and entertainment. One of the joys of cruising is visiting foreign lands, and you never gain much of a picture of what a place is really like if you never leave the harbour area. To get to the heart of a country you are going to have to budget for car hire/cycle hire/ bus fares and taxis. This is money well spent.
- Prepare to be surprised by how much you spend on communication, whether by internet, cell phone or satellite. We have become used to being part of a connected world and from a boat this can be a significant expense.
- You can plan for a monthly budget, but your costs will choose their own timetable. For some reason, boat expenses seem to come in huge lumps, rather than be spread evenly throughout the year. The biggest seem to arrive when boatyard work is being done and one job reveals another, which leads to another, and so on till you suddenly find your bank balance to be worse than zero. There again, there will be weeks on end when you will spend no more than what it takes to feed and water you for the day. Sadly, there's no way to even out the peaks and troughs.

Earning money while sailing

Everyone's dream, eh? A nice little bit of cash rolling into the bank account on a regular basis while the blue seas lap against the bow and the only other sound is that of falling coconuts. Before you get too carried away with the idea of combining sailing with a money-earning venture, note the word 'earning'. It still requires effort, concentration, time and skill. Having a job on a boat is no different from one in an office, except the view's probably better.

If you don't want to bring work into your cruising life, there are many happy cruisers who sail for six months of the year – naturally, the best six months – and return home for the rest of the year to refill the coffers. If you have the sort of work where that is a possibility then it can be a satisfying way of making some money to take to sea. Even better if you can arrange a job share on a six-monthly basis.

But that will not work for everyone and finding work wherever you happen to moor up might be required. Many ingenious ideas have been come up with over the years, and the following is given as an inspiration and not an exhaustive list. Remember, local laws and regulations will have to be taken into account, also visa restrictions, which might prevent any kind of employment. Income tax might have to be paid, and if you are using your boat as a money-earning workshop your insurer (if you have one) might want to know.

CASH IN ON YOUR SKILLS

If you have marine engineering or electrical skills, together with the experience and the toolkit to tackle most on-board problems, then there could be some ready money to be made. Word spreads quickly, particularly where cruisers and live-aboards congregate. And if your charges are competitive, and your reputation is a good one, then you might soon find a queue spreading down the pontoon. However, you will need to promote yourself, perhaps with flyers left in cockpits or cards left in the shower block. The words you don't want to hear are: 'If only I'd known I could have given you a job.' The same would apply if you happen to have a sewing machine and a basic knowledge of sail and canvas repair. One couple set themselves up as experts in the making of winter covers and did great business, all from the cabin of a none too large catamaran. Much of their time was spent stepping over rolls of canvas, but they earned a living and soon realised that there's hardly a boat that doesn't need a stitch or two to keep it together. A refrigeration engineer is never going to be short of a job in the tropics, likewise scuba divers will always earn money from untangling lines from propellers or giving hulls an underwater scrub. Water makers are always failing so you'll be in demand if you know how to fix them. If you can, get testimonials for all the jobs you do, for they can be almost as valuable as the cash.

You'll always come across someone who wants a boat moved and doesn't have the skills, time or inclination to do it on their own. If you can prove you are a capable boat deliverer, preferably one who can produce a couple of testimonials and a few qualifications, then money can be earned that way. Likewise for paid crewing, if you are lucky enough to come across someone who is happy to pay to have you on board. But if you have skills that easily transfer from shore to boat, such as hairdressing, you may be able to create a market. Cutting hair doesn't require a lot of capital investment, or space, making a boat an ideal place for a pop-up salon. Cleaning, babysitting and boat caretaking are regular standbys as quick money earners, but the more inventive have, for example, bought a cheap car and set themselves up as a marina taxi. Needless to say, if you have IT skills and can configure email, Wi-Fi, satphone and a thousand other gizmos, you'll always find someone who will pay you money to get them out of an electronic hole. But make it clear from the outset that this is your job and you expect to get paid.

If you understand how media works, and understand how to harness the internet to promote yourself, there is some money to be made from producing videos for YouTube, writing blogs, or supplying copy to sailing magazines. The magazine market is always hungry for well-written material, especially from unusual parts of the world. They are looking for stories that have a different kind of tale to tell. Magazines have suffered in recent years from the advertising revenue pool draining down the internet plughole, and fees paid are much smaller than a decade ago. But if you have the writing skills and are a natural storyteller, you will find a ready market. Consider reading *Selling Your Writing to the Boating Magazines* by Michael Robertson. As he points out, the raw materials – words – are free. As long as you have the enthusiasm and are prepared to take it seriously and learn the craft, there is a modest amount of money to be earned. More, if you can combine it with photography, which will have to be of a higher standard than a routine snap.

As far as making videos goes, this is a much greater challenge. This is now a competitive business, and although anyone can chuck any old bit of video on to the internet, your storytelling skills, and filming and editing skills, have to be of a fairly high order to compete. As with all successful screen ventures, the most lucrative (through online ads that appear on the same page as the video) have content that can boast some star quality. The most viewed tend to be shot in the most romantic locations with the most vibrant, youthful people, usually dressed for swimming. But even these need to be promoted and a complete mastery of social media is necessary if you want to make any decent money this way. Even so, there are no great riches, and as one maritime YouTuber remarked: 'If you set the rewards against the huge amount of time and effort it takes to produce a polished video, you'd be better off going ashore and getting yourself a job flipping burgers.' The best advice seems to be to make videos if you enjoy them, or make them for the folks back home. But to fund your sailing, forget it.

Blogging has a similar promotional requirement. As with writing for magazines, the words are free but the work comes in the writing and promotion, for without sufficient viewers your advertising income will be pitifully small. Affiliate marketing can provide a revenue stream but this too requires some skill. If, for example, you were writing in your blog about how you'd been out to an island and done a great day's photography with a 'super-duper camera', then by providing a link to a retailer like Amazon, you can receive a percentage of the sale if a click-through from your blog results in a sale. Sounds good. One cruiser reported spending a couple of hours a day developing and servicing this, and three months on had made only eight dollars. However, persistence paid off and several months later he is receiving in the order of hundreds of dollars a month. The price of this, of course, is that you have effectively taken on an office job, you have less time to sail, and the pressing need is always to be close to an easy, reliable and speedy internet connection. Seasoned online workers soon have an encyclopaedic knowledge of every Wi-Fi-enabled coffee shop in every port.

There are many opportunities for online working if you have, say, translational or copywriting skills and there are many websites now that offer working opportunities. As long as the work gets done, and to the right standard, most employers won't care, or even know, where you are. But be aware of one mistake that is easily made: to those on the shore, an excuse along the lines of 'I'm sorry I was late on the deadline but the anchor was dragging' will get you no sympathy.

Then there's always the possibility of renting your own boat out, with you as captain and everyone else paying for the privilege of sailing with you. A well-fitted boat in a good location can make decent money. Although US-centric, the websites boatsetter.com and plainsailing.com give you an idea of current rates.

There can be a lot of regulation, though, before a boat can be chartered and bringing a boat up to the required spec can be hugely expensive.

New online businesses to facilitate the renting of accommodation have transformed the shoreside rental business, such as airbnb.com, and there are now companies offering to rent out berths on your boat as if they were rooms in a country cottage. New players in this field are bedsonboard.com and there will be many others. All require your boat to be fitted out below to a high standard, with fresh towels and bedding supplied, for example. Your boat is not likely to appeal to this market if the heads have a slight leak and the bilges need pumping every hour.

Advice to consider:
'Make your money before you go cruising, and spend it wisely as you sail.'

EASY MONEY – OR MONEY THAT REQUIRES THE LEAST EFFORT TO EARN

A house ashore is rarely anything other than an appreciating asset, but for a cruiser that is not the most important reason for hanging on to some bricks and mortar. There are a good number of miserable folk in harbours all over the globe who sold everything they had, bought the biggest boat they could afford and set off for the horizon. Their story goes something like this: for the first ten years it was great and they sailed the seven seas, but then they aged and the energy of youth seemed lacking. The mainsail was just that bit harder to raise, electric winches were contemplated. The winters on board seemed that bit colder and longer. If they'd had a choice they would have sailed in the summer months and returned to the easy winter living onshore, *if* they'd had a choice. But the home was long gone. They thought of selling the boat, but for some reason it never seemed quite as valuable as they hoped, and the brokers expressed disappointment at the state of the market. So they were stuck. The only safe advice is: don't sell the house. Or if you do, bank the money, invest it, ring-fence it. Think of it as the price of a return ticket.

Many cruisers rent their homes when they sail off. But consider carefully who is going to deal with the broken fridge, the peeling paint, the state of the garden. Unless you can be certain of perfect tenants who will not move on after a few short months, you will probably want to use a management service, which will take all these cares off your shoulders, for a price. It might be a price well worth paying, though. Imagine the stress of being on the foredeck, hauling the anchor in a rising wind, and the phone goes. The tenants can't get the television to work!

But renting your house remains the safest approach. It provides income, and the security of always having somewhere you can call home.

6 Can the Kids Come Too?

You can't leave them behind, but how do you take your kids to sea?

Is the ocean any place for children? This may be the first question you ask yourself when the lure of the sea meets the harsh practicalities of daily family life; the moment when the overwhelming desire to sail away meets the cliff face of practicalities involved in taking your children as crew. At the very best you imagine yourselves as a self-contained family unit, insulated from all the pressures of the shoreside world, watching your children grow and mature in the unique atmosphere the sea provides. And then you remember this morning's tantrum, the frequency of sore throats that sometimes need a doctor, the schooling… and on it goes. Do you take them, or not? Given that you can't just leave them behind, like you might put a dog in kennels, you are faced with the choice of having your great adventure now, or waiting a couple of decades. Difficult.

A generation back, only the smallest proportion of ocean cruisers would take their children with them and parents would wait till their children had grown up, left home and built their own lives. Only then would the elders set sail. It's different now. Adventures are to be had when we want them, not when old-style thinking might suggest patience was a better choice. Consequently, these days the kids *have* to go too. And many will make a great success of it, and remember it as one of the very best periods of family life. But there's no guarantee.

A lot will depend on the age of the child. Teenagers and toddlers do not present the same problems. But the dilemmas that surround taking children of whatever age on a long sea voyage transcend their ages and boil down, essentially, to keeping them safe and keeping them happy, and for the grown-ups to discharge their parental responsibilities to educate and prepare them for a grown-up world. None of these tasks can be lightly undertaken. Nevertheless, there are plenty of ocean sailors who have taken their young families with them, despite all advice to the contrary, and have returned a more solid family than when they left home. Being at sea has a way of bringing people together like no other, and that applies as much to parents and children as any other crew you can think of.

If you were to draw up a list of pros and cons, it might go like this…

On the plus side, you will be together as a family, sharing some of life's richest experiences. The children will learn far more about the world than they would in a thousand geography lessons. They will develop a sense of self-reliance and responsibility, and learn to work as part of a team. They will be divorced from the snares of social media, the wired-up world, and have time to grow their imaginations. They will mature and develop in a way that their peers will not, and with a wider vision of the world. They will walk tall for the rest of their lives, able to boast that they 'have crossed an ocean'. Also, there's no school run to do.

However, there's another side to it. Not everyone likes being at sea and while some children will eventually warm to the idea, others will never understand it, and for them a long ocean passage might feel like imprisonment. The family unit is fine as far as it goes, but without interactions with outsiders, the losses can far outweigh the gains. They will have to leave their friends behind – how are you going to explain that and cope with the resulting tears? Enthusiastically telling them where the voyage will take them might not impress them; they'll simply ask what are we going to do for Christmas? Children do not have an unlimited capacity for invention, and when they've read enough books, done enough puzzles, and the catching of a fish now and again has become routine, how are you going to stop them getting bored? When the wind howls and the seas rise, how are you going to stop them getting scared? And there's schooling – you will be their only teacher. Then there's the safety stuff. Might they fall overboard? What if they get ill and the nearest doctor is 2,000 miles away? What right do I have to place my children at such obvious risk? How do you explain to them that they'll have to leave their pets behind? And what's the answer to the question 'Are we nearly there yet?' when the next Pacific island is 2,000 miles away?

It's all too much, you finally admit. I'm a selfish parent who is going to condemn my children into uneducated isolation where they are bound to get sick and possibly die! And all because I want to go ocean sailing. Oh, and let's not forget the influence of grandparents and older family who might think you're crazy and put subtle obstacles in your way.

If these are the questions you've been asking yourself about whether or not there is any place for children on an ocean passage, you are in exactly the same mental cockpit as the thousands of couples who have thought it through and bravely made the choice to take their children to sea.

We never took our two children across an ocean, but we did circumnavigate the entire UK coastline – a tricky undertaking even for an adult crew, with fast-flowing tides, uncertain weather and unforgiving coastlines. We took them when they were only five and three years old. Many of the problems a trip like that can present are similar to those to be found when ocean sailing.

My wife, Libby Purves, has written:

'You are taking your children away from everything they know – their routines and surroundings, and they have needs and habits; you have to respect that and be prepared for it. The key to keeping them happy wasn't in the boat-craft or visiting exotic locations, but in stimulating their imaginations. We told endless stories – often inspired by our surroundings – which the children would then act out for days. We took a small plastic suitcase full of miniature cars and dolls and dinosaurs, and Rose in particular used these to play out tales and dramas at the table in the galley.

Every night we would carry on with a never-ending saga full of characters like pirates and Bonnie Prince Charlie, and singing endless songs. But we were lucky; we had two children. If you only have one child you have to be prepared to be a second child with them. You can't just expect children to trundle along: you must plan little outings when you get to port, set up hammocks on deck or offer fishing lines, and keep up the mental stimulation with stories, stories, stories.'

And commenting on one family's misfortune to lose their boat after a grounding on a Pacific island, she wrote:

'My eyebrows rose slightly at someone's suggestion that communications and weather forecasting have made ocean cruising feel less risky. Only a fool thinks the sea is tamed. But urban life and motorways are risky, and we impose them on children with far less thought and training than goes into the expertise of navigating and maintaining a seagoing boat. En famille, the inescapable fact is that you as parents take fuller responsibility for children's

There's a job for all ages on a boat – Peter Russell hoists the courtesy flag. (RUSSELL)

well-being than ever ashore. No safety barriers, road crossings, helpful relatives, neighbours, babysitters, doctors, police, teachers. You are also their environment and example; only from the way you interact can they learn courtesy, consideration and resilience. This is true in normal life, but more intensely on an expedition. As the writer Hilaire Belloc said: 'I am not sure that the best thing I find in sailing is not this salt of reality. There, sailing the sea, we play every part of life: control, direction, effort, fate.'

Children on any long trip also learn about the kindness of strangers; in a new harbour you are a petitioner, an immigrant. You warm to a helpful harbourmaster or fisherman, and are inordinately grateful for a seaside B&B allowing a family bath. One of our son's most heartfelt diary entries, in gale-swept Fishguard, was after hot cocoa in the warmth of the sailing club kitchen: "Mrs Chapman let us watch her count potatoes!"

As for education, we took tedious reading schemes and attempted basic maths, but daily life provided elements of geography, history, biology, physics, engineering. Anything a bit hard, a bit uncomfortable, unpredictable, earthily basic and grubby, but rewarding stress and fright with the sudden beauty of a dawn, a dolphin, a dry joke. In soft indoor lives, these things are bracing.'

It is, of course, one thing to sail the oceans with children, but a whole new ball game to do it with babies. In some ways, of course, babies might be easier. For their safety, they can easily be confined in secure bunks with no danger of tumbling out; with toddlers, you can never be quite so certain. There was a time when taking babies on a boat would have been unthinkable, if not irresponsible. But times change and no sooner have they slithered into the world than they are off down to the boat and away across the oceans of the world.

Lying in Ushuaia, I fell into conversation with a young French couple who were clearly sailing on a low budget. For heating during the southern Chile winter (which can be harsh), they had riveted together tin cans to make a chimney and stove on which they burned driftwood. As we chatted, it became clear that the gurglings of a very small baby were heard coming from below. It was only six days old. They explained that they had spent much of the winter in the windy, frosty Chilean channels and only when they thought the baby was due did they sail to Ushuaia where, conveniently, the hospital is a short walk from the moorings. 'Once the baby had been born,' he explained, 'we came back to the boat. Soon we shall set off back to the channels.' All this spoken as if it were the most ordinary thing in the world.

Jess Lloyd-Mostyn and her husband, James, have now been cruising for eight years, in which time they have clocked up over 26,000 miles, made landfall in 36 countries, crossed two oceans and, most importantly, had three babies along the way.

'I was 30 years old and James, my husband, was 42 when we started talking about starting a family. The idea of the "normal" life back in London with kids, a home and a traditional career seemed less and less relevant to us.

There's a traditional way of going about having babies on land, which seems to also involve buying an immense amount of gear. But where was the manual for expectant parents on a yacht? How do you baby-proof and what equipment is really necessary in a home where space is at a premium? What do you do once your little ones are crawling, walking or potty-training?

"Boat kids" are a great advertisement for the benefits of sailing with children. Cruising children are generally friendly, conversational, undaunted by interactions with other adults and relatively hardy. Without exception, children we've met while cruising have looked us in the eye when they speak, can scramble up the mast, on to the boom or jump off the boat with ease and coolness.

When our daughter was born, we had the boat in a marina just to get used to the new arrival in a more controlled way. The usual kit of crib, stroller and car seat weren't going to work on board so we focused on strategies for how to handle sleeping, feeding, carrying and changing. Surprisingly, all of these are fairly simple with a newborn. Our cabin has a wall-to-wall bed so was perfect for co-sleeping with no worry of her falling out. I breastfed her, so that meant there were never any bottles to sterilise or formula to buy. A sling or soft-structured carrier was the easiest way of getting her on or off the boat and for helping to lull her to sleep as we walked the docks. We chose to use cloth nappies and had plenty of water for laundry, while moored in the marina. We began to think that we'd completely got the hang of being boat parents.

But two things changed.

First, the boat started moving and then the baby moved as well. Resuming our lives at anchor with an infant meant that every trip ashore needed a strategy. We had to have a bag packed full of nappies, wipes, snacks and extra bits of clothing. This was when we started using a baby lifejacket, as anchorages are not necessarily still. Even when your journey ashore is calm the wind can kick up, giving you a wet and bumpy ride back, which is daunting with a baby. We had to get used to being at the helm with her strapped to us in the carrier, learn how to change nappies under way and find a safe place for her to doze in, taking into account the heel of the boat and unpredictability of the sea.

Our first passage as a family was the 26-day, 2,850-mile crossing of the Pacific Ocean from Mexico to the Marquesas in French Polynesia. It was then that our eight-month-old daughter learned to crawl, which meant that I saw a lot less sea and a lot more of the cabin than before. However, we made one major concession and enlisted an extra member of crew. It was a smart decision and one that we've found is a good compromise for those who choose not to give up on their larger sailing goals.

Our one major change to the boat has been the addition of baby netting all along the guardrails, pushpit and bow. This allows little ones the freedom to roam without needing a parent hovering over them. A boat is already a remarkably baby-proof environment; there are rounded edges, drawers are fitted with features that stop them flying out at sea, and there are no live electrics or other dangers at toddler height as they'd be a liability out on the water.

Sailing with children brings many opportunities for new firsts. One day I heard James yell, and then our daughter let out a squeal of delight and called me up on deck. Her face is bursting with anticipation of sharing the news.

"A fish!" she beamed, her chest swelling with pride at having caught it. "My FIRST fish!" she cried.'

Jess Lloyd-Mostyn's advice:

- Make sure everyone on board has a properly fitting lifejacket, and let the children help in choosing theirs.
- A playpen or something similar will keep a baby safe below when both parents are needed on deck. A soft sling or baby carrier is great when the baby needs to be on deck with you but you need both hands free.
- When choosing baby netting, get the best quality you can. Ensure it is knotted and not glued – the glue can degrade in hot sun.
- It's worth giving cloth nappies a try. Better for the environment and you've always got clean nappies on board.
- A clamp-on table chair is useful, as that will keep them secure at sea.
- Keeping your kids warm and dry is the first step to making sure they have a good time at sea. Good-quality waterproofs will prove worth the extra expense.
- There are a huge number of sailing families. Don't hesitate to ask others for advice.

By way of reassurance that babies can come through most things at sea, largely unscathed, the return home of the Ingram family after their Pacific adventure might offer some comfort.

They had reached Vancouver on Canada's west coast and left the boat for the winter. The plan was to haul her by truck to Quebec from where they would follow the St Lawrence River, then on to Newfoundland, and across the North Atlantic to home. But unlike on their Pacific voyage, this one carried extra cargo. Robert was less than six months old when they set off.

The Ingrams wrote at the time:

'When at anchor or under way in calm weather, Robert is very happy in his bouncer, jumping up and down in the cabin, in the cockpit or even on the foredeck from the staysail halyard. Otherwise he can sit in his bucket-like chair strapped to the jib sheet winch or in his high chair clamped to the saloon table and watch the surroundings. We also made lee cloths to create a playpen for him on the port saloon berth and across the entire forecastle bunk. The hammock that hangs in the saloon and used to hold fruit has become the toy box, dangling with rattles and teddy bears like a stuffed mobile.

We had been looking forward to the opportunity for some good walking in Newfoundland and got very used to bundling Robert into the dinghy and motoring ashore, installing him into the backpack and setting off. He seemed to love the change of scene and was very content, even when he and his father fell thigh deep into a stinking bog!

As we waited in Newfoundland for an opportunity to make our Atlantic crossing, we had been keeping an eye on the track of Hurricane Katrina (August 2005) and watched in horror with the rest of the world as it struck with full force on New Orleans. Its remnants moved north over the continent and, as it drew level with us, would give us a useful push offshore. The five-day forecast showed nothing sinister, although a long-range hurricane prediction showed tropical depression number 14, not even formed yet and due to dissipate, way to the south and heading for the Caribbean. So, on 1st September, with Robert exactly six months old, we decided to go.

However, just as we realised the threat of that hurricane had passed, the next, which had been pushing up behind, increased speed rapidly. We continued our dash for the safety of the marina at Horta on Faial and succeeded in outrunning it, arriving only 24 hours before it passed just north of the Azores group. Phew!

The relief of arriving safe and sound was immense. We had been at sea for nearly ten days and covered over 1,450 miles, mostly on the wind, at an average speed of more than 6 knots. The last entry in the log reads: "A fairly nerve-racking passage – terrifying. (Katharine)" Robert, however, had taken the whole trip in his little stride. He was unfazed both by being at sea for so long and by any anxiety he may have picked up on. But even he welcomed the change of scene.'

If your children have been used to boats and sailing from an early age, it will help. Pam Wall's daughter, Samantha, was christened when just one week old on a 30ft wooden sloop on a Gulf Stream passage to the Bahamas, living in a bunk with a mesh lee cloth and learning to swim underwater before she could walk. Her brother, James, a couple of years younger, made his first ocean passage from Florida to Bermuda at eight months. Pam and Andy Wall had worked for ten years at building a 39ft sloop, *Kandarik*, when they took off to sail around the world, leaving from Fort Lauderdale. The children were then seven and four, described by Pam as 'children of the sea'.

She says:

'This was the most important and educational experience a family could achieve. It was not considered unusual to us, or different, just an extension of what we had worked to have after many years of hoping we could pull it off. And we did.

It wasn't difficult to explain to our very young children that we were about to take them from home on a long and wonderful voyage at sea. Samantha and Jamie had been so used to going off on long holidays, and cruises to the Bahamas, up to Maine, and also Bermuda, long before we were able to set off for our round the world cruise. They took it for granted that we cast off for some time, and then come home again, only to head off again soon after when we could get away from our jobs.

But, the one thing we stressed to them was that we would not be seeing their young cousins or Grandma and Grandpa for some long time. We were a very close family, and this had to be understood by all of us, not just the children. For us, leaving was just another time to say goodbye to our family, sail out the breakwater, and have the highest hopes of what we would encounter in a world circumnavigation. And you know what? Every single thing exceeded our highest expectations for all four of the crew of *Kandarik*.

The children became so used to this life, it seemed completely ordinary to be getting ready to sail away time and again. I guess that is what comes from taking them sailing when the children are just infants. But it certainly worked as each time we took off for a sailing cruise, they were just as excited as we were. What worked was having them become so comfortable with this type of lifestyle.

Missing the family back home was not such an important question when the children were very young. After all, they had each other and they were so used to entertaining each other and having another child to be with that this was no issue. However, as the two grew older, and more fond of grandparents, cousins, and some friends, it became another important feature of keeping them happy. So, we would have family come to us! My mother, the children's cousins, and even some of their friends would come sailing with us. It was a little tight on our small sloop, but great fun. Of course, it was always sad to say goodbye when they left us to fly home but we knew they would come again. And, truly, Andy and I became their best friends as well, and ever so happily it has always remained that way.

We took 39 stuffed animals with us, all very precious to Sammy and Jamie. We did get pets along the way. In Tahiti we had a darling little white mouse, who we all loved. But it was

◀ *Sandy beaches under blue skies – how could Pam Wall's children possibly object?*

◀ *Make the children part of the crew and teach them the ropes – Jamie Wall all at sea.*

▶ *A sailing dinghy turns any anchorage into an adventure if you have children on board.*

understood before we got him that he would have to stay in Tahiti when we left. We found a wonderful home for him, and it made Sammy and Jamie happy to know if they ever came back to Papeete, Mousy would be there. In Fiji we had a beautiful coloured Kula Bird, kind of like a sparrow in size but brightly coloured like a parrot. He talked like a parrot, ate mangoes and papaya, and was the most wonderful pet. He took things into his own hands when we were preparing to get the anchor up and sail away to New Caledonia and just flew out the hatch and was gone. We knew he wanted to live in Fiji, where he is the National Bird, and he did not want to go to New Caledonia. We were all heartbroken, but glad he would enjoy his freedom.

The things we taught them while we were under way were self-determination, responsibility, kindness, understanding, reading, writing, arithmetic, and of course learning the arts of a sailor. We did not have any official time set for school work, but life as we knew it became the lessons of life. We were so happy to have the opportunity to be our children's teachers, mentors and disciplinarians. Living in such close quarters, you become a very close-knit family and our mores and attitudes became our children's. A wonderful experience for us all. We stopped twice in our circumnavigation to have the children go to real schools, in New Zealand and later in Australia. All the schools were very happy to have them as students.

They met friends, loved the routine of school, and learned a lot about the history of these different countries. They were never singled out as "foreigners" and the funny thing is that they took on the accents of the country as easy as can be.

We made them little bunks with one reading light, a long shelf for books, high lee cloths to keep them snug and protected when sleeping, and we made them Pullman-type curtains that they could close up for complete privacy. And each bunk had a place or locker for toys and stuffed animals, Lego, and Barbie dolls. We also had a very high locker that they could not reach. We had Santa, the Easter Bunny and Grandma and Grandpa put presents in that locker. We had 12-volt Christmas lights, and tiny little Christmas tree and stockings. It was too high for either of them to reach and to this day it is called the Christmas Locker.

We never put netting around the boat. We taught the children from the get-go that always one hand for the ship. Little harnesses were made with crotch straps that had to be worn. But we never used lifejackets as they were too bulky and reduced their balance control. They were taught a great respect for keeping aboard.

There were books, books, and more books. But we did have what we called "Going to the movies" every single day at sea. This was a very special time for all the crew. If the weather was not wet or too windy, each day at 4pm we would all sit together either in the cockpit or down below if nasty on deck. Only Andy would stay up in the cockpit. And I would read a chapter from a good book we all loved. Favourites were *Swiss Family Robinson*, *The Neverending Story*, all the Arthur Ransome books, *The Yearling*, all the Albert Payson Terhune "Lad" books, all the "Black Stallion" books, every single book that Roald Dahl wrote for children of all ages. We would have popcorn made and it was a ritual we all enjoyed so very much. We did not have a lot of games. But we did have checkers, and backgammon on a magnetised board, and we had Lego and Lego and more Lego. Every day the two children would make a great dessert for our dinner. Sometimes the cookies would take all day. The cupcakes were wonderful, and the brownies were made from scratch. Naturally we took a lot of canned butter, eggs, flour, and sugar, and it is a good thing we did... Snacks were apples, tangerines, mangoes if we had any, and once the Doritos were finished we were all very distressed!! We did stock up on canned Crème Fraise! If you cooled it down it was kind of like ice cream when served with those desserts. We would dry apples, apricots, bananas, raisins, all just using flat cookie tins and laying the ripe fruit on deck for two days. They were delicious.

Children getting ill is always a concern. We left home with a huge medical kit that a sailing doctor friend of ours gave to us. We had first responder books, and I even took a three-day Red Cross class on medical issues we might face. However, we always taught the children how to be most careful and prudent about our lives afloat and ashore. We tried to remind them of the importance of taking care of themselves without scaring them.

Andy and I never felt that we were under a greater pressure of responsibility just because we lived and travelled on a small sailboat. It was life for us. It was not something different. We felt the same responsibility for our children as anyone living ashore. Sure, a lot of people thought we were irresponsible, but they did not know anything of how we lived, how we sailed, and how we brought up our children. Being a "child of the sea" I feel is the most wonderful thing a parent can give a child, for the children and the parents. Where else are you living in such a tight-knit environment, where everything that is about you relies on your self-determination, creativity, and knowledge. It is a great atmosphere for raising children and for the parents!

Our experience is that the earlier you take them to sea, the better. It is so easy to have an infant aboard. They don't crawl, they nurse when they are hungry, diapers become a bit of a challenge, but nothing drastic. In other words, they are much easier to look after as infants. As they grow older and can walk, and talk, and need stimulation, then the work begins. But we never minded this. We wanted our children to enjoy and understand, and take part in everything we did as a sailing family. This worked so well, and I can't think of any other place I would rather bring up my children. I feel what we did for our children was give them a fantastic background for responsibility, respect, and reassurance. That is what living on a boat gives to children who are part of a working crew.

If someone said to me I was selfish to take my children to sea, I would look at them right in the eye and say with great authority and enthusiasm, "You are looking at a very selfish parent because I want my children to have as much out of life as possible. And if sailing around the world with two small very young children is called selfish, then selfish I am! I want my children to have as much adventure in life as humanly possible. And what I am giving them in this adventure of a lifetime is the best education, the most interesting and fun life, and the best way of knowing and understanding our globe and people who live upon it.'"

Pam Wall's advice:

- Remember your children are young and need your love and attention just as much as your vessel. But, also remember they are not an object like your boat. Stay an intimate and loving and caring family always. Do things together and teach them the why and the how of what you do to keep your boat safe and sound and cosy. Work together to make this experience FANTASTIC.
- The best thing you can do for your children is to show them the world as it really is, full of wonders of nature, and full of wonderful people. Encourage as much as you can the intimacy of what you find in places and people. What an education you will be giving your children!
- Keep them away from computer screens, and help them see the real world. Today, all too often, the screen becomes a babysitter and your children and you will miss the wonders of the world you see first-hand off the screen.
- Set up achievable boundaries for safety aboard the boat. And make it a fun achievement, not a frightening one for all aboard.
- Enjoy, enjoy, enjoy being a close-knit family, handle the ship as a knowledgeable crew, and do not race from one place to another. Stay and smell the roses, put your children in real foreign schools. They will love it as ours did. Get to know the communities you are in.
- If you take your children voyaging, and you are prepared and knowledgeable yourselves, it will be the best thing in the world a family can do together.

Scott and Kitty Kuhner set off on a circumnavigation in the autumn of 1987 with their two boys, 11-year-old Alex and 9-year-old Spencer. When they returned in 1991, the boys were 15 and 13.

'Kitty and I had previously sailed around the world in 1971 to 1975 and we had put together a slide show about our circumnavigation. We'd told the kids about that adventure and showed them the slide show. Also, Alex and Spencer had grown up sailing with us from the time they were infants. We spent many weekends as well as summer vacations on our boat so they had done a lot of sailing with us, and they had always had fun when we went sailing around home.

They were a bit cautious about leaving their friends behind but we assured them that they would soon make new friends. On the second

The Kuhner children, aged 9 and 11, meet King Neptune as they cross the Equator for the first time. (KUHNER)

day on the ICW (Intracoastal Waterway) we met another boat with kids and they started having fun immediately with their new friends so it all worked out and, in fact, the two boats then travelled south together.

We don't believe that it can be too early to take your children to sea. We met a couple who had sailed from New Zealand, and she became pregnant on the trip and had their baby in South Africa. They left with the baby for the Caribbean when he was only six months old. If one does sufficient planning it is not too early to take infants.

As far as education was concerned, we planned to homeschool them and got our materials from a correspondence school. Kitty had been a schoolteacher before we were married. Also, the correspondence school had everything laid out for us including periodic tests that we had to mail them so the kids could get credit for that grade. We put them in school while we were in Auckland, New Zealand for six months. They loved it and the school liked having them.

Our children, now grown up, they still talk about the places where they have been and many of the local native friends they made in far-off places. When we got home, Alex said to us that he couldn't believe what a narrow view of the world their friends had.'

Make every arrival an adventure. Even Father Christmas made it to Thailand to meet the Kuhner children. (KUHNER)

And the final word must go to the children, the ones who have lived life on the ocean and are now old enough to look back on all its ups and downs. Peter, then aged ten, and Jennie, aged eight, were taken to sea by their parents, David and Jane Russell, on a voyage from the UK to the Mediterranean, which required crossing the Bay of Biscay and long Mediterranean passages aboard *Tinfish II*, a 39ft steel cutter (see page 108).

Jane Russell's advice:

- Whenever possible, anchor in swimming anchorages and avoid smelly marinas.
- Pick the right moments for formal lessons and make the most of learning opportunities ashore.
- Let the children build dens behind lee cloths, and don't be put out if they appear oblivious to the charms of gazing at the horizon.
- Relinquish any expectations of quiet sundowners in the cockpit or similar grown-up scenarios. Those moments do occasionally happen, but probably not when you hope they will.
- Accept that other boats with children on board will always be going the opposite way.

When it came to the Biscay crossing – always an unpredictable passage – it proved that the Russells' decision to take their children to sea had been the right one.

'We tried to time our Biscay crossing to use the diminishing northerlies to get us started and then pick up an easterly flow that was forecast along the Spanish coast. It was a good crossing with the predicted gentle northerlies for the first 36 hours. The first night was magical – no moon, but stars adorning the full dome of a clear night sky, a phosphorescent bow wave and wake lighting our track through the water. At one point we must have gone straight through a large school of sardines or similarly small fish. Each time the bow surged downwards there was a crazy scattering of tiny fluorescent light trails, whizzing chaotically to each side of the hull.

The next day was also gentle and in the morning we were joined by a large pod of common dolphins. They were busy hunting and feeding nearby, lobbing their tails and thrashing the water to corral their prey, but they couldn't resist coming over to say hello. The kids sat on the seat at the bow and chatted and sang as the dolphins crested, dived, rolled and turned on either side of them. I felt quite emotional – these were some of the experiences we had so wanted to share with the children.

Even at this stage the kids had become bookworms. Title after title was being consumed, discussed and shared among us all. It has been a real joy to be able to share books properly with each other in this way. It is something that is so hard to find time for at home.'

Jennie Russell, aged eight when they set sail, writes:

'The longest voyage I had been on before this was a summer cruise to London to see some friends, so this was a massive step up. At first, our parents didn't make it very clear what we were going to do. But once they explained it, they said that we were going away for a year sailing to somewhere with "better weather".

On another sail, my brother had trodden on a locker that my finger was trapped in, and so it nearly exploded and I was in excruciating pain. I was worried how many fingernails I'd lose on a year away. But I just laughed and was excited. I was only seven.

I didn't think it would be very glamorous. I imagined it pretty well, but I couldn't have prepared for the amazing sights we saw, on land and at sea.

I get terribly seasick and I was worried that this would prevent me from enjoying it as much; and there was an element of dread as well as excitement. Also, I worried what injuries I would bring back, or whether we would sink, which wasn't very well thought through as I didn't know much.

I told my friends that I was going but I don't really remember leaving school, I just remember driving over to the boat and not going back to school.

I remember quite a complicated selection process about which cuddly toys I should take with me, including "which can swim?" and "which will all fit on to my bed at once?" Having done this, my bunk was half full of cuddlies, and I had a large picture frame containing photos of me, my friends, and my Brownie group.

Saying goodbye to my friends was very easy as I knew I was coming back, I don't think I had any thought of time, and I thought that I was just going on a really long holiday. However, saying goodbye to my dog, Kendal, was very difficult. As we'd had him since I was four, he and I had grown up together and he was a best friend, and a brother. This meant that leaving him behind was incredibly difficult.

It was fine once we got to sea. I had been provided with a lot of activity books and Nintendo games to play, which distracted me when I was bored. Looking back, I do regret not spending a lot of time on deck while we were on passage.

Daily life was fun. I found it very easy to sleep as I always felt safe and I was frequently lulled to sleep by a gentle swell or the sound of the ripples hitting the hull. I enjoyed a year of Mediterranean diet.

When the weather was bad I would be downstairs throwing up, or my brother and I would be cuddled up in our passage bunks listening to a story book. At anchor, we would all sit down below and play a board game, or go exploring. If we weren't at sea, I would always be swimming, come rain, or shine, or fog, no matter the temperature, I would always be swimming. At sea, I would either be upstairs, looking around or lying on the foredeck, or I would be downstairs playing on my Nintendo.

We filled an entire liferaft case with stacks of books. My brother, in particular, read so much that his suspected dyslexia almost vanished. Even though I was only eight, my parents began to introduce my brother and I to more sophisticated texts in an effort to pull me away from the series of Rainbow Fairy stories. A friend had provided us with a small DVD player, and when we were in a mischievous mood we would sneak it into the forward cabin and watch films into the night. This was also the time that my parents introduced us to the musical *Grease*.

A safe place for the young Russells when the going was rough, and a den to keep them happy under way. (RUSSELL)

My dog was the thing I missed the most about home, and the other half of my cuddly toy collection. I also missed my friends, but my class used to leave small messages on our blog page so they never felt too far away. Before we left, our school gave my parents three maths books each for me and my brother (one for each term), a spellings book for each of us and a science textbook for my brother, which was also used on me. I was fine with my school work, I just got on with it. Compared to living at home, only three hours a day a few days a week was amazing. Compared to the French children, we had to do nothing! However, my brother was never happy to do his work and frequent tantrums/arguments occurred. We certainly did not miss out on school. When I came back I had moved up a set in maths and remained in the same set for English. I slotted straight back into the school system, just with a lot more knowledge about the natural and ancient world.

An advantage of living so close to each other means that you can't escape, so arguments were less frequent, and mostly my brother and I behaved better naturally.

When we got home it was weird, I remember relocating a lot of things that I forgot I had, but it took me a long time to get used to the fact that if you balance something on a shelf it won't fall over, and as I slept a constant lulling, wavy feeling came over me. But it was nice to be back and see everyone again, I got a lot of attention!

What I would say to other children is that there is nothing to be nervous about if your parents have the confidence to take you because they 100 per cent know what they are doing, so nothing will go wrong. You will experience so many amazing things that most people can only wish for. You will never forget the things you have done or seen, and you will always keep in touch with the people that you meet.'

Peter Russell, two years older than his sister, didn't hesitate when the idea of a great sailing trip was mentioned:

'Our parents said something along the lines of "We're going, what do you think?" but they knew I would jump at the opportunity. I said, "Bring it on!" I was massively overenthusiastic about it, and I think that this enthusiasm spread over to my friends; despite being sad to see me go, I think they were happy for me because they knew I was enjoying myself. We all went for one last dinner at a pizza restaurant, which was also a good opportunity for our parents to say goodbye to their friends. We did have to leave our dog behind, although we knew he was happy living on a local farm and that we would be able to see him when we returned. Throughout our trip the farmer sent us email updates about him, including photos.

I didn't know what it would be like so I went and looked at all the photos in the sailing books my parents had, although nowadays I would suggest that children look on YouTube.

I don't think that I was ever afraid, I always had trust in the boat and my parents' ability to sail it, although I think I was too young to realise the magnitude of some of the situations. We moved all the furniture into storage, and were allowed to select a few special toys to come with us. This included things such as a two-litre tub of Lego, and a small model plane.

I remember feeling overwhelmingly excited to be leaving. I suddenly discovered the joys of reading as we had no smartphones at that time. I can thoroughly recommend leaving technology at home, as this encouraged us to interact with the boat and the people and places around us.

Daily life differed little from home life. It was little things like having to do the laundry and washing up by hand that made the difference, and Dad doing the cooking of course! However, the chores were not a negative for me. It made me feel like a useful member of the crew.

Bad weather usually involved making a den down below with my sister and hiding from it. Occasionally we would put on our oilskins and brave the weather to see what our parents were dealing with, and make the odd cup of tea. I would recommend a good set of foul weather gear for the younger members of the crew as this will ensure that they can enjoy themselves in the bad weather, which often provides the most exhilarating sailing.

I passed the time mainly by reading and listening to story books (I recommend anyone to stock up on children's books), I also did things like building model boats from water bottles, splicing ropes, and fishing, all of which provided entertainment. For family fun, board games and occasional DVDs often helped to fill gaps.

We did take lots of books, but having read all the children's books I found myself reading adult books, starting with *Animal Farm* (aged 11), and I think this provided me with a valuable learning experience. In terms of games, we took many board games to pass the time, and they always provided entertainment for the whole family (although mainly in harbour). We took a wallet of films to watch on laptops, however we never took any video games, only a Nintendo DS. The deal regarding these was that they could be used on passage but once they were out of battery they could not be charged until the next port.

I mainly missed the dog, however I did not miss a lot about home, I have loved sailing for a long time and I could not think of a better thing to be doing.

Schooling was never an issue. Once I had settled down (settling me was the hardest part for my parents) I usually worked hard, and I went up two sets in maths by the time I had got home. However, a long-distance cruise is a continuous learning experience, and I obtained life experience I think many of my peers missed out on. By far the hardest bit of homeschooling was returning to school after the trip. All my friends had made new friendships, and I struggled to fit back in and adapt to normal life.

One of my best memories, and one that will remain with me for life, is surfing at 10 knots in huge waves on my 11th birthday with dolphins swimming past the boat. My worst memory is probably the day I fell off a scooter (not a moped, one you push with your foot) and badly grazed my arm. We were in Tunisia at the time and I was worried about going to hospital.

My advice to children of my age would be to throw yourself at it 100 per cent, all the time; and try to leave technology behind as this will make the trip much more enjoyable. But most importantly ***just go and do it***!'

7 Too Old to Go?

Does ocean-going come with an upper age limit?

Not everyone with ambitions to go ocean sailing is going to be able to find the time, the money or the opportunity within the framework of their younger lives. Life is too busy with kids and careers and all the other anchors that so easily prevent us from going to sea. The chances are that for a few decades you are going to have to kick your heels, keep those ambitions simmering but not allow them to boil over. You are going to have to contain yourself, and resolve that one day, you *will* get to sea. But you might be a great deal older than you are now.

There seem to be countless young people who are able to throw off all these burdens with a shrug and get their sailing adventures under their belts by the age of 30, and somehow manage to resume good careers, or so they say. But take a glance around any of the harbours of the world where ocean sailors turn up and you will see more grey hair than you will blonde, and the conversation is more likely to be about the cost of phone calls to home to check on the grandkids, and less about who is dating who back home. Don't worry. A younger generation might think you are never too young to fulfil your sailing dreams, but the truth is that you are never too old either. And like a wine-taster's palate that develops with the passing years, it is possible that the longer you leave it, the better the experience will be.

In the early days of ocean sailing, when a yacht voyaging round the world made newspaper headlines, youth was largely absent. Sir Francis Chichester made his famous circumnavigation at the age of 65, Sir Alec Rose who closely followed him was just turned 60, and Eric and Susan Hiscock, who together largely invented modern ocean sailing by amateur sailors, started when Eric was nearly 50 and lasted until he turned 70. Susan was just five years younger. It is also worth remembering that none of these pioneer circumnavigators had furling headsails, slab reefing, lightweight sails or the battery of navigational backup that we now enjoy. It was a different game back then. If you also add to this the widely held, if optimistic belief that 70 is the new 50, then the inescapable conclusion is that providing you feel like it, and you're fit enough for it, there is no reason why age is any barrier to successful ocean sailing.

But advancing years bring with them their own problems. The legs and arms ache a little sooner, the chartwork may take a little longer, and time has to be found to locate your spectacles, which you were certain you'd left on the chart table but they don't seem to be there.

Eric Forsyth, now well into his eighties, has been cruising for over 50 years, clocking up over 300,000nm. He has two circumnavigations under his belt, four roundings of Cape Horn, and a transit of the North-West Passage. He has made several voyages to Arctic and Antarctic waters.

'Everyone ages at a different rate. Persons of 80 can be more spry than someone of 60. One advantage that age gives you is the benefit of experience, provided one has started sailing early enough. With proper planning, the financial position of older people can be more stable than when you are younger, unless you were born rich. I have noticed when comparing the many crew members that I have sailed with, the stamina to keep going under difficult circumstances often seems to improve with age.

Eric Forsyth – ocean sailing for over 50 years and still loving it.

When we were in our thirties, my wife and I managed to save enough to cruise the Caribbean for 15 months and after that I decided I had seen enough tropical beaches to last a lifetime. Anyway, we were broke and had to go back to work. In middle age, I would take summers for cruising and made voyages that lasted eight to ten weeks. In my sixties, I first sailed through the Panama Canal and started worldwide cruising. Now, in my eighties, I have cut back a bit, leaving the polar regions to others, but making transatlantic cruises. I've made 27 transatlantic passages plus two circumnavigations and numerous long trips. They are still exciting. I try to get to unfamiliar places on each cruise.

Too old for mast climbing? Eric Forsyth, still on top of the world at over 80 years of age.

I suggest cruisers head for higher latitudes at times when the weather there is benign. The way of life of people living well away from the civilisation centres is different and well worth a visit. It is actually easier to stay warm in higher latitudes than it is to stay cool in the tropics. Norway, Northern Scotland, Newfoundland and the Falkland Islands are all wonderful cruising destinations.

My boat, *Fiona*, is pretty much the same as when she was launched in 1983. Changes have been made, of course, but mainly to improve reliability and safety. There have been no age-related changes. I know how to sail and repair her; a change is unlikely until I stop sailing altogether.

Frame of mind is the motivation for sailing. Cruising on a sailboat is illogical but appeals to those who like the challenge of pushing their craft to the far corners of the world.

My own frame of mind can't have changed too much as I still spend about half my life on my boat. I still like to get away from the madness of modern life; the incessant intrusion by the media, politics, and even the traffic.

I have lost a lot of muscle strength in recent years. Lifting a bagged mainsail now is almost impossible. Hauling the main sheet is another activity where I obviously do not pull as well as a younger crew.'

Cabot and Heidi Lyman are now in their seventies and are adding every year to an already impressive list of voyages. As well as a three-year, 30,000-mile circumnavigation, they have made Atlantic and Mediterranean crossings. They are now enjoying what they call a 'slow navigation' of the Caribbean.

'Getting older is not a good excuse to stop cruising, but perhaps pull the adventures back a bit. However, the big advantage of age is that you are perhaps not in such a hurry. I'm probably a little less sure of my physical capabilities at 73 and find it easier to get tired. We like to have a friend or two help us on the long passages. We are always fitter after days at sea so it is good for us both mentally and physically. I take a couple more days now to get used to being at sea, and sleep is important. I worry more, but get greater satisfaction.

I try to "geriatric" the boat every year to make it easier to accomplish the important tasks. This could include a winch to bring the outboard aboard, or creating a step to make it easier to go below. Little things can be significant. I recently added a bow thruster – something I never thought I would do. It adds a measure of safety in tight places.

I decided not to downsize as I got older. I have stayed with the same boat as she fits like an "old shoe". However, 49ft is too big for a couple in their seventies, but *Chewink* is part of the family now after 115,000 miles together.

If I was advising an older person who wanted to take up ocean sailing, I would say, don't go too big. Keep the boat a reasonable size to be easier to handle, and then the problems are slower to develop. I have noticed that older couples tend to go for larger boats and more comfort, but can end up unhappy trying to stay ahead of the maintenance.

In their seventies, but Cabot and Heidi Lyman are still powering on.

You don't have to sail towards the sunshine. The weather moves more rapidly in high latitudes, while in low latitudes bad weather lasts longer. Some aspects of the tropics are more annoying at an older age: officials, safety, the tiring aspects of Trade winds constantly blowing. Quiet nights in a beautiful New England anchorage is to die for.

If I had to pass on one piece of wisdom it would be: "Rewarding adventure is not always to be found where most cruisers hang out."

If there is a VHF net, do not stay long!'

Getting older is no excuse not to go sailing – Heidi Lyman.

Peter Passano is now in his mid-eighties and still voyaging after a career that has taken him to Alaska, across the Pacific, singlehanded around the Horn, transatlantic to Europe and then the South Atlantic islands including the Falkland Islands, South Georgia and St Helena. And Peter is still voyaging.

'Getting older is relative. Over 40 is old to some, whereas others consider themselves ready and able at 80. As one ages, one must be prepared to adjust one's cruising plan to be compatible with one's health, physical limitations, and personal needs. The bottom line is that getting old should not be an excuse to stop cruising. One's cruising plans and itinerary must be modified to reflect reality. Eventually one may get to the point where you are almost relegated to being a passenger, but still able to contribute in a positive way with some jokes or sea stories in the anchorage. The only thing I can think of that might become harder as you get older is how to arrange to get all the pills one seems to take! However, perhaps with a cruising lifestyle, you probably wouldn't need them any longer.

My old sailing partner, Bob, has come from California to cruise on *Sea Bear* three of the last four summers despite being 88 years old, almost totally blind, and very hard of hearing. He is able to steer by feeling the wind on his face, but depends on others to keep a sharp eye out for traffic and other hazards. True, we are three aboard, doing strictly coastal cruising and having the anchor down every night, but we were still cruising and having a wonderful time on the water. Now, as I get older, I more seriously consider taking crew.

If someone asked me to recommend a boat to someone who wanted to do ocean sailing, and they were getting on in years, I'd say certainly a long-keeled, moderate draft, easily balanced vessel with either a cutter rig or split rig, suitable for windvane steering. But basically: KEEP IT SIMPLE.'

Julian Mustoe's passion was to follow in the wake of the famous HMS *Beagle* on which Charles Darwin made the voyage during which were planted the seeds of his hugely important book, *On the Origin of Species*.

Mustoe is in many ways a rare species. He sails simply, with only basic needs, and he is mostly alone. He set sail in 2001 and completed the voyage in 2012, having visited almost every anchorage used by his inspiration, the *Beagle*. His boat, *Harrier*, was an unusual craft, only 25ft and painted bright yellow, like a banana, and carrying a junk sail. It was clearly the choice of a free-thinking sailor, who set off on his expedition the day after his 68th birthday. After a grounding off the coast of Argentina, his boat was lost. Undaunted, Mustoe found himself another – though more conventional this time – and continued on his epic voyage. Although in his mid-eighties, he still lives aboard a modest 26ft boat, which he says meets all his needs.

'There was once a time when I had the sublime confidence of a young man, that life was quite long, and that I would manage its dangers pretty well. With increasing age, one's horizons become shorter and one recalls some of the past close shaves with death. These memories can make you give up and decide to take no more risks, or they can induce a kind of cautious wisdom about continuing to cruise and travel the world. Such wisdom is valuable, and is a source of strength not readily available to a younger man.

With me, this cautious "wisdom of age" takes two forms. Weather forecasts are now much more reliable than they were in my young days. With the passage of time I have become more cautious about risking bad weather, particularly when sailing in pilotage

Mustoe's Harrier – *'A positive frame of mind is an asset.'*

waters. I also take great care not to fall over the side, even in harbour. I do not wear a lifejacket on board, but under way I never leave the cockpit unless wearing a safety harness.

The prudence that comes with age and experience has induced me to multiply the number and positioning of handholds on my deck. I can furl a headsail from the safety of the cockpit but I would like to be able to do the same thing with my mainsail. A reefing boom and a fully battened main would be wonderful. An electric anchor winch would be a welcome compensation for declining muscle power.

A reasonable and positive frame of mind is an important asset in every department of life. Our minds and our bodies are interlinked in many subtle ways, and I find that I think of myself to be less fit and healthy during periods of poor morale. Conversely, experience of good health and fitness is conducive to a good outlook on life. Yacht cruising brings these thoughts and feelings to one's attention quite frequently.

To an older person thinking of starting ocean sailing, I would recommend a steel hull about 35ft overall with no extreme features, with oversized fittings everywhere, an electric anchor windlass, cutter rigged with sails that can be set and reefed from the cockpit. It should have a large cabin and small deep cockpit with an accessible motor and a commodious galley. Modern electronics are a convenience afloat, but they are not essential when sailing across an ocean.

Things like raising the anchor manually or rowing a dinghy a long way become harder when one's muscles lose some of their stamina. On the other hand, one gains more foresight and ingenuity in avoiding laborious anchoring or long trips to the shore. It is a merciful dispensation that cruising does not necessitate a high level of strength and fitness. Hill walkers, sea kayakers and dinghy racers need to be fit in the way that a cruising yachtsman does not.

I wish that I was at an earlier stage in life with everything still to be discovered and experienced. I would say that sailing the oceans is a true adventure, and that it takes time and money. A degree of reflection is needed before embarking on a long cruise. Ask yourself: have you the money, can you afford to invest the time, is your curiosity about the world strong enough to sustain you? If so, the rewards are great, and they are of a kind that can be obtained in no other way.'

Julian Mustoe, turned 80, celebrates the completion of his lengthy circumnavigation.

Jeanne Socrates is a remarkable sailor, now in her seventies and at the time of writing (2018) has commenced her third voyage sail singlehanded, non-stop round the world. As the oldest woman to have already circumnavigated singlehanded, she was awarded the prestigious Blue Water Medal by the Cruising Club of America.

'I think an older person is generally more likely to be cautious and inclined to make sure "all the angles have been covered" before sailing away, or even when approaching landfall. That aspect of seamanship will come more naturally to an older person. We're not so worried about what other people think of us, unlike youngsters!

I haven't had to modify my boats as I've got older. The boat is well set up for safe, short-handed sailing, and I feel there's nothing more needed. The only item I've recently been persuaded by friends to have on board with me is a strong, cordless electric drill adapted to work the winches, none of which are motorised. It's not essential but I do love using it for that very last effort in getting the main halyard well-tensioned so the mainsail is set perfectly in no time at all and it stops at exactly the right time when the torque gets too much for it. So far, I've not used it for furling the genoa but could do so. (I always have to remember to charge the drill's battery as soon as I stop using it, so it's ready for next time.) If the boat is sturdy and well set up and maintained, then you can relax in the knowledge that the boat will take care of you, so long as you do nothing really stupid.

Age is an irrelevant number; frame of mind, being reasonably healthy and being able to trust your boat. Those are far more important considerations. We move a bit more slowly and clearly strength will also inevitably diminish with age and we just have to make allowances for those when sailing. It simply means that certain jobs take a bit longer, which is no big deal.

If you enjoy sailing and want to cross oceans, then go for it, but be well-prepared mentally for all eventualities and do it with a sturdy, well-prepared boat. Size of boat is not too important, although the more sea-kindly the boat, the more comfortable will be the crossings.

The pleasure is of being out in the middle of a vast ocean, crossing it in your own boat, perhaps with an albatross looking you in the eye as it glides close by. That takes a lot of beating.'

8 Keep in Touch...

...with folks back home, and with the weather

Being able to maintain contact with shore from the confines of a yacht is quite new. Those coming to ocean sailing for the first time expect to be able to do it; previous generations would have marvelled at the prospect.

Ship-to-shore communications by radio did not develop till the early 1900s after experiments by Marconi showed that radio waves could be transmitted beyond the horizon, which until then was not believed possible. Radio systems, albeit crude, were certainly established on ships by the time of the *Titanic* disaster in 1912, although there is some debate as to whether the unstructured radio procedures only served to add to the *Titanic*'s troubles by allowing an all-important ice warning to be swamped by passengers' vital traffic, such as updates on the value of their stocks and shares. When taking radio exams, this should remind us that proper operating can help to save life while poor operating can only add confusion.

Long before radio, ships communicated by use of the flags, which might seem crude but were highly effective providing you had good sight of the other vessel, and flags were used by ocean-going yachts certainly within the last 50 years. In accounts of ocean passages by the pioneer circumnavigators, such as Robin Knox-Johnston and Francis Chichester, are regular references to flying the three code flags M–I–K, which meant 'Please report me to Lloyds', the long-established London-based insurance specialists. Lloyds acted as a 'tracking station' not only for ships that they were insuring, but for other vessels reported to them.

In the mid-18th century, Lloyds established a network of stations around the coast of the UK called 'signal stations'. From these lookouts, always sited on prominent headlands, observers would spot passing ships and note the flags they were flying. If close enough, ship and shore could communicate by semaphore. Once the shore station had the message, the challenge was then to get it to London. In the early days this might have been carried by horse and rider to the nearest coaching station, where a coach and four would then take it onwards to London.

Your chart table needn't look like the inside of a spaceship. Badger's *basic chart table served Annie Hill well on all the oceans of the world.* (HILL)

One of busiest signal stations was on the Lizard peninsula, in the south of the UK, and from here it was not unusual to receive a thousand messages a month from passing ships. In 1883, the telegraph finally reached this outpost and the horses could be stood down.

But for yachts to hoist M–I–K in the hope of attracting the attention of a passing ship was always an uncertain business and, to ensure the officer of the watch on the receiving end was fully awake, Knox-Johnston admitted to taking his rifle and firing off three shots, just to be sure. Chichester preferred the use of an Aldis signalling lamp (sending his message in Morse code) and shunned flags, suspecting that every time he hoisted them he looked 'like a ship-wrecked character drawn by Thurber waving a tea towel'. After 1969, the Code of Signals was revised and now all hoists beginning with the letter 'M' are medical. Note that in the case of M–I–K, it now reads 'sputum is offensive'.

The complete code (American version) is available as a free download www.seasources.net/PDF/PUB102.pdf and here you can spend many happy hours imagining the circumstances under which you might wish to fly various combinations of flags. A–D, for example, signals that 'I am abandoning my vessel, which has suffered a nuclear accident'.

The signal flag that is of most practical use today is the yellow 'Q' flag denoting 'I request free pratique', meaning that your vessel is free of disease and you wish to enter harbour. More commonly, it is understood to mean that you have recently arrived and have not yet cleared customs. It is still requested by some authorities, and can be useful in allowing customs officers to spot which yachts need their attention.

A modern communications set-up – SSB, VHF and satphone on Mike and Donna Hill's Oyster 56. (HILL)

A full set of flags is expensive and bulky to stow (although useful for dressing overall at party time) and a set bought cheaply will probably be too small to be of use for sending messages. If you have to choose, carry a big Q flag, and a decent-sized A flag meaning 'I have a diver down' (if you plan on snorkelling or cleaning the below-water hull), which is recognised in all popular diving resorts.

Thankfully, we can consign signal flags (mostly) to history and there is no need for the hapless ocean voyager to sweat over the Code of Flag Signals, memorising it from back to front. And we can be grateful that the radio transceivers are no longer huge grey boxes complete with thermionic valves, such as the legendary Marconi Kestrel, which filled the cabin and every other space with a vast bank of batteries needed to power it. However, these vintage devices did have the advantage that a desperate sailor with a screwdriver and a soldering iron could have a pretty good attempt at fixing a broken one, and many have with great success. By contrast, try opening up a modern radio and see if you can sort out a faulty processor. Nor do we any longer have the patience required to make contact by low-powered short wave radios. Operating these sets was not a simple 'press the transmit button and get an immediate reply'. The operator had to judge the atmospheric conditions, choose his frequency, and then hope that his feeble signal might find its way across a vast ocean and land on the shore station's receiving aerial. And even if that small miracle took place, you might find yourself in a lengthy queue of other ships and yachts, all as keen as you to get a message ashore. So you would 'stand by', possibly for hours, which drained the batteries and diminished your chances of a good contact even further.

It is easy to assume that the more communications you have, the happier you will be and therefore you should fill a shopping trolley with all the communications devices you can possibly afford. This might not always be the case.

On the plus side, it is reassuring for the folks back home to know you are alive and well. And it's always good to chat to someone outside the confines of the boat. Equally, it is good for your peace of mind to know that those left behind are thriving. But what if they aren't, and you are 1,500 miles into a 3,000-mile open sea passage? You are frustratingly unable to help, and it might be another three weeks before you make landfall and can choose to fly home or offer some other kind of support. So, out there on the ocean, you are of no benefit to the unfortunate at home, and half your passage is going to be conducted under a threatening black cloud of concern. In that kind of situation, everyone loses. You might think that under circumstances like this you would have been better off not knowing, and the person back home might have wished they had not dropped you into an unenviable position. Situations like these can make ever-ready communication less advantageous than you might at first think.

It can also be difficult for someone who is living a life on shore to understand the different world in which sailors at sea live. At home, the washing machine might have failed and that would be a major preoccupation. But to you, on board, this might sound paltry set against your current task, which is stitching the storm jib after a particularly nasty blow. A singlehander I know chose never to talk to his wife back home, even though he had a readily available satellite phone. He found it difficult to relate to any of her problems, and she could not appreciate his. This led to friction. Instead they sent loving messages by text.

Next on the list of priorities, after the ability to chat, might come access to weather forecasts. This is, without doubt, of huge value – under certain circumstances. When closing the shore, or planning a track to avoid a risky area, such as a reef, good planning with the latest met forecast makes the greatest sense. But in the middle of the ocean, halfway between Africa and the West Indies, for example, what value is there in knowing what the weather will be like the day after tomorrow? It's not as though you can pull on to the hard shoulder to let it pass. And think of those gloomy hours, or even days, spent waiting for a forecast storm to arrive when ignorance might have led to several extra days of relaxation. To the experienced, the look of the sky, the shape of the clouds, and most importantly the state of the barometer, should be more revealing to a seaman than data down a mobile phone. The pioneer singlehander Blondie Hasler – who invented the self-steering system that bears his name – reported that for his first transatlantic passage he took only a barometer as a weather forecasting aid, but he quickly grew frustrated as he could do nothing about its ups and downs so he chucked it over the side. One suspects if he had been given a satellite phone back then, that would have gone over the side also.

VHF radio

If any radio is essential on a cruising yacht these days, it is the VHF radio. In fact, in some parts of the world, such as Chile, it is compulsory. Any set bought within the last few years will be Digital Selective Calling (DSC) enabled, and this can be of great advantage. DSC effectively gives your VHF radio a dial so you can call up other vessels if you have their number, known as a Maritime Mobile Service Identity (MMSI) number. This means that you can be contacted, or you can contact others, without having to initiate a voice call. MMSI numbers are issued by the communications authorities – in the UK ofcom.org.uk – and programmed into your VHF set, which will normally be also fed by a GPS receiver. This means that should you initiate a distress call by DSC, then not only will your identity be known but also your precise position. To this data you can add the nature of your distress.

Many countries will require you to hold a licence to operate a VHF/DSC set, for which you might have to sit some kind of practical and written examination.

Every yacht intending to make ocean passages should be equipped with a VHF radio that is DSC capable – *and everyone on board should know how to use it in an emergency.*

Pay attention also to the siting of the antenna, for the most sophisticated set in the world will soon stumble if the antenna installation is not up to the job. At its simplest, the higher the aerial the better, and better still if you have two, one of which might be at the masthead while the spare could be on the pushpit or radar arch.

There is a formula for calculating the 'line of sight' range: the distance in nautical miles = 2.25 x square root of the height of the antenna above the sea. A 17-metre mast, therefore, would give you a range of roughly 10 miles, which seems paltry. But remember that a similar yacht will also have a 10-mile range, giving a total of 20, which is better. Shore stations tend to be built on high ground, which adds further range. Atmospheric effects can also affect range, which is why, under certain meteorological conditions, you might be hearing stations 50 or more miles away.

The allocation of channels differs around the world and what applies in Europe, for example, might not be the same as in the US. Make sure you have a set that is easily switched between the two – it usually takes no more than a couple of button presses.

It is when in close situations with a risk of collision, particularly with commercial ships, that VHF DSC really scores. Assuming you are equipped with an Automatic Identification System (AIS), your display will show you the MMSI of the target that concerns you. With that number you can make a DSC call directly to the bridge of the ship without putting out a wider call, which might be misunderstood if there are several ships in the vicinity. Anecdotal evidence suggests that ships are more likely to respond to DSC alerts than to voice calls.

Portable VHF sets, which can be carried in a pocket (but which might still need a licence), are a useful thing to have. If the crew has gone ashore leaving a couple behind on board, it's a safe thing for the two parties to be in contact. The portable set can also be flung in a grab bag in the event of having to take to a liferaft.

SSB radio

At first glance, Single Side Band (SSB) radio might appear to be a technology that is way past its sell-by date. If you have all the money in the world, and the space on your boat for the sizeable antennas, then you can have high-speed satellite and all the communications systems that merchant ships carry and SSB does look like something from the ark. But if you don't have that kind of wealth, then the older technologies still have plenty to offer.

SSB is generally operated on HF, or high frequencies, from 1.5MHz to 30MHz. This portion of the radio spectrum is divided into bands, and within these bands are frequencies allocated to defined users, such as broadcast, direction finding, telex, amateur use and marine. This kind of radio technology has been around pretty much since the early development of radio and although modern sets have a vast array of buttons and dials, they are employing the principles of almost a hundred years ago.

They require some expertise to use and to obtain a callsign you will have to sit an exam, depending on which country you are making application to. The sets are quite bulky compared with a VHF set, use more power particularly when transmitting, and without a proper antenna installation – which will be far bigger than a stubby VHF antenna – you might as well try whistling in the wind. Also, a degree of uncertainty begins to creep in as propagation conditions can vary according to the time of day and many other factors, meaning that a contact made easily one day may not be achievable the next.

So why haven't we chucked SSB in the bin years ago? In some parts of the world we more or less have. An SSB radio in European waters will not attract much traffic. But cross to the US or Caribbean, or cruise the Pacific, or in Australia and New Zealand, and you will find it flourishes. It is the principal way in which cruisers chat to each other. These conversations come in the form of 'nets' in which cruisers gather at the same time of day on the same frequency and exchange their plans, problems and any information they think may be of use to others. In an area where there is criminal risk, the first time you hear about it might be on an SSB net.

SSB thrives on trans-ocean rallies, in particular the ARC from the Canaries to the Caribbean. The fleet consider it not only a social asset, but a safety one too. Given the limited range of VHF, SSB, with its potential range – depending on frequency – of hundreds of miles, is an advantage. With skilful operating and a good installation of radio and antenna, round the world communication can be possible. While VHF requires line of sight, SSB can bounce off the ever-changing electromagnetic layers in the atmosphere to achieve considerable distances.

SSB requires a first-class installation in order to achieve useable results. Also there is the added complication of providing a proper ground plane, or 'earth', and a steel hulled yacht has a great advantage here. Then you need to tune the antenna to match it to the output of the transmitter for maximum transference of power. There's a lot to think about, learn and achieve if installing an SSB rig.

A rough guide to choosing frequencies	
2MHz	200–400 miles
4MHz	400–600 miles
6MHz	600–1,200 miles
8MHz	800–1,600 miles
12MHz	1,200–2,400 miles
16MHz	1,600–3,200 miles
22MHz	2,200–4,000 miles

Apart from voice communication, SSB has other uses. As a receiver, it is possible to collect weather data, which can be downloaded and decoded on a computer to provide weather maps and even satellite images. With the addition of a suitable modem, a transceiver can effectively send and receive emails, albeit slowly. Local broadcasting stations can also provide entertainment.

It is worth remembering, though, that SSB radios are not 'plug 'n play'. Rather like a musical instrument, they reward patience and practice. Many are consigned to the scrap heap because 'they don't work' when in fact it is the operator who is not up to the job.

A useful download is available from the Cruising Club of America, which lists many of the established cruiser nets (although new ones appear all the time) and also frequencies for weather forecasts and weather map downloads: www.cruisingclub.org/pdfs/com_frequencies_nets_wxsched.pdf

SSB may appear to be yesterday's technology but are a useful addition to the modern cruising yacht's battery of communication devices.

Email via SSB

This is the cheapest way to get emails while ocean sailing, and also a convenient way of collecting weather GRIBs (see page 196).

You need an SSB transceiver, well installed with a fully functioning antenna, and a device called a Pactor modem, the P4 model providing the fastest speeds. This device converts the digital form of your email into audible tones that can be transmitted by radio. They produce a warbling sound, which you will be familiar with if you remember the early days of domestic internet connections. You will also need a laptop and some software and ensure that you have a reliable source of power to your transmitter from batteries that are fully charged. When transmitting, an SSB set may draw as much as 20 amps and transmitting data is a particularly heavy user of power. Some European sets may need modification to cover all the frequencies used by SailMail worldwide.

In principle, you establish a radio link from your transmitter to a station on the shore, which in turn is connected to the internet. SailMail has 17 ground stations around the world, but given the nature of SSB propagation, proximity to a station does not guarantee a good contact. It is quite possible that a European yacht will have more luck contacting the Nova Scotia station than the one in Belgium.

The shore stations will be operated by one of two organisations: SailMail and Winlink.

SailMail, a USA organisation, describes itself as 'a non-profit association of yacht owners that operates and maintains an email communications system for use by its members. SailMail supports email communications using every internet communications device in all oceans of the world.'

It cost $275 a year (2018) to be a member and there are strict terms and conditions, which you should read before signing up. SailMail is also of use to those who communicate on email by satellite phone (see below) by offering speedy communications and efficient compression to reduce the on-air time, which is charged by the minute.

Winlink 2000 differs from SailMail by being operated by licensed amateurs. You will need a ham licence to use this service, and this needs time and application, unlike a VHF radio licence, which can be mastered in a day. An amateur radio licence might need several weeks of committed study, depending on which country is issuing the licence.

Winlink 2000 operates in the same way as SailMail and uses the same software, is free of charge to amateurs and has more ground stations, although they tend to be clustered in North America and Europe, and there are only two in the whole of South America, three in the mid-Pacific, and only one in Australia. Winlink is hugely important in establishing communications in disaster areas, such as after earthquakes and tsunamis, where amateurs will be willing to give their time to be of assistance.

- SailMail: sailmail.com has much valuable information about installation and operating.
- Winlink 2000: winlink.org

Ham radio

Many long-distance cruisers choose to obtain an amateur radio licence, which requires study and a practical test (for a licence issued in the UK), although you are no longer required to learn the Morse code. This allows a suitable SSB set to be operated on frequencies reserved for use by licensed amateurs. This is a world that should only be entered by enthusiasts, but those who have done so report many 'on-air' friendships created as they cruise. It is also something of a novelty for land-based amateur operators to make contact with a 'maritime mobile' station, as yachts are designated. A call from a yacht mid-ocean might attract scores of replies.

The amateur bands tend to be busy most of the time and several cruisers report that should they have to issue a distress call mid-ocean, they would do so first on the busier amateur bands rather than hope someone is listening on marine SSB.

Amateurs carefully protect their frequencies and should you try to transmit on an amateur frequency without a licence and proper callsign, you will be on the sharp end of several pointed replies.

Remember that in the event of distress, you are allowed to make a call for help on any frequency irrespective of what licences you might hold. Amateur operators will always respond to a MAYDAY call.

To have a dedicated marine SSB and a ham radio on board might seem excessive. Many ham radios can be 'unblocked' to allow access to marine frequencies, which makes for a more versatile transceiver. But remember that marine equipment is built to a higher specification and will be weatherproofed, where an off-the-shelf ham radio might not be.

Jeanne Socrates, veteran solo round the world sailor advises:

'For me, no one should consider going cruising without an SSB/HF radio. It keeps you in contact with people, gives you plenty of weather information, including real-time weather faxes and satellite pictures of convection (storm formation) in your part of the ocean. It gives you immediate access to up-to-date, local advice on places and any dangers around. Also you can get help with solving problems on board, and being radio, not a telephone, any number of people can chip in to the conversation to help. In addition, you can get free emailing with Winlink (for "hams") or at very low cost with SailMail for non-hams, or for business.'

Satellite communication

The handheld satellite phone will be most people's first choice for ocean-going communication. If you choose the right provider you will have coverage from pole to pole, and no need to worry about the intricacies of the ionosphere as when using SSB. It is as simple as using a mobile phone.

But it is not an answer to all your problems. For a start, the link is fine for voice communication but for data it is so slow as to not allow the use of a web browser. Large commercial yachts might be able to use satellite tracking antennas, which will deliver faster speeds, but these are huge and expensive and way beyond the reach of most cruising sailors. Also, in case of distress, a satphone only enables you to make a call to a single person ashore. SSB or VHF allows you to make a call that will be heard by any vessel within your vicinity, which can be a great advantage if you need assistance. You might have made a satellite call to a coastguard station a thousand miles away asking for help when help was just over the horizon and might have heard a radio call on VHF.

The other snag is that satellite time is very expensive and the technology has improved little over the last 15 years. It is a remarkable, but something of a stagnant technology.

One of the most commonly asked questions is: *should I buy an SSB radio or a satphone?* There is no answer to this because they do completely different jobs. It is not a case of one or the other. If you are going to invest in communications, then you may need both.

SSB

In favour: Can do emails and GRIBs with no data charges, and an SSB allows you to join cruiser 'nets' and become part of the cruising community in places where SSB is widely used, such as the Pacific, USA and Caribbean.

Against: The kit can be quite bulky and for good results needs a proper installation. They can be heavy users of electricity and need fully charged batteries to work at the optimum. You need to obtain a licence, which might require study time. Some skill is needed to get the best results, especially for long-range SSB, and that can take commitment.

SATPHONES

In favour: Easy to buy, easy to operate. You can call anyone directly from anywhere in the world. No fancy installation required but an external antenna is a must if you intend to collect data. They can be used for email exchanges and downloading weather data.

Against: Data comes at quite a hefty price. You cannot join cruiser 'nets' with a mobile phone. Any data connections will be slow and high-speed internet access via satellite will be beyond most people's pockets.

There are four main satellite providers. Iridium and Inmarsat offer the greatest global coverage.

Iridium has over 60 satellites in low orbit and during any call you will be passed seamlessly from one to the next. Regarding data speeds, several figures are quoted but the truth is that the speed does not vary from phone to phone or from computer to computer. With a good connection, the speed will be 2,400 bits per second – this is 4 per cent of the speed of the old domestic dial-up internet connection. With a poorer signal, the connection will appear slower too, but this is because of data being lost or garbled. As a rule of thumb, expect an Iridium satellite connection to convey data at 20KB per minute, and remember you are paying by the minute. This is a strong reminder to keep messages short, to the point, and certainly not containing any graphics. Iridium coverage is truly global, reaching as far as the poles.

Inmarsat employs fewer satellites but in stationary orbit, which means that a clear view of the whole sky is less important. Inmarsat phones are operated in a similar way to an Iridium phone, but both seem less intuitive than the more refined conventional mobile phone. Inmarsat also offers FleetBroadband, which can offer data speeds up to 432KB per second, allowing for limited video and audio streaming. These are used by many sponsored ocean racers providing uploads to YouTube and blogs. Prices start at £5,000 rising to £12,000 for the highest spec systems.

Iridium will work as far as the poles but Inmarsat will fall some distance short, although not enough for it to be an issue for most cruisers.

Thuraya covers mostly Europe, North Africa and the Middle East using two satellites and their coverage has recently been extended to cover East Asia and Australia by the launching of a third. Data speeds can be faster than Iridium at 9.6KB per second and Thuraya handsets have the advantage that they can join land-based mobile phone networks if you are in an area that has a Thuraya partner. Thuraya handsets are sometimes cheaper than those connected to other networks.

Globalstar has 48 low-level orbiting satellites, but no global coverage. Europe and the Med are fully covered, as is Australia and most of the coast of North and South America, except Alaska. From an ocean sailing point of view, it is worth noting that with Globalstar there is not continuous coverage on any of the common ocean crossing routes, certainly not from the Canaries to the Caribbean, nor across the Pacific. If those limitations are not a problem, then the handsets are smaller and cheaper, and call costs can be half those of other suppliers.

Remember also that getting a satphone handset is only the first step. If you want to do emails or download GRIBs then you might also need a modem and associated cables and software (which usually comes as a kit), a laptop and a contract with an email provider.

In a recent survey conducted by the UK magazine *Yachting World*, the vast majority of transatlantic sailors chose the Iridium network and MailASail (mailasail.com) as their internet provider because their service, which includes compression software, spam filtering and blog provision, is built specifically around the needs of boats at sea. OCENS (ocens.com) provide a similar service and is widely used in US waters. They also offer apps and software for interfacing GRIBs with maps and charts. SailMail (sailmail.com) is also in very wide use at a similar cost.

Whatever system you choose, prepare for disappointment. No marine satellite system is going to be as fast or reliable as the broadband at home, and this is worth making clear, particularly to youngsters, before you leave shore.

And the one golden rule is: don't try to get it all working the night before you leave the harbour. Buy it well in advance, play with it at home, have complete mastery of it and many of the frustrations will evaporate.

Frank Cassidy (CCA) and his wife, Lynda, cruised as live-aboards for seven years, usually outside cell phone range. Frank is an engineer specialising in navigation, vessel traffic control and AIS. He has made several ocean passages.

'On our boat, besides VHF, the offshore communications equipment is dual-use SSB/HAM transceiver with an antenna tuner connected to an insulated backstay. This, along with a laptop computer and a Pactor modem, allows me to send/receive emails and download a considerable library of weather data.

When sailing on offshore passages with friends without SSB/HAM, we always make certain that a satellite phone and subscription-minutes are available. I am often the "weatherman" so I bring a laptop that can be connected to the internet using the satellite phone for the purposes of email and weather data. The same HAM Winlink and SSB SailMail software called Airmail can be used with direct internet access via the satellite phone – a radio is not required. It is essential that only low-bandwidth internet sites be used because the satellite data rate is really low and dropped connections are a reality. It is actually possible to go to any site on the internet but that would be a very expensive and painful process.

If one was to do long-term cruising without SSB you would be very much disconnected from the cruising community.

Access to up-to-date weather was extremely important to us and weather data with frequent updates is essential. Forecasts get much more accurate as the time frame shrinks, and the ability to make course change decisions early enough is important. Before the Pactor modem was added we would have to go ashore to get weather, make phone calls or do email to let family/friends know when we started a passage. This was sometimes inconvenient and expensive. Now we can just leave and send an email when we get the chance, and can easily stay in touch along the way.

We never found ourselves in a situation where safety was a concern but knew cruisers who did. The first obvious advantage is being able to contact rescue authorities. However, having access to other cruisers via radio nets and people ashore who might be able to contact people for you and help manage your situation is a big advantage. Doing it all yourself on board in dire circumstances may well be impossible.

A satellite phone is easier and quicker to operate than an SSB but even then the phone may be set up, charged and connected only once or twice a day. But we do not own a satphone. That is because of the cost (initial and cost of minutes) and because we had our radio email system set up and running well. If you are really a long-term cruiser you should have an SSB for keeping in touch with other cruisers anyway. Email and weather data can then be free, or low cost. *But* the initial cost is high. The technically inclined can avoid the Pactor and use newer laptops with the right sound card directly connected to the SSB.

But you can't take it in your ditch bag.

SSB has a learning curve and sometimes can be difficult to get up and running, and it can interfere with other equipment on board while transmitting and vice versa when receiving, but lots of people have done it and gotten the bugs out. Once installed and operating, no particular amount of skill is needed to keep it going, there are no frequent adjustments or tuning requirements – everything is automatic. The most important thing to do is use it frequently enough so that you don't forget how to use it. Of course, if it actually fails it may not be easily fixed on board unless it is something obvious like a fuse or a bad connection.

The advantages of HAM radio are the same as SSB but you have at least doubled your audience of people you can contact when having problems, and you increase the number of frequencies available to you. We sailed with lots of cruisers, some a lot less capable than others; a few had technical backgrounds but most did not and almost all mastered the SSB and most used a Pactor modem and laptop set-up. Cruisers have the advantage of time, and friends to help in getting things up and running.'

Using Wi-Fi ashore

When the internet became widely available and almost every shoreside bar and restaurant set up their own Wi-Fi networks to lure visiting crews, it seemed like some kind of blessing. It worked like this: you would arrive in harbour, get the computer out, see which Wi-Fi networks you could pick up and note the names, which were usually similar to the name of a bar or café. Then, blow up the dinghy, row ashore, buy enough coffee or beer to secure the password and once back on the boat, surf away to your heart's content.

It is now well recognised as a dangerous thing to do.

The problem with Wi-Fi networks that are open to all-comers is that skilful hackers will be able to 'listen in' to your exchanges, which are not encrypted, and glean password information etc – it's called 'Wi-Fi sniffing'. For example, you might be sitting in an anchorage and needing to book flights for which you have to give credit card details – gold dust to a hacker. For yachts at the very top end of the scale, particularly superyachts, cybercrime is now a real threat and is being excluded from some insurance policies due to the fear of hijacked electronic systems, including engine control, being taken over with malicious intent.

For most of us, the apparently innocent guy sitting quietly in the corner of the bar with nothing more than a phone could be the most likely threat. Hacking, these days, requires minimal skill and cheaply bought software. He's created a Wi-Fi hotspot using his phone. He's given it the same name as the harbour and called it Public Wi-Fi and he's smiling all over his face when you try to pay a few bills online and he happily downloads all your traffic to his phone.

Your data is at its most vulnerable when you are under pressure because that's when you're likely to make it easy for hackers. For example, you're in some remote spot waiting for the delivery of a vital spare – a common situation. It's near the end of the working day. You *have* to get a message to them. Under those circumstances, you'll grab any Wi-Fi you can find – we've all done it. But bear in mind it's risky.

There are cheap devices that can greatly extend the 'reach' of your on-board Wi-Fi. They have the appearance of a white fibreglass 'wand' a couple of metres long and mounted either on the stern rail or a radar arch. Height is an advantage although mast-mounted antennae can be less successful due to losses in lengthy cable runs. When connected to a small 'box' these allow weak Wi-Fi signals to be amplified and become useable, and also extend the range of your transmitting power – remember, Wi-Fi is a two-way communication system and it is no use being able to receive a distant station if that station cannot 'hear' you. These boxes in turn create a small Wi-Fi network around the boat, which anyone on board can log into. The networks are accessed usually through a browser needing a laptop or tablet. Some of the more widely available networks might have an app that does the job.

There are rules for staying safe on Public Wi-Fi systems.

- Ask at the bar/desk what the Wi-Fi network is called. Don't assume it's safe.
- Airport Wi-Fi systems can be particularly risky.
- Check that your device requires you to ask before connecting to any network, and doesn't connect automatically.
- Enable your firewall.
- Ensure the address of the site you're trying to connect to is prefaced with 'https'. (Note that there have been breaches even at this security level so it's not a complete guarantee.)
- If two-factor authentication is available on the website, use that. Then, if your passwords are stolen, the thief will not have the secondary code.
- Disable file sharing so your computer does not appear on any other.
- Make sure you have a strong password on your on-board Wi-Fi network. The name of your boat is not a good idea.
- Watch what you send. There's less risk in sending Granny a 'get well' message than in telling someone your bank details.
- Have anti-virus software and keep it up to date.

If you want inter-connectivity, access for everyone on board, and as many channels of communication as are available at the time, then you need a set-up like the one above.

You will need three antennae above decks (if you include a satphone), one of which will be a Marine Wi-Fi; an external antenna to make contact with 3G/4G cellular networks, requiring the purchase of a local SIM card, which is used in a cheaply bought device; a unit that will create on-board wireless access; a satphone; and a router to gather them all together. The laptop can then be fed directly from the router by cable or by joining the Wi-Fi network you've created. Likewise any tablet or phone.

A search will reveal numerous pieces of kit that will fulfil all these requirements but at widely varying prices. Routers with built in Wi-Fi, for example, can be bought from dedicated marine manufacturers at prices approaching £800, but equally devices that perform the same function but, possibly, with a reduced reliability in a marine environment can be had for well under £100.

In summary

WI-FI

For: Only one connection to make. The data is free and usually uncapped, and speeds can be quite high if you can maintain a strong signal.

Against: Not secure, not always available and likely to be switched off at any time. Also the range can be quite small if you are not equipped with a booster.

MOBILE OR CELLULAR DATA

For: The range can be quite large, certainly over 10 miles, and harbour areas tend to have decent cellular coverage. Anchorages possibly less so.

A good 4G signal can deliver reasonable speeds.

You can choose a plan in advance to suit your expected data needs.

Against: If you have data capping, you may run out at a bad moment.

SATELLITE

For: Available anywhere in the world (limited at very high latitudes in some cases).

Against: Very expensive and too slow for browsing. An email system only, and then with great caution in respect of costs.

If you really need satellite broadband then expect to pay $30,000 for a system (Mini-VSAT). Cheaper systems are available for around $3,000 (Inmarsat) but the data charges are higher than for a phone and you need to be able to keep the receiver pointed directly at the satellite – not easy to achieve on a cruising yacht.

New developments

These are coming thick and fast. The growth of 5G with its even higher speeds than 3G will make communications from harbours and anchorages much faster and reliable.

Then comes the 'bonded' internet. A 'black' box combines multiple connections and gathers them into one, resulting in considerable speeds. For example, a modest 3G connection when bonded to a less than perfect Wi-Fi connection can achieve a very fast result.

The ability to connect cruising boats to the internet has come on in leaps and bounds in the last decade or so, and most cruisers now expect it to be available wherever in the world they turn up. The problem is that this is a cat and mouse game in which we are demanding more and more no matter what is provided. It might, sometimes, be better to get used to the idea of being cut off.

Jack and Zdenka Griswold took seven years to complete their circumnavigation in their Valiant 42, *Kite*.

'We have always had a single sideband radio (currently an ICOM 802) and Pactor modem. We have never gone offshore without this equipment and would not recommend doing so. In addition to enabling emergency communications, the SSB, together with the modem, allows us to keep in touch with friends on passage. The SSB makes it possible to talk with groups of people, something a satphone cannot do. We also have an Iridium satphone, which we primarily use as a backup to the SSB, not for routine communications. When in port, we would purchase internet and cell phone service locally. Both are increasingly available and affordable in most places.

Kite *storms along on her Pacific crossing – SSB kept them in touch with the rest of the world.* (GRISWOLD)

Our friends and family ashore found they were able to contact us, although while we were on passage they also understood that we typically check our email no more than once a day, occasionally less. We would sometimes provide family ashore with contact information for an SSB net in case of emergency. On land, we were typically quite reachable via the internet or phone.

We found that we used the SSB daily on every passage. In addition to downloading GRIB files, we generally listened to daily weather nets and checked in to one or more group nets. Some of these were long-standing, well organised and included a number of participants. Some cropped up from time to time, grew in popularity, and then petered out. These nets are extremely useful for information sharing, troubleshooting

The Griswolds' Kite *– note the backstay rigged as an SSB antenna, their main method of communication.*

and advice if someone has a breakdown or other issue, and just plain fun. Unlike a satphone, the SSB makes it possible to chat with groups of people who may be quite spread out geographically. We used our satphone, an Iridium 9555, almost exclusively when propagation was bad, although from time to time it has come in handy as a phone. For example, when we lost our towed water generator in the Indian Ocean, we used it to order a new one from a shop in Australia, which they shipped to us in Mauritius.

The two most important considerations for an SSB installation are the antenna and the ground. On a sailboat, the logical antenna is the backstay. One needs to install two insulators on the backstay to isolate it from the rest of the rig. Any rigger can do this.

As far as the ground, we have a 5-inch-wide ribbon of copper stripping in the lay-up of the hull. This makes an ideal ground plane. The rest of the installation is mostly just a matter of running wires and attaching them in the proper places.

Knock on wood, once properly installed the ICOM 802 SSB is pretty bulletproof, and there are many cruisers and shops willing and able to help if things go sideways. One of us has been a ham radio operator for all of our cruising years. We use Winlink for email and occasionally take part in ham radio weather nets. This was most useful in and around South Africa, where the best weather was provided by the ham SAMMNet, the South African Mobile Maritime Net.

It's easy to get overwhelmed by the options, and these get more complicated every year. When we did our circumnavigation from 2009 to 2016, a good SSB, VHF, EPIRB and GPS is what most of our friends had and they served them well. Some cruisers had no on-board email capability and relied solely on the SSB for weather and communication. In these instances, it's not difficult to arrange with another boat to serve as an emergency contact for families ashore, where that boat then relays the information via SSB on a pre-arranged frequency at a pre-arranged time – a daily net.'

The budget option

If you want a cut-down communications device that does not provide voice calls but can offer messaging, email and tracking via satellite, then devices such as the Garmin InReach have come on to the market and offer a much cheaper way of staying in touch. These are essentially cut-down satellite phones that have no keyboards or voice capability and instead pair via bluetooth with your mobile phone. Once that connection is made you can send and receive SMS and emails (maximum 160 characters), but you cannot download files, such as GRIBs.

The tracking feature can provide continuous updates on your position to folk ashore, who can access your position via an online map. They also have an SOS function monitored by an authorised emergency monitoring centre. The data plans are more affordable than with satellite phones and premium services are available, such as weather forecasts. InReach uses the Iridium satellite network with worldwide coverage.

Similar to the InReach, but based on the Globalstar satellite network, is the Spot tracker, which is widely used both at sea and onshore by walkers, climbers etc. This also allows tracking, SOS, and the sending of short messages pre-installed in the unit such as 'All OK'. It does not pair with a mobile phone so cannot do email or SMS, but is cheaper.

These tracking devices are not a substitute for proper safety equipment, and certainly not for an EPIRB. They are not recognised as such within the Global Maritime Distress and Safety System (GMDSS).

However, the author has found the InReach to be hugely reliable, cheap and easy to operate, and a comfort both on board and for those back home.

Ocean weather

The coastal sailor has no excuse, these days, for being caught out in bad weather. The reliability of weather forecasting over ever longer periods of time has advanced in tandem with the ever increasing power of computers to crunch vast amounts of data in less time than it takes you to think of putting your oilskins on. The result of all this is that at every turn there is a reliable forecast to be had. They come from the coastguard, from broadcast stations, via the internet, plus the hundreds of apps on smartphones and tablets that churn out, often for free, forecasts for days ahead, even including swell heights, visibility and cloud cover. More data than could be imagined even 20 years ago is now a few stabs of our fingers away.

And then you get to sea, towards the ocean, and first the coastguard VHF goes out of range, then the radio stations fade, the phone signal finally disappears, and you are on your own. It might be as little as 30 miles from shore before all these support systems disappear, and the passage ahead of you might be a thousand miles. How are you ever going to guess what the weather might do next?

Ask if you *really* need to know what the weather is going to do? There is a very strong argument that says you might as well shrug your shoulders and resign yourself to your fate. Is there any real advantage in knowing it's going to get rough in five days' time? In fact, the anticipation might spoil what would otherwise have been four days of pleasant sailing. And when the bad weather does arrive you are only going to do what you would have done anyway, and that is take in a few reefs and settle yourself down to cope with it. Remember Blondie Hasler, who took a barometer as a weather forecasting aid on his first transatlantic race and threw it overboard because he was doubtful about the advantage it gave him?

But wanting to know what the weather is going to do is not only so you can spot the bad times ahead. How many sailors have been stuck in the calms of the Doldrums, praying for a bit of a strong breeze, trying to work out which way to head to find it? And what about hurricanes, which, if you know their speed and direction, you can take action to avoid? Well, there's an argument that says the speed of the average cruising yacht is so slow compared to the movement of a volatile weather system that the idea of 'getting out of the way' is somewhat fanciful. Nevertheless, it would be nice to know which way that weather system is going.

Before we look at ways of getting mid-ocean weather forecasts, it might be worth revisiting the humble barometer before we, like Hasler, throw it overboard. It is essentially a simple device, robust, requires no power and no maintenance – an almost ideal bit of kit. If you want to add a little complexity, but a great deal of convenience, a barograph gives a continuous paper trace of the changing pressure, and electronic barographs are now available. Smartphones have barograph apps available.

If you are relying on a barometer, as opposed to a barograph, for weather forecasting, then you need to record the pressure every hour in your log. You are interested in *changes* in barometric pressure rather than absolute levels. Still, it is worthwhile calibrating your barometer before you leave. This is best done when there is a large area of high pressure sitting on top of you. Find a nearby weather observation station, often available on the net. Then compare your reading with theirs and adjust your barometer if necessary. A large area of high pressure means the readings are likely to be the same for several miles around you but pick a station as close to you as you can find and adjust your instrument accordingly. Should you tap a barometer to see if the pressure is rising or falling? That has been much debated. I know an old sailor who is of the view that 'if God had meant us to tap barometers, he'd have given 'em hammers'.

As a general rule, and as you well know from your coastal training, low pressure spells bad weather, and high pressure the reverse – in the broadest terms. But rate of change is more important, and a steady fall in pressure on a sunny day hints that things are on the turn. Incidentally, if you want to know where a low-pressure centre is located, stand with your back to the wind and hold out your left arm – it's that direction. The right arm will point to high pressure. Reverse this in the southern hemisphere.

The rate of change of the barometer can give a good indication of the wind speed you might expect. As a rule of thumb, a 6hPa drop in three hours suggests force 6, and 8hPa drop in three hours would indicate a force 8. (Your barometer will most likely be showing millibars, which are the same as hPa – hectopascals.)

In the tropics, it is easy to become unsettled by diurnal (daily) changes in atmospheric pressure, especially if you are hoping for a change in the weather in your favour. Atmospheric pressure peaks at 10am and 10pm every day – a phenomenon that has puzzled scientists for centuries. The current theory is complex and of no value to sailors. Just be aware that a regular, daily change in pressure is of no significance and after a few days of observation you will learn to ignore it.

Of course, the importance of your eyes cannot be underestimated. A change in the pattern or direction of the swell, the first ripples on the water after a calm, these are all valuable forecasting tools. The sky and the clouds probably reveal as much as a fistful of weather apps to those who know how to read them. If you have been sailing for a while, your experience will tell you how to spot the approach of fronts, or distant fog banks.

But if you feel none of these give you the reassurance you need, where do you turn next? How do you get weather forecasts when ocean sailing and out of reach of land?

You are going to need either an SSB radio or a satellite phone. The satellite device could be a simple communicator, like a Garmin InReach. This can offer basic weather information, or you can be in touch with someone back home who has all the weather data at their fingertips, which they can summarise and send across to you every day. Weather routing services can be expensive and sophisticated in what they can offer, but a competent friend ashore who knows how to read a chart can be useful.

If you have an SSB radio – which need only be a quite basic receiver – your first port of call can be a fax chart. These are synoptic charts covering large oceanic areas and are produced by all the major national weather agencies. They are called fax charts because that is how they were originally distributed and the name has stuck.

These charts are transmitted at regular intervals on shortwave frequencies and a small piece of software will enable you to decode them. You will need a sound card in your laptop and an audio connection to your SSB, after which it is the simplest thing to get fax charts for five days ahead. It takes five to ten minutes to download one chart, but unlike a satellite phone these downloads come free. If you don't have a laptop, there is an app that runs on phones and tablets and all you need do is hold your device in front of the radio speakers and make the audio connection that way – HF Weather Fax from Black Cat Systems. A fax chart, if you have the knowledge to interpret it, can provide not only an immediate picture of the weather at your location but the wider movement of the weather systems around the ocean, which can be a great help in future planning.

You need to know the names of the fax stations covering your area, the frequencies and timings, and these can be found at: www.nws.noaa.gov/om/marine/rfax.pdf

Your ability to receive any particular station depends upon short wave radio propagation conditions, which can vary from day to day. Be prepared to quickly change frequencies to get the best reception and hence the best image.

After the fax chart, your next best friend is the GRIB – Gridded Binary Data files. These are small packets of data and therefore can be downloaded economically through a slow satellite-based internet connection, or downloaded for free with an SSB transceiver and modem. Within these small packages of data there can be a large amount of information such as wind speed and direction, air temperature, cloud cover and swell height, and they are the products of the massive computers that run the world's major weather forecasting models. The most frequently accessed GRIBs, possibly because they are free, are from the GFS, the American Global Forecasting System, which produces four forecasts a day. Although other weather models have their fans, the forecasts produced by the GFS, particularly in the short range, can be relied upon. For areas like the Pacific and mid-Atlantic, they may well be the only forecasts available.

But a GRIB is not a forecast as such. It is just data, and there has been no human intervention in the producing of it. It is merely raw computer output. One of the skills of the weather forecaster is to take this computer-generated output and apply their skill and experience to it, possibly comparing it to other models, before deciding finally what the weather is going to do. So don't expect a GRIB to come up with the truth every time. In fact, many sailors who have wide experience of using GRIBs will tell you that they tend to underestimate wind by about one Beaufort force, but wind direction is usually quite accurate. As a rule of thumb, if the GRIB shows 20 knots, expect 25. Also, the computations are made on the basis of grids that can be 100–150 miles square, and it is quite possible that a small, local disturbance may not show up.

GRIBs are obtained by interrogating a server by email, which is why you need an SSB set that will both receive and transmit, and an appropriate modem (see page 180). The email must be written in a precise form. You must give the co-ordinates of the area you are seeking information for, and remember the smaller the area, the smaller the GRIB file and the less the satellite cost. You also have to indicate the information you are requesting, such as wind, wave, cloud cover, and also at what time intervals – for example 12, 24, 36, 48 hours ahead. If the email is not drafted correctly, if you add spaces where there shouldn't be any, you will not get a GRIB back, so it is worthwhile practising so it becomes second nature.

The precise form of this email may vary from server to server but some, such as weather.mailasail.com explain it well, and the instructions are written with cruising sailors in mind. Their GRIB service is free. Concise instructions can be obtained by sending an email to weather@mailasail.com with a blank subject line. This returns with detailed instructions on how to use this service. Once your GRIB request has been sent, the GRIB returns within seconds. In the above example, it will be as small as 2K bytes – tiny.

Your laptop will now need a GRIB viewer to decode the information within the GRIB and display it in a convenient form, usually on a map. Some chart plotters are able to decode and display GRIB files. Once decoded, you will then be able to click through to see the weather developments in your area as requested at 24, 48, and 72 hours. Wind speed is shown by arrows, and the strength is indicated by observing the 'flights'. A long flight is 10 knots, half a flight is 5 knots.

Always remember that although GRIBs appear on your screen and appear to have great authority, you cannot depend on them 100 per cent. Vast amounts of data are being crunched to produce them and sometimes they will get it wrong. A meteorologist will spot that, but the computer will not.

Consider GRIBs an aid to safe navigation, but certainly not the final word.

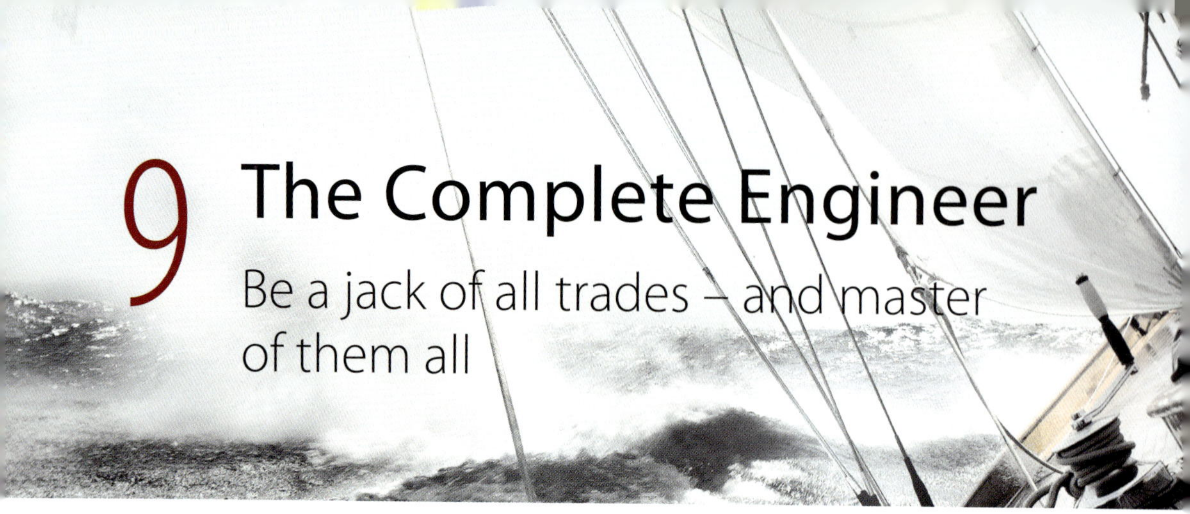

9 The Complete Engineer

Be a jack of all trades – and master of them all

There will be times when you might be far offshore, the nearest land a week or two away, and something will fail to work. It might be a small thing, like an electric fan that seizes, or something more important like a blown alternator or a reluctant bilge pump. The first thought that crosses your mind is likely to be: 'I wish we had an engineer on board.' In fact, you already have, or you certainly *should* have, and that engineer ought to be you.

By engineer I don't mean a super-mister-fixit. You can't be expected to be able to fix anything and everything, or raise seriously broken kit from the dead. But before embarking on an ocean passage you ought to be beyond the stage where the instant something breaks, you panic and look for someone else to help you. You should by now have the confidence to look at the problem in a cool and collected way, and be sufficiently relaxed of mind to be able to think through the issues and how you might solve them. All manner of failures have been fixed by people who have used their ingenuity, and who didn't set off the alarm button when half an hour with a couple of basic tools might have sorted the job.

Sailors tend to be practical people so at least you have a head start. Pulling sheets, raising sails, setting anchors – these are not tasks enjoyed by people who dislike using their hands. Navigation requires a certain mental capacity, so the chances are that you have within you what it takes to be some kind of boat's engineer. If you are lucky, within any crew, even if there are only two of you, one might have a natural inclination towards electrics, another to engines, and someone else might be a good bosun who can whip a rope's end, splice a line, sew a sail. If you are taking crew, it might be worth talking this through before you sail. It would be a tragedy to have to live with a failed generator only for someone on the crew to later mention that they used to be good with small engines when they were a kid.

Can you fix the freezer? Donna Hill won't be smiling if all this has to go to waste mid-ocean. (HILL)

Here's a game to play

Months before you set off, when you are home and in a relaxed frame of mind, take a pile of postcards and on each of them write the name of one system on the boat. For example, your cards might be marked: water maker, sheet winches, windlass, autopilot, vang, cooker, freshwater tap etc. It might take more postcards than you think. If so, you might pause for thought here. Is it possible that you have more systems than you need? And might this be a good time to ditch a few?

Now, gather the crew around the table – doesn't matter if it's only two of you – and one draws a card from the top of the pack. Let's say you drew 'windlass'. The next person has to describe the fault with the windlass, and the next has to say how they would deal with it. Decide among yourselves how to award points.

In this example, you would have to explain how you are going to get the anchor up if the windlass fails. You might suggest the hand-over-hand method – only three points for that, because it's obvious. But perhaps the card says it's blowing F5. What then? With luck, your crew will have figured that a rope, rolling hitched to the chain

You need to be able to fix everything – both above and below the waterline. Alfred Alecio services Ironhorse*'s prop. (ALECIO)*

and brought back to a cockpit winch, might work. Many points for that answer.

Then the next person has to suggest how you might repair the windlass. Has it got power to it? Is there power but the relay is not engaging? Is it something simple, like the clutch was not properly tightened? And if you decide to eventually take it apart, do you have the right tools and where would you start?

Having focused for so long and so hard on this one item of hardware, this is where one of you needs a pen and paper to note all the issues that have arisen. The next time you are on board the boat, you can check all these things so that should the anchor windlass fail, it will not appear like a complete stranger to you.

Then put the cards away. One major failure a night is enough to deal with.

You can play this game with any system aboard the boat, from a complete engine failure to a dripping tap in the heads. When you are in the position of having little fear of anything that might go wrong, imagine how confident you will feel.

Being an engineer

Have you watched a proper engineer for any length of time, a really good one? The first thing I have always noticed is that they seem never in a hurry. They will sit patiently while you outline the problem, take a look at the offending item, and after mulling it over for a time they will decide on a course of action. That is the point at which they will have taken their mind through all the problem-solving skills they have been taught and, hopefully, have come to a conclusion. Then, when the moment comes, and not before, they will pick up a tool – always the right one for the job – and start work. They seem never short of a tool, nor short of a good idea. But the tools are the least of it. Their greatest asset is their experience and their analytical approach. You can buy all the top tools in the world, but if you have no experience of their powers and limitations, you are wasting your money. You are never going to

Donna Hill, mid-Atlantic, fixes the clew, which has pulled away from the mainsail. Do you have the skills to do that? (HILL)

Make do and mend – a mid-ocean repair that got the Hills safely across the Atlantic. (HILL)

become a highly skilled boat engineer, but you can take some useful steps along the way. Not rushing to hasty judgement, and applying a bit of logic, would be a good starting point.

How do you know if your tool kit has all the right tools for the job? Experience will already have taught you a lot and you will have your favourites.

A sailmaker's sewing machine makes easier work of sail repairs for Eric Forsyth and crew. (FORSYTH)

Mike Gill – a complete and oily engineer. (GILL)

For complete confidence, you really need to take your boat apart – then you'll know if you've got all the tools you need! And you'll learn a lot about your boat as well. I freely admit I've had several boats that have had corners into which I've never set eyes, and that's not good. Those out-of-the-way places, such as where the steering quadrant lurks, the bilge beneath the engine, the piping and wiring that hides behind several cupboards and drawers – this is where things can go wrong. Never was the expression 'out of sight, out of mind' more true than on a boat. For example, do you know exactly how the engine is fed from the fuel tank, where the pipe runs, what it's made of, can you trace it all the way, and would you be able to replace it if it fractured? To be able to have such command of all the systems on a boat takes more than a few weekends. It can take years, and the sooner you start the better. Eventually, you will arrive at a situation where you know the workings of your boat better than those of your own body. The ominous grinding sound heard through the hull – what's that? Those who know their boats inside out will say it's only the anchor rocking in the bow roller, nothing much. The tinkle of metal heard falling on to the cabin roof? A search reveals a nut and washer lying in the scupper. It's only a small one, you observe, and far smaller than anything that holds up the rigging. You only know this because you're so familiar with your rig that you can tell in an instant. And then you remember, from months back, that small cleat you fixed to the mast to carry a flag halyard, and how that lower nut and bolt didn't seem to tighten properly when you fitted it. That's where it came from! Breathe a sigh of relief and go below for a cuppa. And so it goes on. Getting to know your boat and every part of it is a huge leap towards a successful ocean crossing.

There is never a moment when some job or other isn't waiting for you – Vicky Jackson gives Sunstone *a lick of varnish.* (JACKSON)

Tools and spares

Tools come in two forms: the ones you use almost every day and the ones you need once in a blue moon. The latter would include major spanners and screwdrivers, wrenches, oil filter removers, heavy hammer and drills. These are not going to see the light of day very often and can be stowed in places that need not offer immediate access.

For most routine jobs that crop up on a daily basis, you only need a handful of tools and these must be somewhere that is quick and easy to access, and preferably as close to the cockpit as you can. My handy kit, easily reached from the cockpit, has three cross-head screwdrivers and a couple of slot-head drivers, a pair of pliers, a pipe wrench for gripping small items, a sharp knife, a head torch and a shackle key. With those few items you can temporarily fix most minor things that are likely to occur under way.

These days, with inverters and rechargeables, it is possible to take an array of power tools with you. Clearly, a power drill is very useful. But multitools that can cut wood and metal have many uses. You might want to consider a battery-driven angle grinder. In the worst case, where your rig has come down and is lying in tangles across the

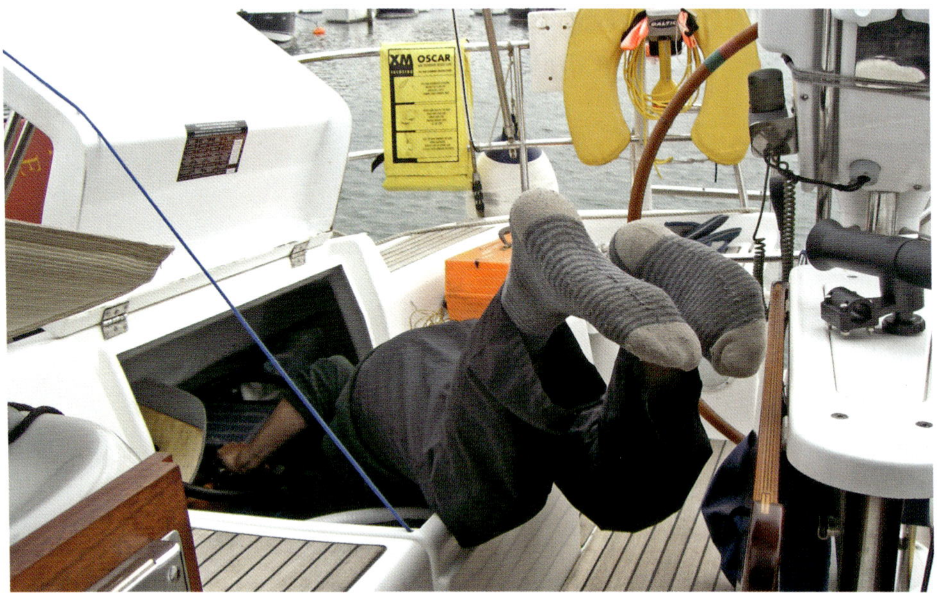

Cockpit lockers really are a devil of a place.

deck or worse, hanging over the side intent on doing damage to the hull, it can be far quicker to cut it all away with an angle grinder than optimistically trying to attack it with a hacksaw.

You also need, in a separate box, items devoted to fixing electrical faults. Apart from fuses, bulbs and batteries and all the usual renewables, you need small screwdrivers with a multiplicity of heads to enable you to dismantle everything from the compass light to the rear panel of the on-board stereo. You MUST have a reliable multimeter and a full knowledge of how to use it. It is the most valuable tool in a diagnostic kit and you will be surprised how many times you reach for it, from when you are uncertain about the state of charge of your batteries to figuring why the stereo isn't working. In fact, of all the faults on a boat, electrical ones are those that seem to cause people the greatest headaches. But electricity behaves not in a mysterious but a perfectly logical way, and fault-finding in electrical circuits can usually be achieved by going through a logical process. Here's how to do it.

Gather evidence: Take the example of a failure I sustained in mid-Atlantic. Not exactly a matter of life or death but a good example of the principles involved in fault-finding. The light in the heads failed. That's all. Nothing serious. But I wanted to fix it. So these are the questions I asked myself: Are there any other lights that are not working? Has anything else in that area failed? Check it hasn't been switched off on the boat's main switchboard. It could be something very simple.

No, it was just that light that had failed. Then examine the light fitting.

Has the bulb blown? You remove it and hold it up to the light (if it's a filament bulb). It looks intact, but to check you use the multimeter to measure the resistance across the bulb. If it's very high, the bulb is blown.

But in this case, the bulb was fine. Now make sure that power is getting to the light fitting by using the multimeter to measure the voltage between the incoming wire and negative. The meter shows 12.6 volts, so no problem there. So, the fitting is getting power, the bulb is not blown, so that leaves only the switch under suspicion. Isolate the power and use the multimeter to measure the resistance across the switch in the 'on' and 'off' position. If it is very high and doesn't change when you flick the switch, then your switch is duff.

Practise the logic and then electrical fault-finding should hold no fears. But some things will still be beyond you. You are never going to fix a systemic failure in the autopilot's processor, but at least you can eliminate a lot of the other factors that might cause it to fail.

What sort of 'complete engineer' am I? Not all that good by professional standards. But I have managed to sort out some quite complex problems at sea, from fixing an entire temporary fuel feed from a tank to dismantling the boat's charging system to find a faulty connection. I was once advised by a sailor who was also a good engineer: 'If something breaks and you haven't got a spare, don't think about what it looked like, think instead of what it did and go from there.' Imagination is a good part of being a decent engineer. I have played the 'what if' game many times, often only in my head – what if this breaks, what if that goes wrong? These are the conclusions I've come to. You might well have far more ingenious ones than I've come up with, and far braver.

- Know where every sea cock is, and have a wooden bung tied to it so that you have something to hammer into the hole if the sea cock should fail. Open and close the sea cocks once a week to keep them moving freely. Likewise have bungs near through-hulls, such as echo sounders.
- Assume that all electric bilge pumps will fail, and check that the manual one works. Then come up with a plan if that should fail as well.
- Know where every pipe clip is that secures the piping to the water tanks. Get used to the taste of salt water so that if you find the bilge full of water you can instantly tell if it's salt water or fresh.
- Dig deep beneath the deck to understand how your steering operates. It's quite simple on a tiller steered boat, but if you have a wheel you should be able to replace the drive chain, or belt. These can be highly inaccessible. It might be an idea to fit a new one just before you leave, then you'll know exactly how it fits if further problems arise.
- What would you do if the rudder jams? This can be very difficult to sort out without going over the side – possibly the riskiest of operations in anything other than a flat calm. Personally, I would never go over the side. Too risky for me, although perhaps not for you. And even if you do, there's no certainty that you can do anything about it. While your boat was ashore, it would have been worth checking how the rudder was constructed, and how it was attached to the boat. Is the rudder-stock held in a tube? How is it held at top and bottom? Do the bearings need lubrication? Such knowledge gives you an idea of the construction and thereby what sort of issues could have arisen, and knowledge of that sort can give you confidence. You might not be able to do anything about it, but you can come up with a decent theory as to what might have gone wrong. Then you can move on.

  At this stage you might start thinking of making a steering oar using a spinnaker pole with a flat board (washboard or leaf of the cabin table) attached. If your rudder has jammed hard over, this might be a waste of time. In such a situation, you'd be better off if the rudder had dropped off!

- I'd assume you'd know how to service the winches and have a decent kit of spare parts. But what if a sheet winch failed completely – do you have a spare block on board that you could rig to bring the lazy sheet across the cockpit so that both sheets can be handled from the one remaining winch?
- What will you do when a breaking wave climbs aboard the boat, deposits itself on the top of the spray hood and opens a long split, allowing spray to dribble below? Do you have spare bits of canvas, and needles, and how's your sewing?
- I have a personal rule that I no longer go up masts. This means I build in a lot of redundancy. I can quickly make a spare main halyard out of the topping lift. I have a couple of spare halyards running forward so I could rig something flying if my roller reefing failed. My boat has single line reefing on the mainsail but I've got a plan, using lashings, for pulling down a reef if the in-boom mechanism fails.
- Can you sail without a mainsail? I once split my main all the way across after an accidental gybe in a katabatic wind (a wind that blows directly down a mountainside, often with force). It split just above the third reef, so it became useless. I could sail to windward with my jib alone, but only just and it involved a lot of speedy and athletic tacking. I wish I'd known that before I had to find out for real.

Be prepared for every kind of task. Chris Marchant rerigs Gryphon II *in Malaysia.* (MARCHANT)

- I was almost defeated by a light weather headsail, which I hoisted free-flying. To get some extra tension in the luff, I applied the winch to the halyard with some force. A short while later, the wind freshened. It is usually a simple matter of letting the sail drop on to the deck but nothing would persuade it to come down. I even swung with my full weight on the luff, but it did not budge. After a futile time spent motoring in circles to wrap it round the forestay – a method suggested in countless magazine articles – I can confirm this has its problems, not least that you're still stuck with a sail hanging from your masthead.

Mike Robinson proving the best engineers can work in the most cramped of spaces. (ROBINSON)

Eventually, I came up with a solution. With a heavy heart I took a sharp knife and cut a gash in the sail, just back from the luff, at about my head height. I then took a length of rope, hitched it to the exposed luff and took it through a turning block to the anchor windlass. Even this strained, but eventually I was smothered in a sheet of collapsing nylon. Job done. It became obvious that in my enthusiastic efforts to tighten the luff, I had winched the eye splice into the cheeks of the plastic block, which had then gripped it so tightly that I thought it might never come down. That particular problem was solved only after I had paused for a cup of tea – many the dicey situation has been averted by the taking of tea.

It is no coincidence that good engineers drink lots of tea.

- On long voyages, I wondered how I would cope without hot food or drink. It would take the mere fracturing of a gas pipe to achieve that. In the end, I've always taken a small camping stove and some spare cylinders.
- Fear of running out of water is entirely justified. I carry water in two tanks and have a very small water maker (half a litre an hour only) and am careful to keep refilling the tanks as often as I can.

Rainwater is hugely valuable and I have a home-made device that can attach to the end of the boom to collect it. Give it a few minutes of heavy rain before you start collecting to wash the salt off the sail. It would be a brave sailor who set to sea without a supply of bottled water carefully stashed away.

- When it comes to the engine, you must be the complete boss of it. I was always taught that given a supply of fuel and some air, a diesel engine will always run. I don't know if that's true, but I'm happy to accept it. Therefore, I make sure I have a full understanding of the fuel system, how the tank is connected to the filters and how the diesel gets to the engine. I know which spanners I need to bleed air out of the fuel line, so that I don't have to spend time groping in the tool bag till I find one that fits. If you work on the assumption that your engine will fail at the worst possible moment, then be prepared to act fast. Be able to change filters without thinking; change the engine oil without having to look in the manual; be able to follow the cooling water system all the way from the sea to the exhaust, paying close attention to the replacement of the impeller. I have a rubber adapter that I can fit to my dinghy pump so I can blow air down the salt water intake to dislodge a jellyfish that might have taken up residence in the strainer. I would never touch a diesel injection pump – far too complex. If you understand the extent of your skill base, then you should also know where to draw the line and simply accept what is beyond you.

Susie Partridge has no fear of tackling a reluctant generator. (PARTRIDGE)

- The main use of the engine on a long ocean voyage is more likely to be for battery charging than propulsion. Only the largest boats have the fuel capacity to make significant inroads into, say, a 3,000-mile Pacific crossing. Despite electrics giving you a headache, you will sleep far more easily if you understand the connections between alternator and batteries, for these are often the root of much confusion. You need to be able to measure voltages across batteries to check what charging voltage is being applied, and if it is insufficient you need to find out why. It is beyond the scope of this book to teach you the often complex workings of a boat's electrical systems, but if you are halfway to mastery of it before you set off you will rest more easily.

- Make sure that the first time you have to look behind your boat's switchboard you're not a thousand miles from land. I know you've been putting it off but sooner or later you are going to have to open that switch panel and have a good look behind it. At first glance it might horrify. If previous owners have bothered, any new wiring will have been well integrated into the existing system. Equally, a professionally installed system might bristle with such complexity that you simply haven't a clue where to start. But all too often you will find the back of your switchboard looking like a ball of string in a kitten's paws. Labelling is often the key. Buy a labeller and mark all the important cabling, especially if you install anything new. A wire that was obviously coming from the GPS when you installed it might not be so well remembered a couple of years down the line. Get over the fear of the switchboard and learn to know your way around it.
- All the electrics may fail. If you have no charging and the batteries eventually go flat, what will you do then? The engine will not start, the plotter will fail. Well remembered if you have a pocket GPS – most smartphones have one. Give more than a passing thought to being competent at astronavigation. It not only gives you the satisfaction of mastering a traditional skill, but when you are coming new to it, it takes an awfully long time to come up with a position. This helps on lengthy passages when there are inevitable periods of boredom.
- If you haven't been able to play my card game as much as you would like before you leave, you can still play it while you're under way. Be careful not to depress yourself, but during those idle moments at the wheel when your brain has dropped into standby mode, just imagine if you had to launch the liferaft now, this instant! What's your first move? Or someone calls 'FIRE!' from the galley? Don't make yourself miserable, and don't let it spoil your voyage. But thinking ahead, working through every imaginable problem before it happens puts you in a hugely confident frame of mind.

And remember, most of the things that go wrong always seem to be ones you'd never thought of before. But that's sailing.

10 Look After Yourself

Keeping well and staying safe

If you're not feeling well, or you don't feel safe, very soon the fun of ocean sailing is going to disappear down the cockpit drains. Your health and general fitness is a hugely important aspect of successful passagemaking. You might imagine that sailing keeps you trim anyway, and it does to a certain extent, but as a total exercise regime there are things lacking. For example, one of the best cures for the 'down in the dumps' feeling is to go for a good, long walk. That is clearly off the agenda.

Your upper body strength, you will find, is greatly enhanced by repeated grabbing, balancing, winching and sail trimming, but for much of this time your legs will be doing hardly any work at all. Many long-distance voyagers find that once they arrive at a distant shore, the business of putting one foot in front of the other on dry land becomes a painful chore and that long walks start to look less attractive.

You might laugh at the idea of having a mid-ocean exercise regime, but it can pay dividends, especially the older you are and flexibility starts to desert you. Muscles and joints that are exercised regularly, and thereby strengthened, are much less likely to develop problems when asked to react in an emergency. You really don't want to inflict a bad back on yourself when you're a thousand miles from land.

When anchored, for example, sailing has provided us with many fitness machines. Paddling a kayak is great for upper body strength, paddle boards for balance and leg strength, and oars for rowing exercise almost every part of the body and in a strong head wind can provide what a fitness guru would call a 'full cardio workout'.

But out at sea it's not so easy. Some recommend yoga, but that can require careful balancing, which would not be easy in a Trade wind seaway. But a word to the idle: if your idea of an exercise regime is pumping the heads, then be reassured that this is the way most people successfully sail the oceans.

However, if you want to take it more seriously than that, avoid the many otherwise reputable fitness trainers who will simply have no idea of what to recommend to sailors.

Eric Forsyth takes a dose of strong medicine while nursing his arm in a home-made sling. (FORSYTH)

Their understanding of a floor that may be inclined at 30 degrees will be limited. But if you can describe to them how you can sit, or stretch out, or balance yourself somewhere safe, it should be possible to come up with some simple stretching exercises. After that you could move on to exercises where you strengthen your muscles by holding them under tension – isometric exercises. If it's calm, you could try resting against the mast and lowering your body till your thighs are parallel to the deck. Hold it for 30 seconds then raise yourself up, and repeat it. Ask an expert for exercises that will work if you are lying in a bunk, or sitting at the wheel. Superyachts carry gym equipment. You might think that on your more modest boat there are items that carry a higher priority.

Keeping well at sea is about eating well. Think about making fresh food last as long as possible. (MARKIN)

Avoid falls and tumbles at all costs. Niki Phillips braces herself for galley work in a rolling sea. (PHILLIPS)

Medicine afloat

In those waking hours that precede any long sailing trip, your mind wanders through all the disasters that can strike. Many of them you will have come to terms with through all the experiences you have accumulated in home waters cruising. But when it comes to nightmares, ocean sailing presents a different challenge, and it is simply that help is so very far away. The Pacific, for example, is a large and lonely ocean where help, if there is any, may be days in coming. In home waters, assistance can be with you within minutes via a helicopter from the shore but there is no such comfort in the midst of the ocean.

You have thought through all your safety practices for man-overboard, storm survival, electrical failure and the rest, but there is one area of concern that you return to, and that is what you are going to do if one of you gets ill. The problem with medical emergencies at sea is that everything is magnified; the distance between you and assistance is greater, the comfort you can provide a patient that much less, the conditions in which you will have to work are far removed from a doctor's clinic. And

Make yourself as secure as you can, especially when sleeping – then the medical kit might never have to come out of its locker.

while all this is going on someone has to tend the boat, otherwise the difficulties can rapidly escalate. Not many medics would wish to practise in conditions such as those found in a tumbling washing machine, but you might have to.

But you are not a doctor, you are a sailor. You have not had the intense training that medical professionals go through but you suddenly find yourself with a patient who needs your care. At best, you did the First Aid course before you left and you've got a few supporting books on the shelf. You may even be carrying a copy of *The Ship Captain's Medical Guide*. The latest edition is available here as a series of downloads: www.gov.uk/government/publications/the-ship-captains-medical-guide

This is intended as 'practical medical guidance for laymen (non-doctors) working on board a ship'.

It is thorough, authoritative, comprehensive but ultimately quite scary. The first chapter, on first aid, is 40 pages long and who wants to be thumbing through a reference book when confronted with a bleeding injury that needs urgent attention?

Sooner or later, you are going to be required to play ship's doctor, and with luck it will be only for something minor, likes cuts, grazes or insect bites. But there lurks at the back of your mind the possibility of serious fracture, heart attack, stroke, poisoning and all the other life-threatening events that fill those waking night-time hours. Not to mention childbirth. So what do you do? Go to medical school for five years? I doubt it. But there are preparations you can make, and if you want to sleep easy, you should. You should also not leave it to the last minute. Those final countdown weeks before a lengthy cruise begins can be hugely pressured. There are stores to take on board, satphones to fathom, software to update and, often right at the bottom of the list, we must remember to do that quick first aid course. Don't leave it to the last minute. It is every bit as important as setting sails and launching liferafts, and I bet you have given plenty of thought to those. Thankfully, death at sea is rare. The most common cause of severe injury seems to be severe blows to the head from a boom. After that comes breaks and dislocations from tumbles taken in rough seas, then galley burns and scalds, closely followed by cuts and rope burns, and bites, stings and cuts while ashore. You might prepare for doomsday but most accidents appear out of the blue. You need to be prepared for the wide range of medical problems that can arise.

Careful! Make sure the blood is the fish's, and not yours.

There is, of course, nothing to prevent you setting off with no training at all and just a few sticking plasters and headache pills in the locker, and many do just that – although hopefully with more than just those basics. But if you want to gain confidence and experience to widen your knowledge beyond basic first aid, then you are going to have to undertake some serious training. But you will not become a doctor. As one trainer said, 'I'm not going to try and make you a medic. But I want to make you realise that if you ask questions and can relay symptoms, then you can go safely offshore and never have an issue.' Of all the aspects of training for medical emergencies, communication might be the most important.

Let's assume you have done a basic course, making sure it is with a maritime trainer who understands the confines of a yacht. The course may have lasted only a day, so the emphasis will be on the word 'basic'. Of the things that are specific to sailing, you will have been taught how to place a patient in the recovery position, especially in a confined place, and how to do CPR (cardiopulmonary resuscitation), which uses chest compressions and artificial ventilation to restore circulation and heartbeat, usually after cardiac arrest. You will also have learned how to deal with hypothermia, seasickness and dehydration, and how to get medical advice by radio. There is a risk that having attended a course like this you feel empowered to deal with any emergency that might occur; this might not be the case.

A typical basic first aid syllabus

- What is first aid, and the priorities within first aid
- Assessment of the patient and what to do next
- Levels of response, and the AVPU Scale – 'alert, voice, pain, unresponsive'
- Unconsciousness and the recovery position
- CPR (including an awareness of AEDs – battery-operated defibrillators)
- Drowning, immersion hypothermia and cold shock
- Breathing difficulties
- Failure of the circulation
- Blood loss and the control of bleeding
- Recognition of internal bleeding
- Angina and heart attack
- Anaphylaxis
- Fractures, including spinal injuries
- Head injury; concussion and compression
- Burns, including sunburn
- Exposure hypothermia and hyperthermia
- Seasickness and dehydration
- Diabetic emergency
- Seizures

Remember, much of this lengthy list is going to be squeezed into a day's tuition so your understanding of any of these topics is going to be limited, and basic knowledge of this kind might well be sufficient to sustain a patient till help arrives in a coastal location, but you are going to need a far wider range of skills if a medical emergency overtakes you far from land.

A point to think about: usually the skipper will either take these courses him/herself, or delegate it to a member of the crew. But what if it is that member of the crew who is struck down? Cruising couples should certainly both take medical training, otherwise it's a big gamble as to which of you is going to care for the other.

It's time to talk to a doctor. James Morrow practises as a general practitioner in the UK and has extensive ocean sailing experience. He sails with his wife, who is a surgeon, and their two children.

James Morrow – a doctor all at sea. 'Hypochondria has no place on a boat.'

'Ocean sailors are, by definition, resourceful, self-reliant and capable of making do and these attributes serve well when it comes to medical needs when offshore. The human body is amazing and usually capable of resolving most things itself, given a bit of time and gentle support. Hypochondria has no place on small boats.

Ocean sailors also accept and manage risk – and this skill should be applied to things medical too. It's easy to become preoccupied with medical what-if scenarios. A good test is to think about the likelihood not just of something happening, but the chances of making a real difference. For that reason, for most people, carrying a defibrillator doesn't make sense. The chances of needing it are minute and if offshore the chances of survival following a cardiac arrest minimal.

Bare minimum knowledge should be a well-taught first aid course. Of all the things you should be prepared for, lacerations and how to manage them come top of the list; how to provide initial first aid using pressure and elevation. Then consideration of closing the wound with medical glue, or failing that, superglue (often found on board and highly effective at closing wounds when used as "spot welds" to hold skin edges together) or "steristrips". Ideally you might use medical sutures, but at a push a sailmaker's needle and thread could be called upon. Local anaesthetic is not essential, though it does improve the situation for both the patient and person doing the suturing.

Recognising the classical features of a fracture is important: pain, deformity and loss of function. You should be able to immobilise the fracture (for pain relief) and if a long way offshore think about reducing (straightening) the bone to prevent longer-term disability. It is useful to think in advance about how you might do this. Inflatable splints are available, but expensive, but usually things like sail battens, wooden spoons or fishing rods/boathooks can be called into action.

Major infections are thankfully rare, but serious. Minor infections like cystitis or conjunctivitis are easily treatable. Being able to recognise major sepsis – a life-threatening emergency with very high fever but cold fingers and toes, confusion, shakes and agitation – and distinguishing this from a cold is useful. Viral illnesses like a cold don't need antibiotics. Major bacterial infections do. It is worth carrying a range of "just in case" antibiotics. Again, the balance between expense, space and potential utility needs to be weighed up.

On our offshore passages the antibiotics we carry are: fucithalmic eye drops (for conjunctivitis), co-amoxiclav tablets (broad spectrum penicillin-based antibiotic with good coverage for respiratory problems, abdominal, skin and lung infections), ciprofloxacin tablets (similar spectrum of use, but also has value for infectious bacterial gastroenteritis where co-amoxiclav may make things worse) and a course of once-daily injectable antibiotics like ceftriaxone. All of these are prescription-only medications in the UK.

Pain relief is probably the most important thing to be able to get right if needed. Simple pain relief such as paracetamol and ibuprofen can work very well, if taken regularly, and should not be overlooked. Stronger pain relief moves into the opiates (morphine derivatives) and can potentially cause issues in some countries. Codeine, tramadol and meptazinol tablets are all highly effective for severe pain, though in the UK are prescription-only medications. Injectable morphine or fentanyl lozenges are extremely effective for rapid relief of severe pain but not all sailors will be willing to obtain or carry them, given the vagaries of regulation regarding opiate drugs across jurisdictions.

Given the age profile of many offshore sailors, the risk of going into urinary retention (being unable to pass urine) is one that needs thought. It is mostly an issue for men at a certain stage of maturity, and largely related to enlargement of the prostate. Untreated, it is not only vastly uncomfortable but can lead to kidney failure and ultimate demise if not managed. The standard treatment is the insertion of a urinary catheter – a bit of kit that I think all offshore yachts should carry. It is cheap, light and potentially a life-saver. Inserting it is relatively straightforward and one of the few interventions that provides almost immediate relief, and gratitude.

You will surely have to deal with seasickness at some stage. Everyone will have their own favourite remedy. For severe cases the risks are of dehydration and stopping the vomiting is key. Tablets may not help as they are not absorbed before vomiting takes over. Patches avoid this issue but don't work (and are not suitable) for everybody. This is one of the few situations where an injectable drug can be needed. Prochlorperazine (Stemetil), haloperidol or cyclizine can all be used. Given an intramuscular injection is straightforward – bury the needle in the upper outer quadrant of the buttock and inject. This location keeps the needle away from any vital structures, arteries and nerves and is suitable for novice injectors.

If someone is dehydrated and not keeping fluids down at all then fluids can be given by other routes. Unless you have a paramedic, nurse or doctor on board you are unlikely to have the experience needed to set up intravenous fluids. But the same fluid can be given through a simple butterfly needle under the skin as subcutaneous fluid (minimal training needed) and done even on a moving boat in someone whose veins are collapsed due to the dehydration. If sterile fluids are not available, fluid can be given by putting a tube into the anus and gently squeezing the fluid (can be straight tap-water) into the rectum.

Anyone who has what it takes to sail on an ocean passage has the aptitude to learn the core skills needed to be a competent offshore first-aider. Any training is better than no training. Targeted training for the needs of those a long way from help is best of all. There are courses for expedition members as well as those specifically for sailors. But even in the absence of specific training, some prior thought about what to do in certain circumstances can help. In the world of medicine, "Don't panic" goes a long way. Very few situations require immediate action and there is usually time to stabilise the situation, then think it through. If the thought of a vast medical kit makes you panic, imagine it is like the rigging on the boat. At first glance to the uninitiated, incomprehensible. However, everything is logical, has its place, and not all of it is ever needed at once. Look at it slowly, think about how it might be used, and recognise that having it gives you options, not a compulsion to use it.

And if you can't stand the sight of blood, get over it! Like a blocked heads that needs to be cleared, needs must. It's ocean sailing, not afternoon tea at The Ritz. Doing your best is better than doing nothing. If someone is seriously ill, and there is only you, then not doing anything is not an option. But remember that you are unlikely to ever have to do most of what you learn. Understanding the principles and being prepared to act is what matters most. Being textbook proficient isn't necessary. Any knowledge gained, or skill learned, is a positive.

Before you leave I would certainly recommend a dental check-up (see Susie Partridge's story, page 223). A thorough medical check-up is largely a waste of time for those in robust good health. For those with chronic medical conditions, or on long-term medications, a targeted discussion around how to manage their condition while offshore makes sense. Having sufficient of their usual medications in separated, sealed and labelled containers is important. As is making sure the rest of your crew know what medications you take, which are vital, and where to find them.

Children are generally highly resilient but are more prone to hypothermia from exposure. Being aware of children's doses of medications is important, as is taking liquid forms for the very young. Older people are more likely to have one or more chronic medical conditions and be on long-term medications. They are also potentially going to be less secure on their feet and potentially more prone to injury and fractures.

If you need to consult a doctor by radio or satellite phone, it is important to remember that not all doctors will be familiar with the reality of treating someone who is ill on a small boat, far from help. And for some doctors, they will not have the necessary insurance cover to be allowed to provide advice outside their home country.

Assuming you have found a doctor who is able to advise then they will need to know:

- Who you are: name, medical experience
- Where you are: how far from external help
- The patient's background: gender, age, significant pre-existing medical conditions such as diabetes or pregnancy
- The general synopsis: 'awake and conscious' or if not report on the airway, breathing, circulation
- What has happened: if an injury, mechanism of injury; if illness, the time frame

Then the specifics:

- Current situation
  Start with the objective: things you can measure, count or see. If possible, report on temperature, pulse, colour, breathing rate. If an injury, describe what you see in simple unequivocal terms, e.g. "His left forearm is bent at an angle halfway between the wrist and elbow with the lower part bent away from the body."

Then the subjective: what the patient is reporting, what you think is going on.

Report (honestly) what you have done so far and what medical equipment you have available e.g. basic first aid kit only, full ship's medical chest.

If you're worried about making a wrong diagnosis and perhaps giving the wrong drug, don't be. It's something every clinician does. The skill is in constantly checking on the diagnosis and revising it as information emerges. A blind adherence to a diagnosis despite information to the contrary is like the sailor who only sees the lights they expect to see, rather than those that are there and so runs into trouble. Given the likely range of emergency drugs on board a boat, there are very limited options for giving the wrong drug and in most cases doing something is better than doing nothing.

Remember that most people are healthy most of the time. Most medical emergencies are easily recognised. A modest amount of preparation and training goes a long way in being prepared. Nothing trumps common sense and a practical approach. Don't panic. There is always time to pause, think and assess before committing to a course of action. In a genuine medical emergency you are more likely to help by doing something than by doing nothing through a fear of doing the wrong thing.

And one question ocean sailors often ask: "Should I have my appendix out before I go?" The answer is *absolutely not*. Removing a healthy appendix is much more likely to do you harm than sailing with it intact.'

Simon Currin is a general practitioner in Wales and also a high latitudes ocean sailor (see page 50).

'I know of boats that sail with no medical kit or expertise and pride themselves on their minimalism. Similarly, there are boats that sail with the kitchen sink of kits. Somewhere in the middle is a compromise that makes the best use of cost, space, expertise and the odds of a medical emergency arising. Remember that you can save life on the basis of a short training course. Understanding of airway breathing and circulation is not rocket science.

Dr Simon Currin: 'Have a plan in place to be able to get the assistance you need.'

The commonest affliction for offshore sailors is probably seasickness. Few folk seem to be aware that the side effects of seasickness remedies can (and do) cause urinary retention, confusion, changes to vision, and heart irregularities. The older the person, the more likely they will suffer. These problems will be compounded by pre-existing illness and other associated medications.

If the crew has no training, and yet has somehow acquired a vast medical kit, then their next most important acquisition should be the equipment to communicate. Modern medics are becoming increasingly fluent in conducting consultations via email and telephone and all sorts of medical issues are now dealt with routinely via such media in my day-to-day practice. What would help a remote medical advisor would be the ability to record and relay simple medical observations such as temperature, pulse, oxygen saturations, blood pressure, urine test strips and blood sugar. Make sure that you have the means to seek advice and be prepared to act on that advice. Nobody is going to expect you to function like a trained physician but you can do a huge amount of good by being the eyes, ears and hands of someone on the end of a satellite phone or an email.

As far as children are concerned, a cruising family should make sure that their kids get their vaccinations as it would be a tragedy to lose a child to measles or meningitis, which are much commoner in some cruising destinations. In older folk, pre-existing illnesses and their treatments are likely to add complexity to their care. For instance, seasickness-induced dehydration might lead to a serious kidney injury on folk taking commonly used blood pressure medications. Know what your crew are taking and make sure you know how to get advice. There is nowhere in the world that Iridium voice or email doesn't work. Invest in good communications and have a plan in place to seek the assistance you need.

Given all the varying infections that can be picked up, particularly in exotic locations, how are you ever going to recognise them and treat them? If you are in a region that has so many infections then it is likely that there will also be access to local medical services, so use them. There are numerous sources of medical advice these days from travel insurers, specialist private advice hotlines, Falmouth Coastguard (see opposite), Geos (travel safety providers) or the family friend back home. The Ocean Cruising Club can, and do, provide significant resources in medical emergencies such as the Port Officer network, which has assisted in providing support to those in medical distress.'

Being able to talk to a doctor ashore is probably one of the very best reasons to carry a satphone. Together with email, you can expect to arrive at a reasonable diagnosis and course of treatment. In cases where you have enough bandwidth, pictures can greatly help a remote doctor in assessing a patient. You may choose to have a tame doctor back home who has agreed to take calls from you in emergency circumstances, but there are now companies that offer, in return for a subscription, what is called 'tele-medicine'. Many organisations worldwide now offer this service.

You can always access, at no charge, the UK's Marine Rescue Coordination Centre at Falmouth, England (+44 1326 317575) and they have the facility to transfer you to a team of duty emergency doctors who will offer advice by email falmouthcoastguard@mcga.gov.uk or by Inmarsat C (AOR-E)423-200-158 (AOR-W) 423-200-159.

If you take repeat medication, then clearly you must carry sufficient stock of it. If you plan to be away from home for a couple of years, it can sometimes take some persuading for your doctor to prescribe in such large quantities. Don't take just sufficient for an ideal passage length – add at least 25 per cent to the amount of medication you need.

And remember that seasickness can cause vomiting, and those taking birth control pills can suddenly find themselves unprotected. A mid-ocean pregnancy might not have been part of your voyage planning.

When medical problems arise

Susie and Tom Partridge were anchored off the Solomon Islands in their yacht, *Adina*, when Tom started to become ill. It was a lonely anchorage with no medical facilities and an intricate exit through narrow channels in the coral reef. Susie now had to face this as a singlehander with an increasingly sick husband, in order to get him to hospital.

'Tom had been lethargic and out of sorts for several weeks and took a very quick turn for the worse. Our initial diagnosis was malaria – he had all the symptoms and we had been in known malarial areas. I emailed a friend we had met in Vanuatu, who was a vet, and had taken a big interest in our trip and like many friends was always willing to do whatever was needed.This friend's knowledge, responsiveness and thoroughness was one aspect of the whole experience that proved invaluable. He gave us his view, and confirmed

Tom Partridge restored to full health, after a close shave. (PARTRIDGE)

it with his GP, who said we should treat Tom for malaria, but also for unknown infections by using high doses of two different broad-spectrum antibiotics, and to get Tom to a hospital as soon as possible.

I had no previous experience of this type of illness and relied upon my instinct and the advice given. I could see Tom was seriously unwell having deteriorated rapidly within the space of a few hours. He had a roaring temperature, was delirious, and not "with it". I started him on malaria treatment and antibiotics. Tom continued to deteriorate and it became clear that we would need professional medical support. I knew it would be unsafe for us to exit the lagoon in darkness and singlehanded given the narrow coral passes, so I planned to depart at first light. In the meantime, I emailed and spoke to family, and our friend the vet, and we agreed treatment for Tom and the best course of action to get help. We considered Tom's condition to be very serious and life-threatening. He needed professional medical support.

The night before we sailed, once I had established a plan of action, I lay awake watching Tom, believing I needed to make sure he kept breathing. I was scared and felt the pressure of being alone and responsible for his life. Once we were under way, Tom's condition improved a little and I believed the malaria treatment or the antibiotics had kicked in. Tom insisted on being in the cockpit with me so I made a bed for him on the cockpit seats and he slept while I sailed.

Before leaving the UK we had to think about how we could be as self-sufficient as possible in every aspect of life on board, including any medical issues that might arise. We undertook a two-day bespoke medical course and agreed the content with the instructor in advance. It included learning how to suture wounds, give injections, use syringes and needles, make basic examinations and we revisited CPR.

During our course we discussed medical kit to carry on board. From this and further reading, we devised a list of what we wanted to carry. We sourced a lot of the physical kit online – for example, neck brace, limb supports, surgical gloves, suturing equipment. We bought extensive first aid kit and over-the-counter drugs from our local pharmacy. For the drugs that were "prescription only" in the UK we saw a private doctor and once he was satisfied we had an adequate understanding of the drugs and training to use them he wrote us a private prescription for everything we wanted. This included an array of antibiotics, steroids, strong pain relievers, tranquillisers, eye medications and more. I created a spreadsheet to track it all.

On board I created a small, quick-grab first aid kit and a larger one containing more serious kit. I stored all of the drugs separately in a lockable case. I also labelled the cupboards in which these kits were kept to make it clear for any friends or family joining us on board and we included an overview of the medical kit in our safety briefing for those joining us for long passages.

Once we left the UK we kept our medical kit topped up, in date and supplemented with additional supplies. It proved much easier to obtain many of the drugs outside of the UK without prescription. We also learned the importance of carrying drugs appropriate for the area in which you are travelling. For example, when we arrived in Vanuatu, where we were to be based for five months, we took advice from local doctors and added the malaria treatment that was being used in the area at that time. We also obtained stronger antibacterial cream for skin infections, and additional antibiotics better suited to common tropical infections than the antibiotics we carried from the UK. This later proved invaluable when Tom fell ill.

We sailed 24 hours to the nearest main town of Gizo where a doctor confirmed that Tom did not have malaria and that we needed to get him further treatment elsewhere. By the time we got Tom to medical care in Australia (via a flight to Honiara, the capital of the Solomon Islands, from where we could fly direct to Brisbane) the infection was passing thanks to the antibiotics – we were still using our own supplies.

The likely source proved to be an infection caused by an abscess in the root of one of his teeth. Tom recovered fully and we returned to *Adina* determined to continue our adventure. I believe that Tom wouldn't be with us today if he hadn't taken those antibiotics. He and I have both looked back at the incident and reflected on the experience, sharing the view that we were indescribably fortunate to have been given the advice.'

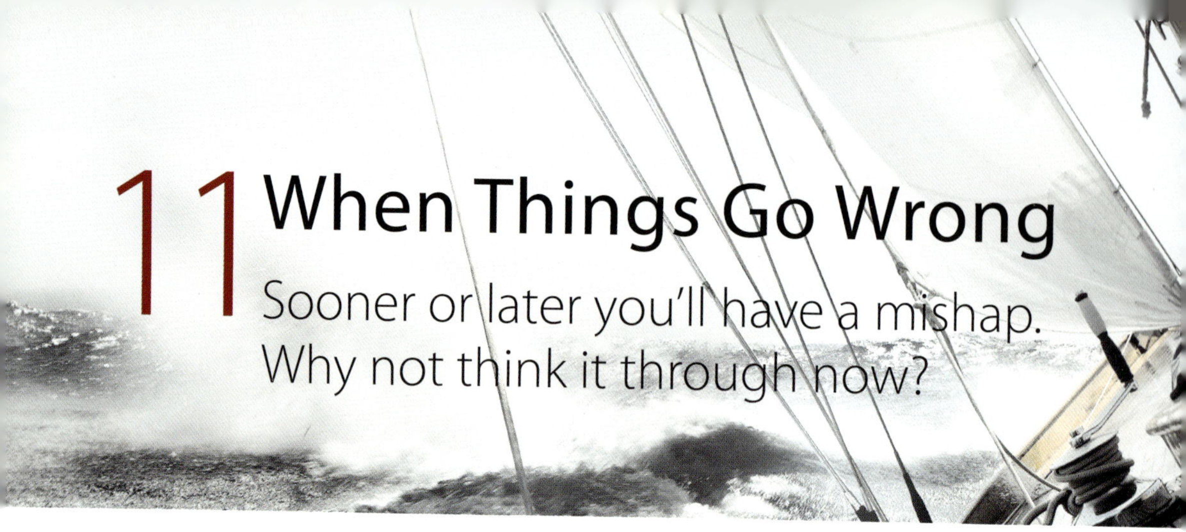

11 When Things Go Wrong

Sooner or later you'll have a mishap. Why not think it through now?

We move on from the make-do-and-mend philosophy to events so catastrophic that not only is your boat and your voyage in jeopardy, but possibly your lives. There are some disasters that seem insuperable, no matter how inventive and imaginative you might be. These are the big ones, the ones that have you reaching for the EPIRB, sensing things are just about to get beyond your control.

As with all boat breakages, cool heads are needed, and often steady hands. But these are difficult virtues to have at your command when true catastrophe strikes. Be reassured, though, that many of the things that can inflict the greatest damage on a boat are very unlikely to happen to you. Always remember the number of successful voyagers who make contented arrivals, perhaps having performed a bit of that make-do along the way. But they got there. They lived to tell the tale. Somehow, they were not swallowed by whales, hit by falling space junk, dragged beneath the waves by unseen forces, or consigned to the fate of the *Flying Dutchman*.

Land may be the greatest threat to the integrity of your boat. There are more than a handful of cases where oceans have been successfully crossed but closing with the land proved to be the most risky part of the voyage. Tiredness might be a factor, but also that sense of deep relaxation at the thought that the voyage is almost complete, and your defences are taking a rest just at the point when you need them most. Strandings on reefs and rocks are far more common than disasters at sea.

All the disasters recorded below are real-life experiences from people who lived to tell the tale. They are far from being an exhaustive list of all the disasters that can strike, but they're enough to be going on with! Don't read these in order to frighten yourself. But don't ignore them either. Thinking through how you might deal with these disasters on your own boat will make you more confident, safer and stronger sailors than before. No two disasters will be the same, but the stories below might inspire you to look again at your own boat, and think about pumps and liferafts and all those things that we profoundly hope we will never have to call into use.

When everything seems to go wrong

If only one thing went wrong at a time, disasters and breakages might be easier to deal with. But when problem piles upon problem until you don't know which way to turn, then it can become truly testing. James Muggoch, a man in his mid-sixties, set sail in his 27ft sloop to cross the Atlantic to the Caribbean, and when he got there he was going to hand over his boat, *Annie of Orwell*, to the Sea Scouts in Grenada. It was a generous gift about which he'd spoken to the Grenadian High Commissioner in advance. In Lanzarote he started to prepare for his voyage by filling his water tanks.

'The first thing I had to do was decant water into the main tanks. In the bilge I found not only water, but running water! A quick taste check and some relief – it was fresh. But where from? First I found a leak in the pipe under the sink, but having fixed it the water kept coming. I found that it was coming from a new tank in the bow, which had been installed without a hose clip on the filler pipe.

Then I went to start the 7hp Volvo engine, but despite an expensive service before leaving the UK it remained inert. Three days later, having been informed that the spares would take two or three weeks to arrive, I asked the marina to tow *Annie* out of the harbour, engineless. I felt that being a sailing boat with a range under power of only 200 miles, I should be able to sail her all the way. I had a solar panel and a wind generator – enough, I felt, to produce sufficient power for the navigation lights and the GPS, AIS and VHF. Then I had to wait for two days while the forecast 38 knot winds blew themselves out, and used up the last of my euros on ten lemons and a Mars Bar.

I raised the sails and we made our way slowly southwards down the coast of Fuerteventura. I had been told of the "funnel effect" of the north-east winds, but my lack of experience showed in that I left the sails up far too long and, as darkness fell, found that I was going far too fast. I had stupidly secured the preventer on the boom so had to cut it loose, and without roller reefing on the genoa I had to go forward to change headsails. I no longer have full use of my left eye following an accident, which meant that I was, to all intents, night blind. Plus, a motorbike accident four years ago injured my right shoulder, which was causing considerable discomfort. Even so I managed to lower the sails, catch my right hand in the mainsheet track, which runs across the cockpit at knee level, fall from the deck into the cockpit on to my head (which still hurt three months later), and have my first, but not last, totally sleepless night of the next 41.

Next morning found *Annie* and me very tired and a bit battered but still, I thought, on course. My head was very sore but had stopped bleeding, though I felt quite sick. Even so, I felt that all was going well apart from the GPS being unable to raise any coverage, so when I saw a large mountain far away on the port bow I thought I'd strayed too far east and was looking at Africa, many miles away.

Then the self-steering came apart, and for about six or seven hours I fought to clear the land, hand-steering and unable to get to a drink or food. Realising that I was in deep trouble, I cut my losses and, ignoring the "voices" that were starting to haunt me, came about on to port tack, managed to fix the self-steering, and went below, leaving poor *Annie* to fend for herself.

I had survived a very bad and ill-prepared start to an Atlantic challenge. The next morning, I saw two large islands dead ahead. The Canaries! I couldn't understand, and still can't, how it happened, but we were right back where we had started two days earlier.

Now out of the shelter of the islands, the sea came up along with heavy cloud cover, which was to remain for the next eight or ten days. My eye problem meant that I couldn't see the compass, the sea, or the sails, and with no stars to steer by I just lowered the sails and went to bed – not the most seamanlike approach, but the best I could do.

At about this time I started to hallucinate quite badly. Days and nights merged into a blur, and controlling little *Annie* seemed much more difficult than I'd imagined back in London. I was managing runs of over 100 miles a day, but with great effort and little sleep as the self-steering needed a lot of attention.

About 500 miles south-west of the Canaries, I was sitting in the cockpit, wet but warm, thinking "I haven't seen a ship for six days" when I realised I was looking straight at what turned out to be the "biggest iron ore transport ship in the world". My thanks to Captain Catalin for that information, and also for emailing my wife in Australia, and for the weather forecast: "Force 8 becoming 9, sea 8 metres becoming 12 to 14 overnight." I said, "Thanks for that."

I had to make a decision between bailing out and going to the Cape Verdes or turning right and going on to Grenada. So I tossed a coin. Then I did the opposite. Carry on it was. By this time my hands were very sore with rope burns, my left shoulder had reacted to the fall a week earlier and was killing me, plus boils and salt water sores were making life very uncomfortable when I sat down. With 35 knots of wind over deck I lost a jib halyard up the mast where it became tangled round the radar reflector. Everything was soaking wet with a lot of water in the boat mainly coming in through the main hatch and possibly through a leaking seam where deck meets hull.

The next day was quite a day. I'd just opened the main hatch and removed the top splashboard when the largest breaking wave so far came aboard. It washed me back into the cabin, loads of water, floorboards washing around, all electrics out and the sound of rushing water behind the cupboards over the sink. I was bailing like mad with no 12-volt pump and the hand pump out in the cockpit. I sprayed the electrics with WD40 to dispel the sea water and carried on bailing, though I was tiring quickly. Suddenly, I could smell burning, and to my horror saw smoke and flickering flame from the electrics. I turned the batteries off, which seemed to do the trick, but I was left without any of my 12-volt system. I was then relying on my handheld GPS and VHF and a handheld strobe light.

Annie was still sailing, but more and more water was finding its way below. I went outside, choosing my moment with care, and realised that, as *Annie* had gybed under the force of wind and wave, the preventer had ripped a stanchion clean out of the deck leaving a triangular hole big enough to put my fist through. I was at a fairly low ebb and, thinking I was sinking, put out a PAN PAN call to see if there was anyone about. I really had had enough, and after more bailing changed it to my first (and I hope last) MAYDAY call. After several repeated calls there was still no response – not surprising as I was about 800 miles from Africa and 1,800 from the West Indies. I realised it was down to me.

I pulled myself together and lowered the sails, which stopped a lot of the driving waves over the deck, and, taking the claw hammer, smashed out the cupboards and headlining over the sink. Peace and quiet returned as the wind dropped and the sun came out. I pumped *Annie* out and tried to tidy up, noticing that the cooker had come off its gimbals (no more hot drinks or food) and the chart table had collapsed. The seas had gone down a bit, so I tried to block the hole with Plastic Padding by tying my feet to the starboard handrail and lying across the boat, but the waves and the difficulty mixing the paste with both hands while gravity was trying to pull me overboard proved too much and I had to leave it. I deployed the sea anchor and took the night off, going to bed to lick my wounds.

From then on things got slowly better. The Trade winds kicked in; not the benign soft breezes I'd hoped for but robust force 6–7 with warm sunshine and clear skies so I could, at last, steer by the stars. With the better weather came more sleep, and with more sleep came an end to the "voices". I've since learned that I'm not alone in being visited by these things and I hope I never am again.

There were ups and downs over the next few weeks during which I was becalmed for three days, which was worse than the storms. In the calmer conditions I rewired the VHF radio and managed to reinstall the cooker for the last week … coffee!

I held back for the night when 25 miles off Grenada so as not to make landfall in the dark, and at about 0500 got under way for the final day's sailing. At 0730, much to my surprise, the radio, which I had left on down below, came to life with a girl's voice saying: "Morning Grenada – this is Yachtnet radio – come in please." I was beside myself with joy. "Hello *Annie* – welcome to Grenada. We are all waiting for you."

Annie and I sailed the last few miles at speed. About half a mile out a police launch came up behind us. I couldn't make out what the officer was shouting and called for them to come closer, to hear, "Put some bloody clothes on!"

I'd forgotten I'd been naked for over four weeks!'

If James Muggoch's story proves one thing, it is that how you deal with problems as they arise, and how you dig deep to find the inner strength to cope with them, can often dictate the success or otherwise of an ocean passage. At times, it seemed as if James was like a boxer, coming close to being floored by every blow. But how he got to his feet and arrived in good order after the sail of a lifetime serves as a reminder that on any ocean passage there are bound to be a few knocks, and it is how you recover from them that counts.

The worst nightmare

To have a member of the crew go overboard is probably every cruiser's most recurring nightmare. More so if you are sailing as just a couple. Imagine the helplessness of that situation. It is beyond the scope of this book to tell you how to rehearse man overboard practices and what methods you should employ – let's assume you have given it plenty of thought before setting sail.

But sometimes unexpected events overtake you and suddenly someone is in the water. Luckily, Tony Gooch lived to tell the tale.

'It happened in April 1997 when we were about three days, 400 miles, out of Caleta Hoppner on Staten Island heading for Buenos Aires.

Our boat, *Taonui*, was a 42ft aluminium German-built sloop designed for long-distance ocean voyages particularly in high latitudes. She had completed a circuit of the Americas before we bought her. We took delivery of her in March 1996 and sailed from Germany, through the Panama, down the Chilean channels and then down the Antarctic Peninsula.

Running north we were overtaken by a deepening low that caused havoc onshore and to nearby shipping. We ran before it for 36 hours before deciding to stop and let it blow over. Lacking experience with *Taonui* in these conditions we hove-to and then lay a hull. Now we know we should have just kept sailing or deployed a series drogue. We had a couple of knockdowns during the night.

In the morning the storm had passed and the wind and seas were down. I went on deck to check the boat before getting sailing again. All looked in good order. The boom vangs on *Taonui* go to the rail on either side. Going forward along the starboard side, I unclipped my life harness from the jack line to step over the boom vang. At that moment I was thrown overboard as *Taonui* was lifted up then rolled upside down by what must have been a big rogue wave. We know the boat went upside down as Coryn, who was below in her bunk, was thrown against the cabin roof leaving three holes in the headboard lining, one for her head and two for her knees.

The mast broke at the lower spreaders, probably as the boat righted herself. If I had still been attached by my life harness and tether I most certainly would have been caught up in the mast and rigging and likely drowned. As it was I was caught by the wave and tumbled and tossed. From my surfboard riding days, I know what the inside of a big wave is like – fizzy air, crazy turbulence, hard to know which way is up. I came to the surface to see *Taonui* way upwind, probably 150–200 feet (45–60m), maybe more. She looked like a stricken bird with her broken mast. I reached down to pull off my boots, only to find they had been ripped off by the wave. I started to try to swim but in reality I can't have made any progress.

Coryn made her way over the lifted engine floorboards and into the cockpit, blood from her lacerated head obscuring her vision. Downwind she could see a little yellow blob. I guess we both sensed that the boat was drifting down to me. Coryn threw the Lifesling in the water and it drifted down towards me. I swam to it, or it came to me. Coryn pulled me back to the boat and I climbed the boarding ladder on the stern. If we did not have a boarding ladder it is doubtful that I would have got back on board as by then I was getting cold and exhausted. If the mast had not broken and become an effective sea-anchor, it is unlikely that I would have made it back to the boat.

The mast was banging on to the side of the boat so after a few hours of recuperation I lashed the mast to the boat. We waited until later that day to start work on pulling pins to get rid of the broken mast. When all was clear we started motoring towards the shore 400 miles away.

We should have kept sailing longer, letting the windvane do all the work with only the staysail pulling her along. We should never have let ourselves get tired to the point where we just wanted to stop.

We should not have hove-to, and certainly should not have lain a-hull. I had not enough experience in high latitude sailing. We should have deployed a series drogue, With a series drogue in place, the boat would have been stern to the rogue wave. We likely would have had a lot of water in the cockpit but would not have been rolled.

We were in the wrong place at the wrong time.

Boats that sail in high latitudes should be strongly rigged. Ours was not. The mast and rigging was suitable for the Med or mid-latitudes, but was not strong enough for high latitudes. The replacement mast and rigging has survived at least half a dozen solid knockdowns in the course of three subsequent Southern Ocean circumnavigations.

I would recommend all hatches, dorades, cockpit locker lids and the like must be positively shut. Often overlooked is the main hatch horizontal closure.

The lids of all below deck top-loading lockers must be able to be secured. As a guidance, imagine the boat on its side or upside down.

Consider lashing netting or similar over the chain in the anchor locker. In a knockdown, and particularly in a rollover, the chain will fly up against the anchor locker lid.

All floorboards, and particularly those over the engine, should have positive latches to hold them in place in the event of a knockdown.

After a knockdown, monitor the engine fuel filters as it is likely that water or dirt in the bottom of the tank will have become mixed in the fuel.'

That sinking feeling

We joke about 'that sinking feeling', but those who have experienced it for real do not find it funny at all. There can be multiple causes, collision being the most obvious, and that might be with whales, debris, and the most frightening of all, sunken containers that have fallen from ships and lurk just below the surface, as deadly as a mobile mid-ocean rock. There are as many as five million containers on the high seas at any one time, and some are bound to go astray. The danger for yachts is that there is no way they can be detected in advance, certainly not by radar, but anyway you're not going to cross an ocean with your radar running full time. That means that the heavy, heart-sinking crunch is probably the first hint that a lurking container is in your way. Some containers, especially those carrying perishables, are built as tightly sealed units and these may take many months to sink. Others may be damaged as they tumble from their ships in a storm, and with luck will become punctured (the walls of an average container are not very thick). In that case, they might fill and sink within days.

Be reassured that according to *Yachting World* magazine, in the Clipper Round the World Race no boat has ever had a close encounter with a sunken container, let alone hit one. The World Cruising Club also reports that in 30 years of rallies and events, no yacht has ever collided with a container. Nor could any of the marine insurance companies that the magazine spoke to recall handling a claim by a yacht that had been hit by a container.

It's one way of sinking that you can put to the back of your mind.

A failure of anything below the waterline that can cause ingress of water may go undetected until it is too late. Almost without warning, you can be set on a road to a full scale sinking and an eventual decision to abandon ship. Sea cocks, or the pipes connected to them, rudder bearings torn from the hull, stern glands that 'pop', log and depth transducers that fail, all these can lead to a rapid ingress of water. Although the last two might sound minor, remember how much water enters the boat in a short time when you pull the impeller to clear the weed. Keels that are attached by bolts don't have to work loose by very much before water starts to creep in and its source is almost impossible to detect. Bow thruster housings can come under repeated assaults if you are pounding to windward for any length of time. A properly maintained bilge pump of an adequate size will deal with some of these, but not all.

But flooding and eventual sinking can happen in a far shorter time than you might imagine, and the real reason may never be discovered.

Les Crane's *Monterey*, a 56ft Farr Pilot House sloop, had cruised extensively off the NE USA, through the Mediterranean and back to the USA via Las Palmas in the Canaries, and the Caribbean. In 2017, she left Antigua bound for Bermuda in the inaugural Antigua/Bermuda Race. There was a crew of six, all experienced sailors. Less than 300 miles to the finish, Les was joined on deck by one of his crew.

The $300 pump that Les Crane wishes he'd had. (CRANE)

'Shortly after James joined me, he called out saying there was water in the forward head. I investigated and, presuming it was due to the toilet intake valve being stuck open, called for the helm to stand the boat up as I opened the sea cock and pumped the room dry with the shower pump. Returning to the galley, I was surprised to see water over the floorboards. I opened the engine compartment and found perhaps a foot of water in the leeward corner. Calling all crew up, I closed the sea cocks on the through-hulls as we tried to identify the source of the water. We had a laminated chart of the boat's plumbing with the sea cocks highlighted. Regrettably, many of us need reading glasses and a large-print, numbered list would have ensured nothing was missed.

We knew that *Esprit de Corps IV* (*EDC*), a Volvo 60, was about 5 miles behind us and *Spirit of Bermuda* 10 miles behind. Before leaving Antigua, we had had some issues with the boat's VHF and had replaced and tested the antenna. The VHF worked fine in communications with another competitor during the race but it took some "local knowledge" to ensure it was working properly – the push-to-talk button was fickle. Kit got on a handheld and hailed *EDC* with no response. At this point, we were merely looking for them to come and stand by as we attempted to solve our problem. I got on the satellite phone calling Rescue Control Centre (RCC) Bermuda to alert them of our situation and our position. Meanwhile, Jock and Cam had been trying to use a large manual pump without success. They then got the flares out and set off a red. The boat was filling surprisingly fast — much more than would be explained by a broken or detached hose.

I told Kit to up the broadcast level to "MAYDAY" and had Jock send up a parachute flare. Bob and Cam got the liferaft ready but were under instructions not to launch it. The parachute flare did the job. Jock called out that he could see *EDC*'s lights shift toward us. Shortly thereafter, they came up on the VHF.

While it was still pitch dark, the weather conditions were benign with an 8 to 12 knot breeze but there was a swell that prevented *EDC* from coming alongside. We would need the liferaft to transfer to them. The boys launched the raft. Of course, it inflated upside down. As Jock and Cam drew the lanyard in, Bob and I were able to get on the sugar scoop and muscle it upright in the lee of the boat. We were now safe. I went below again to reassess the situation. The boat was bow down with 3 feet (1m) of water in the forward cabin. With the volume of water in the boat, it was now totally impossible to determine the source. I could not see anything that could be done and was concerned that the boat might become unstable as it filled with water. The boat was replaceable, while someone getting trapped or hurt was another matter. I decided to abandon ship and get everyone in the eight-man raft.

We cut loose and drifted away from *Monterey*. *EDC* came near, we caught their line, pulled to their stern and were helped aboard. They were well prepared and welcomed us with jackets and warm liquids. We stood by *Monterey* with her lights blazing like the *Titanic* until 0700, by which time the bow was awash.

In no time at all we had gone from a tranquil sail to the deck of our rescuer and fellow racer *Esprit de Corps IV*.

The boat sank in water about 2 miles deep. We will never know the true causes of the sinking. A blown stern gland was one possibility, or a structural failure of the bow thruster. We had sailed 40,000 nautical miles on the boat and had spent 14 wonderful summers aboard. It is a loss we will not get over.'

Les Crane's gorgeous Monterey *before her tragic loss.* (CRANE)

The saddest sight – Monterey *dips beneath the waves as her crew watch on.* (CRANE)

Lessons Learned by Les Crane

In advance of a significant offshore voyage, we should have conducted a flooding drill in addition to a man-overboard drill. The flooding drill should be carried out while at a dock with a fresh water supply to fill the bilges and test the pumps. Testing infrequently used pumps is crucial. Time is very short. In our case, we had 45 minutes of desperately trying to save the boat. Once the water level is significant, it is very difficult to trace the source.

The crew should be divided into three groups, each with a distinct responsibility. They should not leave that responsibility until complete. We suffered from people moving from one function to another.

Group 1 – Source of flooding

- Identifying the source will get more difficult as more water enters the boat. Early identification is key. Have a large-print, laminated, prioritised, numbered list and map of all sea cocks and other possible sources of flooding.
- Open and close each sea cock during the drill.
- Be familiar with all other possible sources of flooding such as the stern gland, bow thruster and rudder tube gaiter.
- Be equipped with a powerful waterproof torch.

Group 2 – Pumps

- Know the locations and switches for all bilge pumps and their overboard outlets. Change from float to manual switches.

Group 3 – Communication

- Know how to access your current position.
- Train with the ship's VHF and handhelds.
- Train with a satphone. Ensure that the satphone has all emergency numbers pre-programmed.
- Do a test call to authorities.
- Know how to locate and identify nearby boats on the AIS.
- EPIRB: Know how to activate the EPIRB.
- Flares: Know how to access flares and be prepared to set them off.

All – Liferaft

- Know how to prepare and launch the liferaft.
- Have someone responsible for putting passports, computers and phones in grab bags.
- Put crew jackets in a garbage bag.
- Be equipped with a powerful waterproof torch.

Lightning

Storm tactics are widely discussed among ocean sailors, but mostly they refer to the wind and waves variety. But electrical storms are just as threatening on many oceans of the world, particularly in the tropical areas. The science is complex, but where you get massive amounts of hot, moist air rising over a warm ocean to produce electrically charged clouds, you have the potential for electrical storms. Some of these spark between clouds and are no threat, even if a little unsettling, and 80 per cent of all electrical storms are of this nature. It is the remaining 20 per cent we have to worry about. These are the ones where the bolt of lightning, only an inch wide, can be up to 5 miles long and travel faster than a bullet from cloud to ocean. And there you are, out there, where the only finger for miles around is your metal mast pointing directly at the wicked, black thundercloud directly overhead. You may see the bolts of lightning approach, hear the sizzle as they hit the water, and wonder if the next one is going to get you. So you start counting, knowing that the sound of thunder travels more slowly than the flash of light, and only when the crack comes at the same time as the flash do you know that you are getting perilously close to being struck.

And if it does strike, what then? What effect can lightning have on a sailing boat? You assume the electrics may be fried, but will all those metal skin fittings be blown off the hull and you have a sinking situation on your hands? Will it inevitably lead to fire? Is there any way to protect yourself and your boat? And can lightning strike twice in the same place, despite old wisdom confidently saying it never does?

HOW LIGHTNING STRIKES

It starts with a thundercloud, which carries a huge electrostatic charge and is looking for ways of discharging itself to earth. It begins by emitting 'fingers' of negative charge of 100 million volts relative to the ground (according to the US National Weather Service) and 'tests' the ground beneath it for somewhere to strike. These negatively charged fingers attract positive charges from the ground, which appear more readily on tall structures, especially if they have a point to them, like a church spire or a yacht's mast.

So you now have fingers of energy moving towards each other and at some point they will meet, usually at about 100 to 300 feet (30–90m) above the ground. Once that connection happens, a floodgate of energy opens as the negative charge from the cloud starts to travel to earth. But as that happens, a much larger current, called the return stroke, travels the other way, from ground to cloud. This transfer of energy emits light, and the lightning strike you see is as the energy passes from the positive ground to the negative cloud. This might seem counter-intuitive as you think you observe the lightning passing from cloud to ground, but the energy is, in fact, passing the other way and the whole process may take place in millionths of a second so the eye is not able to discern the precise detail of what's happening. And it's a considerable amount of energy. The voltages can be as high as 20 million, the current 200,000 amps, but for no longer than a few microseconds. Given those figures, it is difficult to see how any yacht could be protected, and it makes laughable the idea that dangling a frying pan over the side is going to do any good.

PROTECTION

Be clear – there is no system that will guarantee you will never be the victim of a lightning strike. There is nothing that is going to render a strike totally harmless. All the methods so far devised seem plausible, but when dealing with the transfers of energy on the scale we are talking about, much of the science remains uncertain and anything that offers a guarantee should be viewed with suspicion. But if you feel happier by having done something, there are options.

SHOULD I FIT A LIGHTNING CONDUCTOR?

In fact, you already have one if you have an aluminium mast, or even a wooden mast with a metal track for the mainsail – the jury is still out on how carbon fibre masts would behave. The difficulty is getting that vast amount of energy that strikes the mast safely to earth, causing no damage along the way. The obvious method is to provide a conductor from the base of a mast to a large area of metal that is immersed in the sea. This will also discourage any attempts by the charge to travel through the rigging, which might weaken it due to the heating that results from the passage of large currents. For this reason, any devices that you hang over the side as a grounding plate might lead to other problems later on. Also, there is a theory that grounding your mast in this way may make you *more prone* to a strike – there is a lot about lightning strategies that remains uncertain.

If you have a metal keel then you might attach a conductor to that, which in turn could connect to an exposed metal keel. But any old bit of wire will not do. The minimum size of copper cable should be 35mm squared, or even better 58mm squared. If you think this over the top, take a look at the thickness of the copper conductor that runs down the side of a church spire.

If you are going to install a ground plate (which is not the same as an earthing plate used as part of an SSB radio installation and is not designed for the task) then it should be about a square foot in size. If you have no exposed metal keel or ground plate, all metal objects in the boat, including the engine and propeller, can be bonded together and the exposed underwater surface area can have the same effect as a single plate. But the connections must be made with great care, with bends made with as large a radius as possible to prevent 'flashovers' where the lightning jumps from one place to another seeking the path of least resistance. The difficulty is also ensuring minimum resistance where the cabling meets tanks and through-hulls. Any resistance will produce great heat when large currents flow, leading to the possibility of fire. It should be noted that because of the uncertainty of the science, and the impossibility of gathering observations during a strike, there remains an argument that says the worst thing you can do is connect to your keel. More confusion.

There is a widely used device that looks like a wire brush, often seen at mastheads. This claims to inhibit the build-up of static at the masthead, and consequently those 'streamers' that form in the early stages of the strike. The manufacturers make it clear that this is 'not 100 per cent effective in preventing a lightning strike … but controls the causes of lightning strikes'.

Nick Charman was sailing his Tanton 43, *Fera*, a cat-rigged ketch (with carbon masts), in Swedish waters when lightning struck.

'Around midday, a small squall approaching from ahead had some thunder under it. I was taking the usual precautions of putting the small electronic devices (VHF, mobile phone, EPIRB) in the oven, and I was in the very act of opening the oven door when we were struck by lightning on the foremast. There was an extremely loud crack and bright light.

I rehearsed in my mind how to launch the liferaft should it be necessary. Things had taken on some urgency now, and happened in very quick order. Was anyone hurt? Apparently not – they were shocked but not injured (there were children on board). Many alarms were going off. The engine was still running – was it OK, or about to seize up? "It must be the charging voltage alarm," I thought. Was water coming into the boat? Bilge board up – no sign of rising water, thank goodness.

Smoke was coming into the cabin from forward. Tentatively I opened the access to the foremast foot and the smoke was thicker. I could see clearly burnt wires and charred insulation, but no flames so no fire. I opened the forehatch to clear the smoke. Was the VHF working? It was. The aerial was on the mizzen and was apparently undamaged.

I checked the bilge again – still no rising water. Then I checked the engine. Oil pressure was good and, amazingly, the voltmeter showed the alternator still charging the battery. All engine alarms were still sounding. The boat's course had gone awry but Stella dealt with it having disconnected the autopilot and was hand-steering.

Not knowing what might happen next, I decided to alert the rescue authorities while I could. Sweden Rescue was clear and supportive, promising immediate help if necessary.

Until the boat had been lifted, inspected and checked below the waterline, we could not possibly consider her seaworthy. Once safely tied up, I called and signed off with Sweden Rescue. So there we were and we stayed until all the damage was assessed and fixed; and as things have turned out, with all the work to be done, it was the end of sailing for *Fera* that season. The total cost in replaced electrics and electronics was in excess of £40,000.'

(OPPOSITE) Fera, *before her lightning strike. (CHARMAN)*

What to do in a thunderstorm

- Put on lifejackets and have in mind where the grab bag is located in case you have to take to the liferaft.
- Get all your portable electronics, especially satphones and trackers, and put them inside the galley oven. The very best protection will be found in a microwave oven if you have one. The Faraday cage effects will mean that any electrostatic charge will appear on the outside of the oven and not inside it. This is the same protective principle that says you should stay in your car in a thunderstorm.
- Any electronics that can't go in the oven, unplug the power leads and any antenna.
- Do not grab two metal objects at the same time – for example, the steering wheel and the backstay.
- Get everyone below and keep them in the centre of the cabin rather than to the sides.
- As the thunder rumbles around, try and comfort yourself with the thought that you *did* remember to include lightning strike in the insurance.

Steering/self-steering failure

Ask any ocean sailor who is their best friend, and they will point with great pride to the stern of their boat, waving their finger in the direction of the self-steering.

Whether driven by electricity or the wind, they are as good as another crew; never complaining, never needing food, caring not about the weather, happier the stronger the wind blows, and willing to stand watch 24 hours a day. Of course, history says that the electrically driven self-steerings can sometimes be a fickle friend, and stories of their antics and failures are legion. But for those who choose to have their boats driven by the wind, talk of failure is much rarer.

Self-steering, of any kind, is a comparatively recent invention and much of the development was done by model yacht enthusiasts. The device invented by Blondie Hasler, which used a trailing paddle to provide power to move the rudder, was the first to come into widespread use, but not until the 1960s. Even now, many of the self-steerings currently being made operate on the principle Hasler first employed, which was to use a 'servo paddle' that trailed in the sea to provide power to move a rudder.

In choosing between electrical and wind-driven, it is worth knowing the plus and minus points of each system.

Self-steering looks after itself for thousands of miles, but could you fix it if it went wrong? (GRISWOLD)

THE WINDVANE

The wind is free, and a properly designed and installed windvane will see you safely across the oceans of the world. Indeed, you may have trouble remembering when you last touched the wheel. They need no external source of energy, such as electricity.

However, when there is no wind they will not steer you, nor will they steer when you are under engine.

They cannot steer a compass course, only a course relative to the wind.

They can have a temperament, and it can take some time to get the best out of them, although it is often the balance of the boat that is at fault rather than the self-steering. Some liken the experience of using them to learning to play a musical instrument.

THE AUTOPILOT

This is a very simple device to operate, often requiring no more than a stab of a button to keep the boat on course. They can be set to steer to a compass course, or follow a mast-mounted windvane. They require electricity, and over the length of an ocean passage this can be a considerable amount of power, which must be replaced by solar, wind, or use of the engine.

Failures are often impossible to repair at sea. Some mitigate this by taking two complete autopilots with them – one as a spare.

There is a neat blend of the two, which you might consider. The windvane's paddle mechanism is very efficient at converting the forward motion of the boat into power that can be used to move the wheel or steering quadrant. The windvane itself, though, is usually a finely balanced device so that it can easily be moved by the slightest breath of wind. If you want your windvane to steer the boat in calm weather, or steer to a compass course, you can remove the windvane and attach in its place a cheap and lightweight tiller pilot. This tricks the windvane into thinking that there is a breeze and it steers according to the course you set on the tiller pilot. Tiller pilots cost a fraction of a powerful autopilot, and use a tiny proportion of the electrical power because the windvane mechanism is so easily moved. A lightweight model will often do the job. Carrying two of those would be a small expense and could be a saviour.

But whatever kind of self-steering you have, it is worth having at the back of your mind that it is going to fail, and will probably let you down at the worst possible moment.

It happened to Rosemarie and Alfred Alecio, who were on passage to La Réunion, east of Madagascar, in their widely travelled 38ft gaff cutter *Ironhorse*, a heavy boat with no wheel steering. She was fitted with an Aries self-steering, but such a failure could have happened to any of the popular makes of windvane. It was on their third day at sea, at dawn, with a boat speed of 6 knots and winds of 20 knots, that Rosemarie heard a loud bang from behind her.

'Just as Alfred shot into the cockpit, hardly awake, I pointed to where the bang seemed to have come from. When we looked over the stern we saw the Aries paddle had sheared off completely and was dangling behind, tethered by the line that attaches it to its frame, and being dragged through the powerful ocean waves. Alfred donned his lifejacket and, boathook in hand, climbed out over the stern to try to rescue the paddle, me in a panic as to the wisdom of this in such rough conditions. It proved an impossible task, and even though we carry a spare paddle, replacing the broken one was just not on and would have to wait until conditions were much steadier.

We looked at each other, Alfred reading my thoughts, and commenting that at least we had not lost our main rudder as had happened to good friends only a few weeks previously. They had had to abandon their yacht when 1,000

Ironhorse *powers along, until Rosemarie heard a loud bang behind her.* (ALECIO)

miles from both Cocos Keeling and Rodrigues. Luckily for them, another yacht was only a day or so from where they were and deviated to take them on board. Although we were not in their situation, we have never needed to steer *Ironhorse* by hand for any length of time. It would be quite demanding. There is 18 tons of her to control with a tiller, and no wheel-steering nor all the gearing that provides. Alfred looked devastated – a rare happening.

We were now west of Mauritius. Port Louis, the main port on the north-west coast, was over 45 miles north-east of us, and the nearest place we could make for. We debated the wisdom of doing so.

I checked the instruments. We had about 102 miles to go for the waypoint on the north coast of La Réunion with the marina 10 miles beyond. Impossible to steer all that way, I thought, as we were already experiencing how demanding it would be, and for such a distance it would require extraordinary effort and impossible tenacity. The question was, of course, for how long

Running repairs are a feature of all ocean passages. Here, Alfred put a few careful stitches in the staysail. (ALECIO)

could we steer her bulk in these increasingly heavy seas?

Alfred was on the tiller while we considered our options. "Can you take her again for a few minutes?" he asked. I did so and he jumped down into the boat, fiddled about in the bosun's bag, and returned to the cockpit with some short lengths of line and a couple of pulleys. "Just let's see if we can set something up," he continued, threading rope through a pulley and passing it behind me, which I couldn't follow since my job required full concentration. I was already worried as to how much longer I could hold her steady for we now had 22 knots of wind and the swell was noticeably bigger. But he continued to work around me, passing a line behind my arm then winding it around the tiller as I steered, before fixing something on the sidedeck. Another knot being tied, after a "by eye" measurement of length and… "OK, let's see how this might work. It should make the steering lighter and I'm just wondering if it's possible for us to cope – between us – the rest of the way."

He sat beside the tiller – which was now wearing this contraption of lashings and blocks

– and picked up the loose end of the rope coiled around it and led through pulleys fixed across the sidedeck. He pulled it towards him, moving the tiller apparently more easily, then releasing it to move it the other way. "Have a go and tell me what you think."

I took the rope and sat where he'd been, then pulled and released. It certainly was much easier although it still needed some effort, especially when working against the weather side, and my poor little arthritic finger joints clearly didn't like it. The rope was already rubbing my skin and I imagined how it might be after a few hours. At the speed we were making in these stronger winds, and having computed that we had at least another 22 hours to reach the waypoint, I said: "I'd better find our gloves."

"Go and make us a cup of tea," said Alfred, "and let me try again." Well, we're Brits, for goodness sake! After another few minutes, he reckoned he could do two hours at a time. I questioned that, passing him his cuppa and offering gloves, both of us immediately realising that it was impossible to hold a cup or anything else and steer as well. We considered heaving-to from time to time – perhaps to eat or sleep – but decided we should aim to continue non-stop if it was physically possible, agreeing to get drinks and snacks during our breaks.

Half an hour later, he called me. "Two hours is too much," he admitted. So I prepared to take my turn, with us both agreeing that one hour was sufficient, not so much because of the physical demands of working the pulleys but because concentrating on keeping the course was very wearing.

We steered for an hour, then rested for an hour. Interestingly, both seemed to race by. The concentration of steering occupied us full time with no lull or boredom, and our rest time – such a luxury – seemed to pass incredibly quickly. After having managed several stints, with my fingers feeling sore and my right shoulder aching, I found myself wondering if I could last the course. We had covered less than half the distance, and I wondered if I should suggest heaving-to so we could have a proper rest. But Alfred's encouragement and enthusiasm kept me from that, and I continued with gritted teeth, determined not to let the side down.

By now we were well into the night, not having slept at all since the previous night, and part of the steering rope was beginning to show signs of chafing – we know the signs well on a gaffer! I worried that the line would need replacing.

By midnight we were only 20 miles from our waypoint, with the bright lights of La Réunion's north coast clearly visible ahead. It was obvious that we would be way ahead of our planned dawn arrival. But what encouragement, and what a boost to determination – less than three more hours of "hard yakka" (Australian for hard work).

And if we needed to heave-to for a few hours to await daylight, that would be more than welcome.

The wind remained just aft of the beam for most of the time and, as we continued along the north coast, our concern was how long it would take to find some lee so that we could comfortably get to the foredeck to drop the hanked-on headsails and reduce our speed. It was not until we were within a few miles of the north-west tip of the island with its brightly lit town slopes that we felt some protection from the land, and we were able to slow down. Then, having pulled the main in amidships, *Ironhorse* slowed almost to a stop, comfortably bobbing slowly back and forth in a semicircle. Finally, we could relax.

"We've made it!" breathed Alfred. "I'm really proud of you," he added, hugging me as we both collapsed on to the cockpit seat, delighted that our 70-year-old bodies were still up to it. As he went on to mention something about "...repairs later", we both became aware of a bump-bumping around the stern. "What now?" I thought, as he took a torch to check. "Hey, look!" he exclaimed, "how about this?" After a rough ride of over 100 miles, our broken Aries paddle was still attached.'"

It was Alfred's skill, and quick thinking, that enabled him to jury-rig a block and tackle that would enable them to hold that weighty tiller and keep the boat on course in a steep, following sea – a point of sailing on a gaffer that makes weighty demands on the tiller and rudder. Short watches, hot tea and determination saw them through and Rosemarie later noted, with satisfaction, that their '70-year-old bodies were still up to it'. Sadly, though, for *Ironhorse*, this story does not have a happy ending (see page 253).

Self-steering failure is something you should plan for, but it is difficult to know how. It is likely that failures will occur in the most testing conditions, and since all these devices hang over the stern, an immediate repair will probably be impossible. All windvane self-steerings have some kind of paddle, which are vulnerable and might collide with floating debris, fishing nets or sea creatures, and they are deliberately built with a weakness so that when something is hit, the paddle becomes detached from the main mechanism to prevent further damage. This is often in the form of a tube, and a couple of these must be in your spares box. It might be best to practise replacing it when the boat is on dry land so that you are not having to figure it out as the wind is rising.

Failures of electrically driven autopilots are more problematical. A windvane can usually be fixed, if you have the spares, but a modern autopilot is a sophisticated creature driven by a small computer. You are never going to be able to repair that. Some apply force to the rudder by means of an electric motor, which again it is doubtful you will be able to service. Others can be hydraulic, and failure of a seal is something you can prepare for. On a modern, lightweight boat, an autopilot works extremely hard. I once took part in a transatlantic race when half the fleet of 40 boats were forced to retire entirely due to autopilot failure.

If you aren't willing, or are unable, to have your steering done by the wind, plan for electrical failure. Make sure the helming position is comfortable so you are able to sit there for lengthy periods of time. Make sure there is somewhere to safely place the essential mug of tea. And try to ensure there is some shelter. It is not the action of holding the wheel or tiller that tires people, it is often the relentless assault by wind and rain, coupled with the draining effect of the concentration required.

Piracy

Let me tell you about my pirate experience. I was about 200 miles off the coast of West Africa, heading south in very light winds from the Cape Verde islands, aiming to cross the Equator and then make a starboard turn for Brazil.

Night had come rapidly, as it does in the tropics. I noticed, astern of me, a red and green light and two masthead lights in line. In other words, a ship was coming up behind me on exactly the course I was sailing. A radar fix showed it to be about two miles behind. Something about it seemed odd. Nervously, I covered my stern light with a sail bag. Half an hour later he was in exactly the same position, hanging on to my coat tails. That was when I got seriously nervous. We were close enough to land for it to be a real possibility that this was pirates and this was one of their known hangouts.

I couldn't make much of an alteration of course as I was flying a poled-out headsail, so I plodded on, and so did he. As midnight approached, the wind dropped to almost calm and I hardly had steerage way. There was no point motoring as he could easily outrun me. Eventually, I lost my nerve, showed him my stern light and called him on the radio. It was a while before there was an answer. Eventually a somewhat gruff voice replied, 'I see you'. He then went on to explain that he was a slow-moving survey vessel and thanked me for alerting him to my position.

That's how easy it is to get spooked in waters that have a reputation for being home to the bad lads of the sea. But how real a risk is piracy?

There is no real answer to the question as the danger varies day to day, month to month. But there are clearly certain parts of the world where extreme caution is needed, and places where it would be foolish to cruise. At the time of writing (late 2018), Southeast Asia, parts of the Indian Ocean and West Africa are places where the strongest warnings apply, but even the Caribbean comes with a certain element of caution. The infamous Somali pirates, who relish capturing a yacht if no bigger catch presents itself, now have much reduced operations in the face of international naval security efforts, and now confine themselves to operating closer to their own shores, making the Indian Ocean a safer place. However, the Red Sea remains a danger and few yachts will be brave enough to attempt a transit, thwarting many an ambition to return to Europe via the Suez Canal. However, in recent years, with a reduced threat of piracy, some yachts are attempting the passage, about a dozen in 2018. None reported any problems. Some try to organise convoys on the safety-in-numbers principle and there are Facebook pages for those who might want to join.

An invaluable source of latest information can be found here: www.noonsite.com/General/Piracy with links to piracy reports and experiences. Advice for UK nationals, available to everyone, is given here: www.gov.uk/guidance/sea-river-and-piracy-safety and regularly updated.

Although the information is directed at commercial shipping and not yachts, these regularly updated reports will give a good indication of those parts of the world where piracy is active: www.icc-ccs.org/piracy-reporting-centre/live-piracy-map.

SSB radio nets may operate in piracy-prone areas, certainly in the Caribbean, and if you find a local net you should join it. Not only will you share the experience of others, but if you are feeling threatened there are others who know your position and can act on your behalf.

Is there anything a yacht can do to protect itself from pirates trying to board it at sea? It's doubtful. Yachts don't have the speed to make an escape, and don't have things like power hoses, which commercial ships have used to great effect. Some companies will provide you with a weapons-trained crew; there is even a foul-smelling liquid that you can spray on pirates to deter them, but these seem rather fanciful solutions. You are here to enjoy the ocean, not engage in warfare. If you are considering getting into a fight, mark the words of one security expert: 'A combination of a yacht and pirates will only end one way, and this is the people on the yacht getting killed or captured.'

The best advice, in what can often be an impossible situation, is to:

- Keep a good lookout at all times, especially for small craft who might be following or trying to keep pace with you. Be aware, though, that these can be innocent fishermen on minimal incomes who will often close on a yacht to beg for cigarettes.
- Large ships have a safe area built into them where they can retreat to raise the alarm. If you have a large enough yacht, you might want to plan in advance how you might achieve something similar.
- Bad weather could be your friend. Most pirates using small skiffs rarely operate in winds above 25 knots, according to reports.
- Hide a VHF radio. Pirates will destroy any communications equipment they can see.
- If you can broadcast a MAYDAY, give your vessel's name and position and any information that might help in a rescue.
- If the pirates get on board, don't fight. Give in. Do what you are told.
- You can argue long and hard over whether or not to carry firearms. Cool heads say you should not.

There are some simple rules:

- Do some research among the locals and discover which anchorages are safer than others.
- Make it as difficult as possible for them to get on board. Don't leave the dinghy down at night, and raise any boarding ladders.
- Keep a handheld VHF in your bunk to raise the alarm. Know where you can grab a parachute flair, which will not only signal an alarm but might deter thieves before they get on board.
- Difficult though it is in tropical areas, lock yourself in at nights and place an alarm in the cockpit, such as a motion sensor connected to a klaxon, which might alert the entire anchorage.
- If you can find room for a concealed safe, fit one.
- Leave old credit cards and mobile phones lying around. Split your cash into two. Hide the larger portion and be prepared to hand over the smaller.
- Hide anything that could be used as a weapon against you, such as galley knives.
- If the anchorage has a reputation, you might ask neighbouring yachts if they'd like to be part of a VHF watch system.

Boat security needs to be considered every bit as much as boat safety. Pirates, robbers – call them what you will – do not always strike on the high seas. In poorer parts of the world, an ocean-going yacht is seen as the height of wealth, and potential rich pickings. Robbery while at anchor is a far greater threat than piracy, and robbery with violence is rapidly becoming more common.

Advice given by the Greek coastguard in the past has been:

- Don't go close enough for them to board. If they get on your boat it will become your responsibility to get them safely to land.
- Keep the boat under observation, report its position and stand by until help arrives.
- If they appear short of water, provide some, and lifejackets if they look in need.
- Only attempt to rescue them if it is clear their boat is sinking.

Although not piracy issues, Mediterranean sailors will be aware of small, overloaded boats carrying would-be immigrants to mainland Europe from North Africa. It is difficult for a well-meaning skipper to make the right choices when presented with one of these, remembering these can be desperate people who might resort to violence if it proves to be the only way they can achieve their ambitions.

Abandon ship

There are times when disaster strikes, the human will to survive takes hold, and somehow you extract yourself from the perilous position in which you suddenly find yourself. These are the moments where experience, ingenuity and preparedness all come into play. But also good fortune can play a part. We've all been in some kind of situation where the day has been saved by a lucky find at the bottom of the spares box, or an ingenious thought that suddenly crossed the mind of a member of the crew. That is called good luck.

But what happens when the luck runs out? When whatever you try to do results in failure, not due to any fault of yours but simply because on this occasion the dice have not fallen in your favour.

We heard earlier from Rosemarie and Alfred Alecio, who lost their self-steering while crossing the Indian Ocean, about how invention and determination got them safely through (see page 244). Their much-loved boat, *Ironhorse*, was a 38ft gaffer. They were heading for South Africa, intending to make an Atlantic passage back to the UK, and were 150 miles south of Madagascar when their luck finally ran out.

'During the night, a brand-new 20mm 316 stainless steel mast through-bolt, replaced during our haul-out before we left Thailand in January, sheered clean through at the mast top, sending the inner stay and staysail over the side. With the mast's main forward support lost, we were left with only the smaller forestay to the end of the bowsprit, designed simply to carry the small yankee jib. This was not the result of negligence. Indeed, Alfred had always been more than cautious. Any suspicion of weakness in any equipment and it was repaired or replaced immediately. We were always working to ensure *Ironhorse* was in tip-top condition.

Alfred lashed the unused topsail halyard to the bow for extra support, wondering how long it would hold. Certainly, with the 4- to 5-metre seas and 25 to 30 knots of wind, the possibility of the mast falling was very real, especially with predictions for much stronger winds upward of 40 knots.

Unbelievably, another major problem hit us the following day when our rudder suddenly stuck fast. We immediately hove-to, drifting with the east-going current, but despite our efforts over the next few days it remained immovable.

We were carrying supplies on board sufficient for more than three months, so were in no immediate danger. Like all cruisers, we'd experienced numerous equipment problems during ocean passages and none had beaten Alfred's ability and resourcefulness. Now, after a couple of days of deliberations and little sleep, he had no solution and we began discussing the unthinkable and abandoning *Ironhorse* together with all our worldly goods and priceless souvenirs from our travels.

Then, the Dutch crew of the sailing yacht *Avanta*, whom we had never met but who were within 8 miles of us, contacted us, having noticed on their AIS that *Ironhorse* was making no progress. On learning of our dilemma, they kindly offered to take us on board as far as Durban, about 900 miles away. We eventually accepted, and they informed Durban Rescue Services of the situation.

Alfred and I prepared our small dinghy for launching and packed a few vital possessions in dry bags – documents, a few clothes, our computers, phones and cameras. Alfred also made preparations to scuttle *Ironhorse*, but I persuaded him to leave the actual deed until certain of our safety. Thank goodness I did.

We had never used a dinghy in mid-ocean and only now appreciated the physical demands of battling against swell, wind and breaking waves to get heavy bags into it, as well as ourselves. We drifted down to meet *Avanta* but with no ladder or steps to assist, getting a foothold up to the height of the sidedeck was impossible. They indicated their swimming platform aft, so we slid back to try there, grabbing a thrown line as we went. Perfect for climbing aboard in a calm anchorage, it was positively lethal in this seaway. Eventually we were forced to accept that it was impossible and Alfred, with considerable strength, pulled our water-filled dinghy back to *Ironhorse* once more. We were grateful she hadn't been scuttled earlier.

A nearby ship, MV *Bittern*, eventually came into view, having learned that our rescue had failed, and offered to give us a lee so we could try again. *Avanta* and her crew stood by. The *Bittern*'s captain suggested that a heaving line to our helplessly drifting *Ironhorse* might hold us in the ship's lee, giving time for us to try again to get across to the *Avanta*. Unfortunately, the crew's enthusiastic efforts brought *Ironhorse* too close to *Bittern* and, anticipating the inevitable, Alfred rushed to cut *Ironhorse* free again, but seconds too late.

It was a whisper of a touch, but the impact was precisely on to the end of her bowsprit, which, like a matchstick, was broken clean off, flying high into the air before disappearing into the waves. The forestay, with jib attached, immediately flew aft towards the mast, flapping madly and horizontally across the sidedeck, effectively closing off our route to where the dinghy was still leaping about. Free again, *Ironhorse* moved back and, bereft of forward support, the mast jerked within its tabernacle, slackening the mainsail, which flapped uncontrollably.

Alfred was on the bow and I on the forward end of the port sidedeck. I looked to our solid pine mast and its obvious wobble in the seaway.

"It'll come down, get forward of it!" screamed Alfred. We watched it sway for a few more seconds. The halyard that Alfred had set up was still holding.

"We MUST get into the dinghy!" screamed Alfred, as we watched that hefty pole sway, jolted to a stop by the shrouds and stays at each flop. The upper holding points were all held by new through-bolts identical to the one that had broken days before. What if they were also to fail?

"Get to the bows!" he ordered, and nervously I did so as quickly as the rolling and bucking allowed. But the swaying mast was clearly going to distract us from getting into the dinghy.

The knife came out again and he sliced through the halyard, forcing the issue, and now, with no forward support, the violent, incessant movement of the hull jolted the mast. I froze and watched helplessly as the great mass fell slowly astern, exactly along the meridian line – mast, topmast and spreaders, port and starboard shrouds, light boxes, radar dome, aerials and a mass of halyards. The higher part crashed over the strong metal pilot house, splintering the solar panels fixed on top, but the roof remained intact. Dust clouds rose as the shrouds crashed along the sidedecks and, relieved that it had fallen away from us, I remember staring at the bottom of the mast and thinking how it all looked as perfect as when it was stepped back in January. The Thai coin placed beneath, traditionally for luck, lay there still.

With the 22ft solid wooden boom having tucked itself squarely beneath all the mess, everything was held steady from rolling, which I'd thought might affect her stability. Nothing moved, and hull-wise she looked and behaved as well as ever. However, our route along the sidedeck to the dinghy was totally blocked by the shrouds, halyards and violently flapping jib.

"We *have* to get into the dinghy – *now*!" And, struggling to get back around to the sidedeck, I realised the only clear way off was over the sheer of the bow. No scuppers and no footholds. I looked down at the dinghy, bouncing around, rising and falling with the swell, and sheering off at all angles at the end of the short line. I searched uselessly for somewhere to put a foot on the outside of the hull so that I could lower myself and time my dropping into the constantly moving dinghy. The dinghy would rise past the rail, then jolt away and drop way down again. The idea of getting outside the security of our wonderful solid hull and rails horrified me.

Exasperated, Alfred rolled himself over the rail, managing with great strength not only to reach the dinghy but to continue holding it into the hull for me. Quite a feat, I realised later, as the rail was way above his head.

"Use me as a ladder," he ordered and, blindly, over I went. With luck on my side, and his firm body to give a foothold, I somehow landed beside him.

Ironhorse, to which we were still tethered, was now picking up the wind raging around *Bittern*'s stern and was being blown on to us.

"I'm cutting us free!" yelled Alfred above the noise, setting us adrift in the ocean and, as another wave broke into the dinghy, on towards *Avanta*, still outside *Bittern*'s lee. Her bucking and rolling was as bad as ever.

"Doesn't look any easier," shouted Alfred, as we watched her approach and tried to imagine just how we could muster strength to board her. Alfred and I were becoming physically exhausted.

Then, when she was within about 30 metres of us, *Avanta* suddenly began motoring away. *Ironhorse* and *Bittern* were now over 100m away. Then I spotted the ship's crew unrolling a ladder, which dropped down amidships. (We learned later that the Captain ordered this when *Avanta* motored away from us.) "Make for *Bittern*!" I yelled, and we paddled towards her as though our lives depended on it, as indeed they did. Her lee made things easier as we got closer.

Despite extreme exhaustion, with our eyes on that ladder, we somehow found new strength. As *Bittern* rolled threateningly towards our tiny dinghy, the lower part of the ladder (made of rope with hefty wooden steps) tumbled into the swell that raced along the hull from bow to stern, then was jerked above us, before being flung back down. Then a thin rope slid down past the ladder and I grabbed it, holding us close to the hull. Two safety lines were lowered to attach each of us to *Bittern*. Safety was high above us, *so high* above us. All we had to do was get on that ladder and climb up there. Timing was crucial, and Alfred repeatedly urged me to "go for it". Ensuring that my feet were fully free from between bags and dinghy tube, and finding strength I wouldn't have believed I had, I pushed off from the dinghy, which miraculously provided resistance to send me off. Then I was on the ladder.

The shouts continued from above. I looked up, and up, and up... vertically for ever. I could see the faces of six or seven men. Prone on the deck, head and shoulders over the side, they yelled encouragement. I was on the last lap, but what a distance between each rung. But hand over hand, step by step, and hearing the guys above urging me on, the adrenaline must have kicked in big time, keeping me going up and up for ever. And then strong hands grabbed me, hoisting me over the last step and on to the deck. It felt like terra firma.

"OK, your man coming too," said a tall, smiling young man in a gentle foreign accent, guiding me to sit away from the edge. Amazingly, Alfred managed to tie all the bags to a line for lifting on deck before he himself finally climbed to safety. I ran to him and we hugged, holding each other like we had to for ever, before thanking the crew.

Then, as reality began to set in, Alfred and I looked below. Mastless, sails now billowing a-top the coach roof, but still floating high as always, *Ironhorse* looked very sad and rejected, and it remains an abhorrent vision for us both. She had looked after us perfectly for more than 65,000 wonderful miles and we had abandoned her in mid-ocean. We both felt we'd somehow let her down.'

It can all come good in the end – if you're very lucky

Don't worry. Despite all the stories you've just read, even when disaster appears to be staring you in the face there might always be help at hand, sometimes arriving from the most unexpected sources at the least likely moment.

This story of reassurance comes from Niki and Geoff Phillips, whose second east–west crossing of the Atlantic was in their 39ft Westerly Sealord.

They were sailing from Bermuda to the Azores and were a thousand miles from the nearest land. Then…

'We anticipated seeing little traffic on this route, let alone another yacht, but at around 1400 on our ninth day at sea, an orange sail was spotted three miles or so off our starboard bow. After a quick scan with the binoculars, we altered course to intercept, suspecting that all was not quite right.

The orange sail soon revealed itself as a jury-rigged storm jib and we recognised her as *Mirabel II*, a 36ft Westerly Corsair with a singlehander aboard – we had seen her back in Bermuda.

Under reduced sail, we approached her and could make out the skipper on the aft deck. His storm jib was set on a spinnaker pole stayed with various lines on the foredeck, pulling the boat along at about 1 knot. The motion was horrible as she rolled in the swell. Obviously she had suffered damage from the dismasting but, while looking in a bad way, she was still afloat and the skipper appeared in control.

We checked how much fuel we had on board and considered what assistance we might be able, or be asked, to provide. The skipper appeared to be tired and rather knocked about, and was hanging on to the guardrails as his mastless ship rolled uncontrollably in the swell. In good English fashion, I shouted "Good afternoon, are you okay?" to receive the reply, "Can I come with you to the Azores?"

Of course he could, but we were unsure whether he really wanted to abandon ship. We could see that he had sustained some head injuries and suspected he might be suffering from mild concussion, in addition to the inevitable fatigue following the shock of the dismasting, then the effort of cutting the rig free and getting the jury rig set up in those conditions, and all singlehanded too!

Several alternatives were discussed (not easy shouting over the wind and swell) but

Mirabel II rolling horribly under jury rig, the skipper preparing to abandon ship. (PHILLIPS)

the skipper was adamant – he'd had enough! He knew, as we did, that the jury rig would not stand up to a blow, and also told us that his engine was out of commission. We were primarily concerned for his safety and, whatever his decision, would not have left him out there without at the very least standing by.

The skipper had done his sums; his ship was tired, having completed many ocean miles over a good number of years, and was already in need of an extensive refit, never mind an entire new rig. His decision was undoubtedly the right one. "The boat is finished" were his words as he calmly contemplated making preparations to abandon his floating home.

If we had any doubts, the skipper's offer to jump overboard and swim towards *Spirit of Penmar* confirmed his firm intention to abandon his ship. "No!" we both shouted.

There was no reason to rush but we sensed that, having resolved to leave, the skipper wanted to transfer across as soon as possible. It was agreed that this would best be achieved via his liferaft, which was lashed to the deck and appeared to be unharmed. It was duly launched, but the canopy didn't inflate and

All's well that ends well. Geoff and Niki (left and centre) successfully land Richard (right) in Horta, Azores. (PHILLIPS)

it remained inverted until he managed to get it alongside and right it on the rise of the swell.

We looked on as he made a number of trips below to retrieve his personal belongings and the hurriedly assembled remnants of his "home". Eventually, as the raft slowly drifted downwind towards us, we felt desperately for the skipper who, before abandoning ship, had cut the hoses to scuttle his cruising home of many years.

Once alongside, everything was brought on board and the liferaft slashed to send it to the bottom. Our new crew member, Richard, seemed okay if pretty exhausted, but mainly just relieved to be aboard and "alive". Under way, none of us looked back. Niki went below and contacted Falmouth Coastguard via satellite phone to report the incident, and she also put out a DSC safety alert to any other vessels that might be in the area regarding the stricken *Mirabel II*, as we assumed she would probably take some time to sink.

I'll never forget the positivity of Richard, sitting on the aft deck surrounded by his sodden possessions but already planning the next stage of his life. Over a brew, he recounted the rig failure and the trauma of the night before and how he couldn't believe his luck when, just 12 hours after the incident, he sighted a sail on the horizon that then altered course towards him.

It took Richard a couple of days to recover from his experience before taking a watch.

An experienced voyager, he had lived an extraordinary life full of ups and downs and we were never short of conversation over those long ocean miles. From time to time Richard would, understandably, agonise over his decision to abandon *Mirabel II*, but any doubts he may have had were dispelled after five days when *Spirit of Penmar* was assaulted from three sides with large waves during a fair old blow. Richard reflected that *Mirabel II* and he "might not have made it in this".

It's also surprising to note what a "shipwrecked sailor" considers essential when abandoning ship. We'd just run out of marmalade, of all things, when we discovered that Richard had brought a jar with him, along with digestive biscuits, peanut butter and potatoes!

Following an emotional arrival in wonderful Horta, and with *Spirit of Penmar* safely tied up alongside the famous harbour wall, Richard went ashore to call friends and family. Within hours he had arranged a flight to the UK. Two days later we said our goodbyes, and not without a tear or two.

For us, arrival in Falmouth a month or so later saw the completion of our Atlantic circuit – so wonderful to be back in home waters. One calm, misty morning found *Spirit of Penmar* anchored in a peaceful spot up the Lynher River in the Plymouth backwaters. A pretty little Halcyon 27 came to anchor nearby with a singlehander on board, who rowed across to see us. We had arranged to meet Richard to say hello and to hand over some of his gear, left with us for safekeeping. I'm pleased to report that all is well and Richard is busily getting his new love ready for further adventures. You just can't keep a good man down!'

12 And When It's All Over

Coming down to earth and hitting dry land

You remember the anticipation, the excitement, the fear, the uncertainty as you made the decision to embark on ocean sailing. But how does it feel when it's all over?

You look back on it now as a truly magical time when, despite the doubts, you were overwhelmed by the sense of adventure. You have braved the worst weather and enjoyed the best; you have sailed to places that you once thought were beyond your dreams; you have visited far-off lands that have opened your eyes to worlds of which you knew nothing before. And you have achieved all this through your skills and determination as an ocean sailor.

But now, home shores are beckoning. Your bows are once again pointing at that same harbour from which you left all those months or years ago. The GPS says less than a hundred miles to go. You'll be alongside tomorrow, tied up in your old berth, being greeted by some of the people who came down to wish you farewell. How will it feel? Will you be overjoyed that it's all over, and sigh with relief? Or are you somewhat fearful of what life back home is really like? All manner of thoughts that have not crossed your mind for months or even years start to flood in. Will the tenants have left the house in good order? Will the dog want to know me? How high will the pile of bills be? What if I suddenly find I don't like home anymore?

We have had some great company throughout this book of cruising people who have roamed the oceans of the world. But even they had to face the reality of life back home. As a final note, they tell us their feelings when the big adventure is suddenly over.

Jane and David Russell

From a practical perspective, the coming home is the start of the next phase, the next learning curve, the next adventure. You hit the ground running. You switch back into the land life you know so well. The first time you drive on a motorway or city freeway you have to fight the feeling that everyone is going to die because manoeuvring at such speeds feel insane. But mostly you just get stuck back in as if you've never been away.

Friends and family love you, but they also hate you; from their perspective, they have been grafting and toiling while you have been swanning around the world sending postcards from paradise. Even your nearest and dearest will not necessarily want to hear too many details about your adventures. Don't expect to be the returning heroes for more than about five minutes. But over time they will come to ask more questions, so don't lose heart if they seem pretty disinterested at first.

From a personal perspective, the changes you see in yourself are likely to be profound and permanent. I don't think you can cross oceans without coming face to face with challenges that strip back all pretence and lay your true self bare. You might fight that process to begin with, but in the end you find a peace within yourself. It's an inner centre of calm, whatever gets thrown at you. Perhaps it's a kind of wisdom. It's certainly not a cocky confidence, more a quiet but firm self-belief. And what it means is that you don't look at the world, or other people in the world, in quite the same way that you used to. Sometimes that can feel lonely and it can feel as if fellow ocean cruising friends are the only people who you can really connect with, so it's good to keep some of those connections going through the years. But mostly it is an inner, steadying constant that equips you well to learn and develop and thrive in any walk of life that you choose thereafter.

I can't think of any ocean sailors I know, of any age, who haven't continued onwards with interesting and fulfilling lives. You might argue that if they cross oceans they are wired that way to start with, and maybe that is partially true. But I think the longer term crossing of oceans is something that tempers your very soul into something more resilient, more patient, more adaptable, more forgiving. In short, it is life changing. And it seems to be enhanced, not diminished, over time.

Donna Hill

Following each transoceanic passage, I felt without purpose. Even depressed. I correlate the empty feelings to how Olympians must feel when the Games come to an end, soccer players after competing for the World Cup. Fortunately, my depression never lasted long. I always got attached to another plan.

At the end of our circumnavigation, we realised that to continue the adventure, we would need to leave family and loved ones again. We weren't willing to do that. We rejoiced in what we had done and were ready for new challenges. Returning home, we discovered that friends could not relate to our former lifestyle. Suddenly, conversations focused on topics other than sightseeing, exotic islands, anchorages, hiking, safaris, whales, sunsets and green flashes.

To share the same life-changing adventure that we had, I wrote two travelogues. Reliving these adventures through writing helped to transition from blue water sailing to a land-based lifestyle.

Eric Forsyth

After the tranquillity of an ocean passage, getting home can be hectic. You will crave for the peace and quiet of the boat. Instead of gradual decompression, you will be faced with immediate problems: getting the boat fixed up, dealing with accumulated mail and messages, bills, traffic, and all the trivia of modern life. Friends will ask what you have been up to. When you tell them, they will look bemused and ask, 'Did you run into any storms?'

Nicola Rodriguez

I wrote the last chapter of my book *Sail Away* with tears falling down my face. It was a catharsis, of sorts. It helped with the grieving process and a difficult re-entry.

When we first returned, I anticipated we would be off again within three years, at most. If I had thought eight years later we would still be ashore, I would have crumbled. We have kept the dream alive, John by selling blue water boats, and me by writing about sailing. I met a cruiser who mourned the anniversary of her return, to the hour, every year. While away, I found this sad but once home I understood. After seven years of marking the anniversary, I thought enough and focused on planning the next cruise.

This is what I wrote: 'For me, there were days on the school run when I felt I was being buried alive. The enforced return to routine can be debilitating. Whilst living on a boat, cruisers become used to open spaces, physically, emotionally and metaphorically; so going for walks or runs in large open spaces is a great panacea. Whereas on the boat one could wear shorts and T-shirts, old clothes must be de-mothballed or a new wardrobe acquired, which can be expensive. Stocking up a kitchen can be a gradual process, helped by unloading foodstuffs from the boat.

Every little helps at this time of transition. Lugging laundry to laundrettes that beat up your kit is part of the cruising life. A washing machine is one of the perks of living at home.

Although re-connecting with friends can be a joyful experience, it can also be a drain on your depleted reserves. You will be the novelty treat at dinners, which is fun but exhausting at a time of change. Some friends may seem interested initially, then glaze over. Most cruisers experience this and revert to small talk, leaving their extraordinary experiences for evenings with other cruisers who can talk up and down twenty Caribbean islands or across thirty atolls in the Pacific in a sentence.

Don't let go of letting go. You have lived the dream, you have been it.

Tom and Vicky Jackson

Every long-term cruiser we know who has 're-entered', no matter how long ago they were cruising, says, 'I'm so glad we went when we did. Things are so different now.' Everyone thinks things were better when they were cruising and have got worse since. Of course, the radical improvement in communication is the primary factor that makes re-entry very different now than it was. Most cruisers are no longer incommunicado for very long periods. We even know cruisers who have continued to run their businesses from their boats for years while long-term cruising.

Tom and Susie Partridge

We returned to England in May 2017 after over four years away. We were excited to be back near family and friends yet sad to be leaving a life we loved. While we had a plan of what we wanted to achieve over our first months back in England, we felt apprehensive about how it may all turn out.

Big changes in technology struck us. Several times over that first summer we felt like foreigners in our own country – asking shop assistants for help, reading information signs diligently to work out how things worked and where to go to find what we needed.

We found London, our home city, overwhelming at times – the crowds, the pace and the seeming lack of engagement. Having established a routine of morning walks we were struck by how 'shy' English people are. We had become accustomed to offering a smile and a friendly greeting to all and sundry. Back in England, people would look down or look away and hardly raise a cheer – thank goodness for friendly dogs always happy to wag a tail!

One of our biggest learnings from living on a yacht came from the fact that you have to think about what you can carry – you take only the essentials. So, coming back to land we took the same attitude and decluttered. It's been a revelation – no more stuff for the sake of it, we've saved money and it's good for the environment!

What do we miss? Exploring new places, meeting new people, and the freedom and simplicity which sailing brings.

Mike and Devala Robinson

On ocean passages we entered a 'bubble' that stretched to the horizon and it's hard explaining that to family and friends who haven't sailed offshore. For long periods of time, days at a time, we were the only people in the world enjoying our vista. Approaching land, there was often a feeling of resentment – we would now have to share our own private world.

This was mixed with feelings of relief, and a sense of achievement – we had 'done it', again, without any major mishaps – which would stand us in good stead for the next time. And of course, landfall promised the joy of an uninterrupted night's sleep. It's funny how quickly we almost 'forget' what we'd achieved, a sense of unreality about it.

The people you meet as you voyage far and wide will be people you will never forget. (GILL)

Over time, ocean passages became less daunting, a different way of life that we quickly settled into. Though we never lost our respect for the elements, modern day weather forecasting, pulled in once or twice a day, usually allowing us to skirt around the worst. Friends rarely realise that and we got used to questions about storms and disasters and could sense a slight disappointment when we had little to report.

Of course, friends' (and family's) lives have moved on without us, something of a rude awakening! It's taken time to catch up with them and where they were in their lives after our nine years away.

At the end of our circumnavigation, our challenge is not to lose the wanderlust and curiosity that made us want to set sail in the first place. Our experiences circumnavigating have made us more likely to say 'yes' to opportunities and invitations – no matter how unlikely or improbable.

Mike and Hilde Gill

Depending how long you have been away – we were cruising for seven years – don't be surprised if the family molecule has somewhat reconfigured in your absence. The hole you left is unlikely to be the same shape on your return, and you will have to earn and adjust your position in the new shape. However rewarding, it may not be that straightforward.

Ocean voyaging is a project in itself. Once over, there's the risk of anomie and listlessness. Some get depressed. Depending on your personality, it is probably worthwhile generating some ambition and plan for what you will do on return before the project ends.

Pam Wall

When we first came home we were very sad to get off our boat and know that our adventure was complete. While we were so happy to see family and friends, we were sort of strangers. No one was really that interested in what we had accomplished, and everyday life ashore was more important to those who had never had that experience. I cannot blame anyone. Our life was so bizarre and so out of touch with the reality of what was happening that the interest just was not there.

Our children did not fit in with school back home. They never minded being foreigners in another country's schools, but they felt they were in their schools back home. Andy and I were grateful being home and able to work and begin to replenish the kitty for future cruising. And I must say it was lovely to have my own shower, running hot water, and our own car that we did not have to borrow or rent. We were very lucky to find jobs right away and to fit into the life that we had left behind.

Our sailing did not end, our lives were forever looking for being on *Kandarik* again. You never know what will happen in your future. My husband suddenly passed away as we were planning a third Atlantic Circle, and a few years later my darling daughter, Samantha, passed away. The lesson is: GO WHEN YOU CAN, not when you are ready!! You will never really be ready, and the adventure of life does not wait!

Suzanne Hills and Chris Cromey

Before we sailed off, we purchased a small rural plot of land at our destination of New Zealand to enable us to slip back into land life easily, and we wouldn't have to jump into the sudden shock of city or suburban living and full-time jobs.

We have continued living as we did at sea by conserving resources and keeping our lives simple, and by being selective about what we plug in to. We've gained the good things of land living, like a vegetable patch and community connections, but so far avoided the busy nature of normal modern life.

Although we have a stunning view of the nearby Tasman Sea, we built our tiny house with its back to the sea and the front door opening to the forest. Eight years of blue water cruising has left us with a lifelong craving for green!

From friends, the common response was, "Wow, you should write a book." So in the first year back on land, I wrote a children's book based on our journey and relived our adventure. Not only was this an enjoyable reflective process, but the book itself is a precious personal memento of those years at sea.

Annie Hill

So often when I've been cruising, people tell me about 'it's all very well, but it's not the Real World'. My own view is that whenever I get back to the Real World, I can't wait to escape it and get away from the sheer insanity of it, back to a sane life. What's Real about people striving all their life to pay off a house that they will never own, because they always want something bigger and better? What's real about working all your life – particularly for someone else – all the while promising yourself that one day you will live. And then to find that when that day comes, you are too infirm or timid to follow that dream. Or that the dream doesn't appeal anymore. Or that, worst of all, the dream proved to be a disappointment, so you feel that it's all been for nothing.

To me, life ashore was no longer normal and I didn't want to pick up the pieces. My friends, generally, said, 'Oh, I want to hear all about it, but first, I just want to tell you about…' The truth is, most people aren't that interested and if they aren't sailors, they are simply bewildered. Has my view of ocean sailing changed? Not really. I (patronisingly perhaps) feel sorry for those who have never crossed the ocean relying on a sextant and regret that the anchorages are so full, and the boats are so big and so ugly, but I still feel that Conrad was right about true peace being found 1,000 miles from land.

A Christmas dinner round the cabin table. Memories to last a lifetime – Nordlys *in the Pacific. (RIDOUT)*

Kevin and Theresa Ruscoe

We had spent years dreaming of, saving and preparing for our sailing adventure and very little time considering our life after our voyage had ended. From the outset, our cruising time was limited. We had agreed to move to Australia (Theresa's homeland) and decided that spending two to three years getting there would be preferable to a long-haul flight. Our plan was always to resume work upon our arrival.

We did indeed sail into Sydney Harbour about three years after leaving the UK. Theresa believes that our time cruising taught her a great lesson in accepting and dealing with what cannot be changed; complaining won't improve the weather and stressing won't improve Brazilian Officialdom!

We never did resume our 'normal' life as our son was born two months after our arrival in Sydney. I was offered work with my previous employer and certainly found resettling into life in a suit to be challenging.

Before we left the UK, a friend and consummate sailor said to us that, when we're done, no one will be particularly interested in our journey. With the exception of a couple of close family members, our friend was right. I think it is difficult for non-sailors, or people who have no keen interest in travel, to appreciate the impact that cruising can have on those of us fortunate enough to set off.

Ultimately, we continue to look back upon our time sailing and visiting so many new places as an absolute gift and privilege. Though our next voyage is still years away, we are looking forward to our next adventure.

Chris and Lorraine Marchant

We returned home in autumn 2015 having been away for six years, during which time we circumnavigated, covering more than 50,000 miles and visiting more than 32 countries. We felt a great sense of achievement having completed what only a few people manage to do each year. For us it was the journey of a lifetime; the seas we had sailed and the variety of places visited did and still does feel mind boggling. The life is very addictive. We had sold our house before the trip and ended up with three small properties, two of which had been rented out for part of the time we were away and none of which we wanted to live in. This has all meant that for the last three years we have actually been very busy: selling our boat, moving house twice, selling property, buying our present home and re-acquainting ourselves with life back in the UK. I think if we had not been so busy we would have got bored.

Now we are healthy (after a health scare) and sorted out domestically, we can answer those who have asked us 'what next?' With a new but slightly smaller boat we aim to set off to the Caribbean again, hopefully leaving the boat there as a winter retreat for a few years, and perhaps venturing up the east coast of America. We tend to get itchy feet and do miss the cruising life: the people, the passages, the landfalls, the challenges and the new experiences. One day we will buy a dog and settle down to some serious gardening, but the day has not arrived yet.

Final Words

I wonder if some of those responses surprised you? Were they more downbeat than you expected? Certainly, there was little talk of the popping of champagne corks or the lighting of cigars. In fact, there wasn't one mention of a party or a welcoming home.

And that is often how it is. You sail across the oceans of the world only to find that while your experience has been totally immersive and, at times, overwhelming, while you have been away the world has been getting on fine without you. To sail around the globe is hard work, but it is not a kind of labour your friends will understand. They'll assume you've been on holiday. They won't understand that the confines of a yacht relate in no way to the comfort of a cruise liner. In fact, they will hardly be able to relate to your experience at all. After my own Atlantic passage, a friend asked me, 'did you put in somewhere every night?' I didn't know how to begin to come up with an answer, and neither will you. My world and their world were so far apart. So be ready for the strange questions people will ask. You may have crossed the entire Pacific but someone is sure to remark, 'I suppose there's always a lifeboat close by'.

You have to be patient. In fact, patience is the key, and proper reflection and appreciation of a lengthy voyage takes time. I once knew a wise old sailor who had made thirteen singlehanded crossings of the north Atlantic in a 26 foot boat and had learned many lessons along the way. At the end of my own solo Atlantic crossing, he was waiting in the quayside to meet me. He reached out his hand and congratulated me and said, 'You won't think much of your voyage now, but it *will* grow on you. And he was right. For several days after my arrival I thought nothing of the up and downs of the previous month and busied myself with repairs, shopping and sleeping. But I didn't understand the nature of the experience I'd had. It was several months before I was able to fully appreciate, and enjoy, what I had achieved.

So don't expect an immediate pay back for all the hard work you have put into your ocean passage. There will have been ample rewards along the way, and even more in the months and years to come. My friend was right; like a fine wine, or a good fruit cake, the passage of time only adds to the flavour of the experience and the maturing cannot be rushed.

When it finally hits you, when you fully understand what a profound and rewarding experience your ocean sailing has been, then comes the tricky bit because, without the slightest shadow of doubt, you will want to do it all over again.

Your friends back home might not quite understand, but sights like this will stay with you for ever. (PHILLIPS)

Bibliography

INTRODUCTION

The Royal Cruising Club:
www.rcc.org.uk
Here you can search the Club's journals going back to 1883 and glean much useful advice and information.

The Ocean Cruising Club:
www.oceancruisingclub.org
Here, non-members have access to *Flying Fish*, a quarterly account of members' voyages, as well as an active forum and other cruising information.

The Cruising Club of America
www.cruisingclub.org
An impressive amount of information, from radio communications to safety and seamanship, is available to non-members.

The RCC Pilotage Foundation
www.rccpf.org.uk
This is a huge resource covering PF publications and updates to their pilot books (available from www.imray.com). The website maintains updates and corrections as well as pilotage information recently received.

1 ALONE ON THE OCEAN

Tom and Vicky Jackson
www.sunstonesailing.com

2 WHERE IN THE WORLD SHALL WE GO?

World Cruising Routes, Jimmy Cornell (Adlard Coles)

World Cruising Destinations, Jimmy Cornell (Adlard Coles)

The Atlantic Crossing Guide, Jane Russell (Adlard Coles)

The Pacific Crossing Guide, Kitty van Hagen (Adlard Coles)

Ocean Passages for the World (NP 136), UK Hydrographic Office www.admiralty.co.uk

Pilot charts (as above) or free download from www.offshoreblue.com/navigation/pilot-charts.php

Cruising Under Sail (somewhat vintage but the advice is still good), Eric Hiscock (Oxford)

Voyaging Under Sail, Eric Hiscock (Oxford)

Kevin and Theresa Ruscoe www.sapphireoflondon.org

Noonsite www.noonsite.com
An invaluable research resource, particularly for entry requirements etc.

Tom and Susie Partridge www.yachtadina.co.uk

Mike and Devala Robinson
www.searover.co.uk

Chris and Lorraine Marchant blog
mailasail.com/gryphon

3 IT'S TIME TO BUY

Voyaging on a Small Income, Annie Hill (Tiller Publishing)

The Ocean Sailing Yacht, Don Street (Norton)

Cost Conscious Cruiser, Lin and Larry Pardey (Pardey Books)

4 THE BOATS THEY CHOSE

Max Campbell video at www.youtube.com/watch?v=tNVVmZBX3wo

One Wild Song: A Voyage in a Lost Son's Wake, Paul Heiney (Adlard Coles)

Rachael Sprot
www.rubicon3.co.uk

Richard Woods
www.sailingcatamarans.com

John Charnley
www.discoveryyachts.com

Metal in Boats, Vyv Cox (Crowood Press)

Hand, Reef and Steer, Tom Cunliffe (Adlard Coles)

Practical Junk Rig, HG Hasler (Adlard Coles)

Voyage of Egret
www.nordhavn.com/egret/

5 HOW MUCH TO GO OCEAN SAILING?

Terysa Vanderloo and Nick Fabbri
www.yachtrubyrose.com

Mike and Windy Robertson
www.logofdelviento.blogspot.com

Selling your Writing to the Boating Magazines, Mike Robertson (Force Four Publications)

6 CAN THE KIDS COME TOO?

Voyaging with Kids, Mike Robertson, with Behan Gifford and Sara Dawn Johnson (Pardey Books)

Kids in the Cockpit, Jill Schinas (Adlard Coles)

One Summer's Grace: A Family Voyage around Britain, Libby Purves (Hodder)

Jessica Lloyd-Mostyn
www.water-log.com/a-family-at-sea/

Pam Wall
www.pamwall.com/photography/

7 TOO OLD TO GO?

Eric Forsyth
www.yachtfiona.com

Voyage of the Harrier, Julian Mustoe (go to Amazon)

8 KEEP IN TOUCH...

RYA Handy Guide to Marine Radio (Royal Yachting Association)

Marine SSB Operation, J Michael Gale (Fernhurst Books)

Jack and Zdenka Griswold
www.sailmagazine.com/cruising/a-seven-year-circumnavigation

Reeds Weather Handbook, Frank Singleton (Reeds)

Hurricane Survival for Small Boats, Richard C Dumas (Kindle)

First Aid at Sea, Douglas Justins and Colin Berry (Adlard Coles)

9 THE COMPLETE ENGINEER

Nigel Calder's Cruising Handbook, Nigel Calder (McGraw-Hill)

Boatowner's Mechanical and Electrical Manual, Nigel Calder (McGraw-Hill)

Marine Diesel Engines, Nigel Calder (Adlard Coles)

The 12 Volt Bible for Boats, Miner K Brotherton (Thomas Reed)

Understanding Boat Plumbing and Water Systems, John C Payne (Sheridan House)

10 LOOK AFTER YOURSELF

Ships Captain's Medical Guide, free PDF chapter downloads are available here www.gov.uk/government/publications/the-ship-captains-medical-guide

National Formulary (ask your doctor for a recent copy)

Wilderness or expedition medical guides:

forum.oceancruisingclub.org> medical matters

cruisingclub.org> resources

11 WHEN THINGS GO WRONG

Understanding Boat Corrosion, Lightning Protection and Interference, John C Payne (Sheridan House)

Lightning and Boats, Michael V Huck Jr. (Partners Publishing Group)

Self-steering for Sailboats, Gerard Dijkstra (Sail Books Inc)

Self-steering Without a Windvane, Lee Woas (Seven Seas Press)

12 AND WHEN IT'S ALL OVER

Books by Pam Wall
www.pamwall.com

Yanmara, Ship's Cat, Suzanne Hills (A M Publishing, New Zealand)

Sail Away: how to escape the rat race and live the dream, Nicola Rodriguez (Fernhurst)

Index

abandoning ship 235–6, 253–6, 257–60
Agulhas Current 45, 48
AIS systems 59, 178, 237
Alaska 44
Aleutians 42–3, 44
aluminium boats 107–8
American Global Forecasting System 196
anchoring 52, 64, 83, 135, 138
Angle of Vanishing Stability (AVS) 82
Antarctic passages 49–50
antibiotics 218, 224, 225
antifouling 32–3, 138
Arctic passages 49–55
Argentina 33
astronavigation 210
autopilots 243, 249

babies, cruising with 148–9, 150–1, 155
barometers and barographs 194–5
Beagle Channel 33
bed space 86
bilge pumps 206, 237
boat types
  basic/low budget 89–93
  catamarans 100–4
  gaff rigs 111–14
  luxury boats 96–9
  metal boats 105–10
  motorboats 119–22
  ordinary boats 94–5
  unstayed rigs 115–18
  yacht broker advice 122–4
Brazil 30, 33, 132
buying a boat
  anchorage 83
  bed space 86
  cabins 84–5
  centre-boarders 78
  cockpits 83
  comfort 69–70, 71, 74
  could you love her? 73–4
  engines and electrics 84
  hatches/ventilation 85
  hull and rudder 74–8
  is your current boat suitable? 72–3
  keels 77, 78
  list of considerations 87
  living costs 69
  manageability – winches and halyards 83
  multihulls 79–80
  propellers 80
  a sailors' guide 68–71
  sales pitches 66–8
  size of boat 74
  spreaders 83
  stability/stability curve 81–2
  stowage 85
  surveyors 80, 82–3
  see also boat types

cabins 84–5
capsizing 23–232, 81, 100
catamarans 100–4
  see also multihulls
centre-boarders 78
children, cruising with 144–6
  advice to consider 144–6, 150, 156
  babies 148–9, 150–1, 155
  on board entertainment 146, 154, 160, 163
  formal education 147, 153–4, 157, 161, 163
  health and safety 145, 149, 150, 154–5
  health on board 220, 222
  sailors' stories 146–59
  young sailors' stories 159–63
circumnavigation 56–7
  sailors' stories 57–65
clothing 8, 163
cockpit, checking the 83
'Coconut Milk Run' – South Pacific 34–40
Code of Signals 174–5
collision/danger warnings 178, 182
collisions 232–3
communication
  Code of Signals 174–5
  consulting a doctor 220–1, 222
  costs 139, 183, 184, 189
  email 180–1, 185, 192, 196
  flags 173, 174, 175
  HAM radio 181–2, 186
  internet 184–5, 187–90
  mobile or cellular data 189, 192
  Pactor modems 180, 185, 186, 190
  radio 65, 173, 175–82, 183, 186, 190–1, 195–6, 250, 251
  sailors' stories 185–6, 190–2
  satellite phones 40, 59, 181, 182–5, 186, 189, 191, 192–3, 195, 223
  signal stations 173–4
  SSB 8, 40, 46, 178–81, 182, 183, 186, 190–2, 195–6, 250
  VHF/DSC radio 177–8, 251
  Wi-Fi 187–9
  see also weather forecasts
condensation problems 43
conductors, lightning 239
crew considerations 53, 55, 60–1, 64, 96, 169
crime 30, 38–9, 45, 58, 98, 249–52
cyclones
  see tropical cyclones

Denmark Strait 51, 52
Digital Selective Calling (DSC) 177
dinghies/RIBs 138, 253–4, 255–6
  see also liferafts

disasters, tackling 226–7
abandoning ship 235–6, 253–6, 257–60
coming to the rescue 257–60
flooding and sinking 232–7
lightning and thunderstorms 237–42
man overboard 230–2
piracy 249–52
sailors' stories 227–37, 240, 244–8, 253–6, 257–60
steering/self-steering failures 242–8
Doldrums 14–15, 30, 41

El Nino years 35
electrical systems, boat 84, 205, 209–10, 238, 240, 249
electrolysis 107
email 180–1, 185, 192, 196–7
employment whilst cruising 130, 137, 140–3
engines 84, 209
EPIRB (Emergency Position Indicating Radio Beacon) 8, 92, 192, 237
Equator, crossing the 30–1
Equatorial Current 30, 44

the Falklands 33
family and friends at home 128, 136, 137, 139, 152, 160, 163, 176, 186, 190
fax charts 195–6
financial considerations 58, 69, 126–9, 171
boat types 90, 96
cards and cash 134–5, 136, 139
earning money whilst cruising 130, 137, 140–3
equipment 133–4
food and drink 131, 132, 135, 136–7, 139
insurances 131, 134, 137
marina bills/mooring costs 128, 135, 137, 138
raising money 130, 133, 134, 137, 140–3
renting/selling your home 134, 143
repairs and fitting out 130, 131, 137–8
sailors' stories 129–37
second hand goods 137–8
summary of 139
what about the unexpected? 128, 139
what do you need? 127–9
first aid training 216–17, 219–20, 221, 224–5
fishing 38, 59, 132, 149
flags, signal 173, 174, 175
flooding and sinking 232–7
food and drink 5–6, 40, 52, 62, 131, 132, 135, 136–7, 139, 154, 208
fuel supplies 40, 51–2, 59–60, 64, 84, 122

gaff rigs 111–14
Garmin InReach devices 192, 195
Global Maritime Distress and Safety System (GMDSS) 193
Globalstar 184
gnomonic charts 18–19
GPS (Global Positioning System) 7, 18, 49, 89, 133, 192, 210
grab handles 84–5, 170
GRIBs (Gridded Binary Data files), weather 8, 180, 183, 185, 186, 196–7
ground tackle 51–2, 64, 135

hackers, computer 187, 188
hallucinations 228, 229
halyards 83, 207
HAM radio 181–2, 186
hatches, checking 85
health on board 213–15
children and older people 220
consulting a doctor 220–1, 222
cuts/lacerations 217–18
dehydration 219, 222
dental health 220, 225
exercise on board 211–12
first aid training 216–17, 219–20, 221, 224–5
fractures 218
infections 218–19, 222, 223–5
medical kits 37–8, 62, 154–5, 219, 224–5
medications 218, 219, 220, 221, 223, 225
sailors' stories 223–5
seasickness 100, 219, 221–2, 223
voices and hallucinations 228, 229
high latitude passages 49, 232
sailors' stories 50–5
when to go? 50, 166
home, returning 261–72
homesickness 65, 152, 161, 163
horse latitudes 15
hulls and rudders 74–8
hurricanes 17–18, 25

ice navigation 26, 50–3, 54–5
Immarsat 184
Indian Ocean 44–5, 57
sailors' stories 45–8, 57–8
insurance 131, 134
internet 184–5, 187–90
Intertropical Convergence Zone (ITCZ) 14–15, 41
Iridium 184

Japan 41, 42–3

katabatic winds 52, 55, 207
keels 77, 78

licences, radio 177, 181, 182
liferafts 32–3, 235, 237, 258–9
see also dinghies/RIBs
lightning and thunderstorms 237–40
luxury boats 96–9

MailASail 185
maintenance/boat jobs 27, 46–7, 69, 84, 105–6, 167
boat switchboards 210
do-it-yourself engineering 198–210

electrical faults 205, 209–10
engines 209
financial considerations 130, 131, 137–8
problem-solving skills game 199–200, 210
rudder jams 206–7
sails and halyards 207–8
servicing winches 207
sewing skills 207
steering systems 206
tools and spares 204–5, 207, 208
man overboard 230–2
marina bills 128, 135, 137, 138
Maritime Mobile Service Identity (MMSI) 177, 178
MAYDAY calls 182, 234–5
Mean Maximum Iceberg Limit 26
medical insurance 131, 134, 137
medical kits *see* health on board
Mercator maps 18
metal boats 105–10
mobile/cellular phones 189, 192
monsoon season 43, 45
motorboats 119–22
Mozambique Current 45
multihull boats 79–80, 100–4
multimeters 205

navigation 7, 38, 210
see also GPS
Ninigo Islands, Papua New Guinea 40
North Atlantic Ocean 20
high latitude passages 50–1
NW Europe to Caribbean 22–5
USA to NW Europe 25–9
when to go 21–2
North Pacific to Alaska 41
sailors' stories 42–4

ocean currents 16–17, 30, 44–5
OCENS 185
older people, cruising for 164–5
adding equipment 167, 170, 171–2
health on board 220, 222
sailors' stories 165–72
strength and fitness 166, 167, 168, 171, 172
weather 166, 167, 169–70
outboard motors 138

Pacific Eddy 45
Pactor modems 180, 185, 186, 190
Panama Canal 35
pests/insects 62
pets on board 152–3
pilot charts 12–14, 26, 54–5
piracy 45, 56, 58, 249–52
planning, passage
measuring distance 18–19
pilot charts 12–18
reference books 11–12
where to go? 9–11, 20–65
plotters/GPS 7, 18, 38, 49, 89, 133, 192, 197, 210
providers, satellite 184–5
provisions *see* food and drink

radio communications 8, 65, 173, 175–82, 183, 186, 190–2, 195–6, 250, 251
reference books 11–12
refitting 124, 133, 137–8
refrigeration 63
renting/selling your home 134, 143
rhumb lines 18–19
RIBs/dinghies *see* dinghies/RIBs
Royal Cruising Club 4, 5
rudder jams 206–7
rust 105–6

safety and security
circumnavigation 56, 58, 59
computer hackers 187
cruising with children 145, 149, 150, 154
equipment 134
luxury boats 98–9
MAYDAY calls 182, 234–5
piracy 45, 56, 58, 249–52
Red Sea and Suez Canal 45
South America 30
South Pacific Islands 38–9
UV rays 59
SailMail 8, 180–1, 185
satellite phones 40, 59, 181, 182–5, 186, 189, 191, 192–3, 195, 223
Scoresby Sound 51, 52
sea cocks 206, 236
seasickness 100, 219, 221–2, 223
security *see* safety and security

shipping containers 232–3
Single Side Band (SSB) communications 8, 40, 46, 178–81, 182, 183, 186, 190–2, 195–6, 250
sinking, flooding and 232–7
'skeleton coast' 29
sleep/sleeping arrangements 8, 86
solar power 46
South America 30
South Atlantic Ocean 29
crossing the Equator 30–1
sailors' stories 31–4
South Pacific 34–5
sailors' stories 35–40
spreaders 83
stability, boat 81–2
steering failures 242–8
storms, electrical 237–40
stowage 85

tankage 84
thunderstorms and lightning 237–42
Thuraya 184
tools and spares 204–5, 207, 208
torches, waterproof 236
Torres Strait 45
Trade Winds 15–16, 43–4, 167
trading with locals 40
tropical cyclones 17–18, 41
typhoons 17–18, 41, 42–3, 44

unstayed rigs 115–18
Uruguay 30
UV/sun protection 59

vaccinations 222
ventilation, checking 85
VHF/DSC radio 177–8, 251
Viking Route 50–3

washing/personal hygiene 7–8
water supplies 7–8, 59, 63, 84, 208–9
weather forecasts 47, 55, 176–7, 179, 180, 182, 186, 193–7
Wi-Fi 187–9
winches, checking 83
wind roses 12–14
wind vanes 133–4, 243–9
Winlink 2000 181